World University Library

The World University Library is an international series
of books, each of which has been specially commissioned.
The authors are leading scientists and scholars from all over
the world who, in an age of increasing specialization, see the
need for a broad, up-to-date presentation of their subject.
The aim is to provide authoritative introductory books for
students which will be of interest also to the general
reader. Publication of the series takes place in Britain,
France, Germany, Holland, Italy, Spain, Sweden and
the United States.

Frontispiece Roman bridge
at Alcantara in Spain.

J. P. V. D. Balsdon

Rome: The story of an empire

World University Library

McGraw-Hill Book Company
New York Toronto

Photoset by BAS Printers Limited, Wallop, Hampshire, England
Manufactured by LIBREX, Italy

Contents

Introduction   7

Part 1: Growth

1 The First Empire: The Republic 241-27 BC   16
   History   16
   Administration   43

2 The Second Empire: Augustus and his
   successors, 27 BC-AD 193   68

   The new system   68
   History   87
   Administration   126

Part 2: Decline

3 The Third Empire: Septimius Severus   196

4 The Fourth Empire: Diocletian and Constantine 217

   The division of the Empire   217
   Diocletian's reorganisation of administration   219
   Christianity   228
   Barbarian invasions   234

   Epilogue   240

   Bibliography   247

   Acknowledgments   252

   Index   253

Though the distinction is not necessarily in every case exclusive, there are two sorts of imperialism: mercenary imperialism, and the imperialism of fear.

The European empires overseas which flourished in the nineteenth century and have now generally dissolved were mercenary empires. Trade went before the flag. Traders discovered the existence overseas of rich sources of natural wealth which invited the kind of exploitation of which a higher civilisation alone was capable, and of great stretches of rich uncultivated or inadequately cultivated land which cried out for settlers. Trading companies established themselves, soon – if not from the start – with the support of their home governments. In this way the colonising power acquired possession of overseas territories which it came to administer through civil servants of its own in the joint interest of the native peoples and of the settlers. In every case the colonisers brought with them a superior civilisation which they communicated to the native inhabitants: law, education, hospitals, agricultural and veterinary science. Also, with differing degrees of effectiveness, they brought the Christian religion. Considerable fortunes were often acquired by the colonisers, both by those who traded and by those who migrated and made new homes for themselves in colonial territories.

The wiser colonising powers came increasingly to appreciate that their government and administration was a kind of trust which must come to an end at some time or other. More and more they thought in terms of responsibility for the native people whom they governed. Members of these peoples, whom they themselves had educated, were increasingly associated in administration with the civil servants sent out by the imperial power. Responsible local authorities were created or recognised, and elected parliaments were introduced. The task was not easy and often it was not wholly successful because what was being effected or at least aimed at was a social revolution, the replacement of a kind of feudalism with both law and religion (on which law was based) personified in the tribal chief-in-council, by a western European type of democratic organisation, a revolution the like of which in Europe had been accomplished over centuries of time, often through internal and external wars, but whose achievement in the colonies was attempted by persuasion over a few decades. The task was the harder because European administrators found it easy to appreciate and to start building on the many excellent features of tribal rule; but they had to persuade the tribal councils, responsible men, to stand down in favour of a new, quickly-educated, often falsely Europeanised town-dweller; and, as all history, particularly Roman history, shows, an antagonism exists between the countryman and the town-dweller. At the end the administrators of the imperial power were withdrawn and the former colony, now an independent sovereign state, was left to govern itself.

The transition from colonial status to independence was not always a smooth one. Once the prospect of independence approached, those then in the ascendancy in the colonies were impatient to throw off the restraints of the imperial power and have freedom to act before their rivals could challenge them. The colonial powers, on the other hand, were sometimes over-cautious, demanding too high a standard of political advance in a world itself advancing at breakneck technological speed. History, which is a wise judge, will appreciate how reasonable were the feelings of either side.

Fear was never a motive of such imperialism in its early stages. Britain was never likely to be attacked by Canada or by India, France by Algeria, or Holland by the Dutch East Indies.

It was only when colonial empires grew and came into conflict with other colonial empires or expanding powers that fear – sometimes bred by jealousy, sometimes not – became a motive of imperial policy, because colonies came to assume significance in world politics and strategy, as did Aden for the British, once the Suez canal was opened. And the ending of Germany's role as a colonial power in east Africa after the 1914 war was a repercussion of European power-politics, motivated by feelings of revenge on the part of other colonial empires, particularly the British, in Africa.

Fear, however, is the explanation from the start of another kind of imperialism in the modern as well as in the ancient world. One power sees in the existence of another, often a neighbour, a threat to its own independent existence, a threat which conquest and subjection alone will remove and must attempt to remove for ever. Once conquered, that country must be absorbed and ruthlessly controlled.

Fear, as will be seen, was the mainspring of Roman imperialism in its early stages, down to the ruthless extermination of Carthage. *Mais l'appétit vient en mangeant.* Romans acquired a greed for empire, pride in its possession and a kind of arrogance; they expected everywhere to be treated as the master race that they were. And it did not take them long to discover that there was money in empire, money for the State which enriched itself by provincial taxation and money for individuals, not for traders and business-men only but, on an even larger scale, for Roman administrators who cared little for the letter of the law to which they were nominally subject.

Where the Romans came, they came to stay. They had no con-ception of such a thing as a trust, no eye on a day when they would retire and leave their provincial subjects to govern themselves. If asked why not, they would have retorted that they offered their provincial subjects something far better, the opportunity of sharing in the government of Rome and of the Roman empire itself. It was not difficult for a native to gain Roman citizenship through public, particularly military, service and, once a citizen, he or his des-cendants, granted the ability, could rise to the highest posts in the Roman government and administration. In Palestine, St Paul, a native of Cilicia, and the chief captain were equally proud of the fact that they were Roman citizens. So when the day of the Roman aristocracy, which won the empire, was at an end, men bred in the country towns of Italy took over. Then emperors came in succession from Spain, Africa, Syria and finally, in the last desperate years, the Balkans. So, also, did numbers of great generals and administra-tors. This, the Roman would have said, was Rome's great achieve-ment; it took a good native and made a good Roman of him.

The Roman empire was born in fear and it perished in fear. The fear at its beginnings, from the first moment when the city's expansion from a few acres of land on the Tiber started, was the fear that, if its neighbours were not the victims of its own expansionist urge, it would be the victim of theirs. How well based, at the successive stages of Roman expansion, this fear was, we can only guess.

On the other hand, there is no guessing about the fear at Rome's latter end; that was real enough – the fear of those who were overrun and pillaged by barbarians who outnumbered them, sweeping in from over the frontiers; the fear of their own armies, watchdogs which had turned into wolves; in parts of the Empire fear of Nature herself. When Lepcis Magna in Tripolitania was devastated by tribesmen from the interior in AD 363, the encroachment of sand from the desert had already started. By AD 533, the city was buried under sand-dunes.

By the time the Roman empire fell, it had enjoyed seven centuries of life. No other territorial empire in history has lasted even a portion of that time.

In describing the Roman empire there is a difficulty about words at the start. What in modern empires have been called colonies in the broadest sense of the word, were called provinces (*provinciae*) by the Romans. *Provincia*, in fact, meant 'an official posting', 'a job to do' (as today we say 'That is not my province'), and Roman magistrates were allotted provinciae long before the birth of Rome's territorial empire. For instance, if one of the two consuls was given the responsibility of holding the elections, that was his provincia. So it was in a secondary sense that the word came to be used of a specific tract of territory under the regular government of successive magistrates sent out from Rome.

A colony, on the other hand, was a privileged town in the empire, one which had been founded by a special settlement of Romans or Latins, or an existing town which had been given the status of such a settlement, which meant that its inhabitants had Roman or Latin citizenship. A colony was always a town.

The inhabitants of overseas colonies in empires of the modern world have either been natives or non-natives, the latter having come out as traders, professional men, artisans, businessmen, or farmers. In the colony they have been foreigners and not necessarily citizens of the colonising power. There were, for instance, and are, Indians in east Africa. For all such persons in the provinces of the Roman empire, in the absence of any satisfactory term, the word 'settler' will be used in this book, but in the full consciousness that it can in many cases be a misleading term.

The Romans called natives of the provinces (Spaniards, for instance, in Spain or Greeks in Greece) 'foreigners' (*peregrini*) or, more flatteringly, 'allies' (*socii*). The word *provincialis* (a provincial) denoted a Roman resident in the provinces, in contrast to *Italici*, who were Roman citizens living in Italy. Settlers, then, were provinciales, if they were Romans; but so were natives on whom Roman citizenship was conferred. On the other hand, a settler who did not possess Roman citizenship (an Egyptian Greek, for example, who had set up in business in Marseilles) was a peregrinus, a socius. This is a field in which consistency in the use of modern words for Roman things is impossible; but generally in this book a distinction will be made between 'natives' and 'settlers'.

The word 'empire' in Roman history is used in two senses. You may speak or write, as this book will, of the Roman empire in the territorial sense in which in modern times there have been German, Spanish, Portuguese, French, Dutch, Belgian and British empires. But in 27 BC, at the end of the civil wars, over two hundred years after the territorial empire came into existence by Rome's acquisition of her first provinces (Sicily, Sardinia and Corsica), the central government at Rome itself changed from being republican, and from then onwards there were emperors. So the word 'Empire' – technically 'the Empire of the Caesars' – is used in another sense. In 27 BC the Republic ended and the Empire started.

Floods are news, as slow-moving water is not; and it was with the dynamic of imperial vicissitudes that the ancient historians concerned themselves. Peaceful administration, being static or slow-moving, was no news at all. So no serious account of such an administration was ever written by any ancient writer.

Yet historians like Tacitus in the second century AD, Cassius Dio in the third and particularly, in the fourth century, Ammianus Marcellinus, an active soldier, were not without experience of provincial conditions, and Velleius Paterculus, who published his slight account of Rome in AD 30, brings a breath of fresh air into history by the unconcealed expression of his personal feelings – that 'Germans were born liars', for instance – and by vivid descriptions of events which he witnessed as a subaltern. He stood on the bank of the Euphrates in AD 2 and watched the meeting of Gaius Caesar and the Parthian king, 'an extremely tall young man'; in AD 5 he saw an elderly and distinguished German canoe himself across the Elbe, simply in order to discover what Tiberius looked like. He shook Tiberius' hand, declared that the Germans must be mad to fight the Romans and, on retiring, said that it had been the happiest day of his life.

There is Tacitus' biography of his father-in-law Agricola, whose life was chiefly spent in provincial administration and military command. There is the picture of Roman administration which is given by the Gospels and the Acts of the Apostles, a picture the more valuable from the fact that it constitutes a worm's eye view. There is the priceless record of imperial constitutions in the Theodosian Code from the start of the fifth century AD and the codification of the law under Justinian at the beginning of the sixth. And there is the correspondence of two men during the time that they were governing provinces, the private and official correspondence of Cicero in Cilicia in 51-50 BC and the exchange of letters between the younger Pliny in Bithynia and Trajan in, probably, AD 109-11. On the dark side, there are the records from the Roman law courts, in particular the vast catalogue which Cicero compiled of Verres' crimes.

Day after day, year after year, towns had their lives and provinces had their lives, the lives of the people who inhabited them. Apart from the great events which reached the history books small changes were taking place all the time. A new road was built, or a school; or water was brought in by a new aqueduct. Troops moved into a new barracks, then moved away again and were replaced by different troops. Industries started up, so that things were made on the spot and no longer had to be imported from Italy or from somewhere else overseas. New religions arrived, strange exotic priests, inviting enquiry, making converts. There were the annual local elections, public benefactions, endowments, the excitement of the regular and special festivities and games. There was interest in local people who did well, whether they stayed at home and made money or whether they went out into the big world to be soldiers, even great statesmen in Rome, and who never lost their affection for the places where they were born, as Mediterranean people never do today. On retirement they sometimes came home to live out the rest of their lives, and perhaps perpetuated their names by some new building or, it might be, a charitable endowment for the local children of the poor.

There were contractions and expansions of population, disasters from flood or fire or, in the latter days, invasion and assault by barbarians – times when, rather than be robbed of all he carried, the fugitive buried his money underground in a carefully marked spot, hoping – forlornly in the event – that he would return one day in happier times and recover it. Though already the coinage itself, gold excepted, had steadily been adulterated.

About such things, which were the life-blood pulsing through the arteries of provincial life, the history books written in antiquity have little to tell us and we owe our knowledge to the archaeologist and his spade: to inscriptions, funerary reliefs, graffiti on the walls, mosaics, coin-finds, papyri in Egypt. Houses, frontier defences, even great cities have been born again from below the earth and the sand. Monuments have even been reconstructed in something like their original splendour, like the Stoa of Attalos in Athens, and as the great Severan basilica at Lepcis Magna will soon be standing again thanks to the generosity of the Libyan government and the oil companies and the skill marshalled by the University of Philadelphia.

What the eye has once seen, the mind can understand. And, as such a book as this attempts to show, it is not necessary to travel over the vast extent of the ancient Roman empire in order to see the surviving evidence of its greatness.

Part 1 Growth

1 The First Empire: The Republic 241-27 BC

History

Eastern Mediterranean peoples had felt the effects of the great eastern empires of the historical period. The Jews from Palestine were taken into captivity in Babylon; and, though mainland Greece fought off the Persians at Marathon, Salamis and Plataea, Greek cities in Asia Minor were Persian subjects before Alexander; and Egypt became a satrapy of the Persian empire. Then in ten years Alexander King of Macedon, fought his way through the Persian empire, as far as India. The tables were turned, and the whole of the known East was subject for the first time to western imperialism. Persia had disintegrated; so, on Alexander's death in 323 BC, did Alexander's empire. It fragmented into the Hellenistic kingdoms, their kings being for the most part Macedonians, descendants of Alexander's marshals: Macedonia under the Antigonids, Syria under the Seleucids, Egypt under the Ptolemies, and later Pergamon. And a theory of history as the story of a succession of empires, each of restricted length, became current. Within a few years of Alexander's death the question was being asked: when will it be Macedon's turn to be conquered, and who will be her conqueror? In the event Rome was to conquer Macedon; and the Roman Scipio Aemilianus was in the tradition when he burnt Carthage to the ground in 146 and asked, with tears in his eyes (for the barbarous Roman was apt to weep when destroying places): 'When will it be Rome's turn to fall?'

In the event Rome came near to disproving the theory. Her empire dated from the first defeat of Carthage in 241 BC. It grew through the centuries and split in the end into a western and an eastern empire. The western empire 'fell' in AD 476 in the sense that the child Romulus Augustulus was sent into retirement by the Gothic leader Odoacer and after this there were no more Roman emperors in the West. The eastern, Byzantine, empire lasted for nearly a thousand years after that, until AD 1453.

The problem of the Roman empire is not why it ultimately fell, but why it lasted so long. In a sense it never fell; it fragmented.

When the city of Rome was taken by Alaric in 410, Constantinople, built on the ruins of Byzantium, was nearly a hundred years old and Rome was no more than one of the two imperial capitals, a city which for the last century or two had hardly set eyes on a Roman emperor. It was, it is true, the see of the Pope, the Church being by now authoritarian, having taken over the notion of Rome as centre of the universe; but Christianity was universal, not a particularly Roman religion and in the East there were those who disputed the supreme authority of the Pope in Rome.

The fragmentation had been going on for a long time, for more than two centuries. Bits fell apart; then they were patched together again for a time, only to fragment once more. Even after the barbarian invasions, when there were Goths, Huns and Germans everywhere, patches of highly civilised Roman life still survived. And the invaders themselves had to build on what they found; they accepted existing Roman law and Roman systems of collecting taxes; they adopted Latin as the easiest language for communication, just as, realistically, English has to be accepted today in India. And Christianity could be a common bond uniting conqueror and conquered. There were Christians in the empire who so disliked the rule of Rome that they saw little that was alien in the conquerors who, after all, were often fellow-Christians.

Rome's first expansion and its explanation

In the early days clever Greeks, contemptuous of the Romans as 'barbarians', ascribed Roman success to luck and consoled themselves with the illusion that, if Alexander the Great had chosen the West instead of the East for his conquests, Rome would have been stifled in infancy. Romans themselves had doubts. When the first spate of conquests was over, they reflected that Rome, like any other individual, had passed beyond its childhood and vigorous young manhood; its old age could not last for ever. Indeed, more than most other people, the Romans were haunted by the thought of their own decline. Yet, challenging history and challenging providence, Rome called herself eternal, 'Roma Aeterna'. And

providence has had no alternative but to concede the claim. Is not the Pope today, like Julius Caesar, 'Pontifex Maximus'?

What was the secret of the Roman success?

Its first chapter, spanning nearly five hundred years from the foundation of the city by Romulus, supposedly in 753 BC, was the conquest of Italy.

Rome shook off, then mastered, the Etruscans. She shook off the Gauls, who had captured and pillaged the city in or soon after 390. She reduced the Latins from equals to dependants. She emerged victor from three grim wars with the Samnites, a people as tough and resolute as herself and, beyond Samnium, came up against the Greek cities on the south coast of Italy.

One of them, Tarentum (Taranto), in 280 BC appealed for help to King Pyrrhus of Epirus across the Adriatic, who came to its assistance, hoping perhaps to acquire south Italy and Sicily as an addition to his own kingdom, and expecting to frighten the Romans

These figures of two warriors carrying the body of a dead comrade surmount the lid of a bronze urn from the necropolis at Praeneste (Palestrina); perhaps fourth century BC. The urns are generally engraved with stories from Greek legend and the lids sometimes show warriors, or sometimes a nude female acrobat.

by the sight of his elephants – which, so far from inspiring terror, provoked Roman wit; the Romans, seeing them for the first time in Lucania, called them 'Lucanian cows'. Pyrrhus returned home undefeated, but the fact that he was not victorious was enough to startle the courts of the Hellenistic monarchs. Pyrrhus' fate was a first shiver portending the great earthquake to come.

In the middle of the second century BC, when Carthage had been eliminated and the absorption of the Hellenistic kingdoms into her world-empire had already started, the Greek Polybius, held as a hostage for seventeen years in Rome, himself experienced in the politics of a smaller world, published a history of the creation and growth of the Roman empire down to his time.

Like a good historian, he had all the time at the back of his mind a question to which his book must supply the answer: what was the secret of Roman success – so far, success in conquest? He found a number of sensible answers. Romans won wars – often after disastrous defeats in early battles – because they were resolute fighters, well armed and with a fine military organisation. The legion, fighting in maniples, three successive lines, each of which advanced through gaps in the line ahead, enabling that line to draw back, and confronting the enemy with three successive waves of fresh fighters, was a more powerful unit than the Hellenistic close-packed phalanx. Also it manoeuvred and deployed more easily in difficult conditions on broken ground. It was an army of the Romans and of their Italian allies. The allies provided the best cavalry, for the Romans themselves were never distinguished horsemen.

Besides a good army system, the Romans had, Polybius thought, an admirable government, whose three elements, the senate, the magistrates, and the people in their voting assemblies in the city, were so well balanced in their powers that none of them could ever be strong enough to dominate the other two.

Armies and governments are material, visible things. What is more difficult to comprehend is the spirit of a people. The key to this Polybius found in the loyalty, the discipline and the religious

A Roman family group. The husband reclines on a couch as men always did at dinner. His wife sits on a chair, as Roman women once did. But by the late Republic they, like men, reclined.

devotion of the great Roman families. This was the *pietas* which in his epic Virgil was to make the distinctive quality of Aeneas, Rome's mythical Trojan ancestor: loyalty within the family and loyalty to institutions, to the religion and traditions of the state. The Roman governing class was very small indeed, a limited number of families living in and around the city of Rome itself, land-owners, none of them particularly rich. From boyhood in the *tablinum* of the noble house, a Roman accustomed himself to the death masks of his ancestors and, as soon as he could read, to the inscription below each, recording distinguished service to the state. He was brought up in the belief that his life was to be devoted to a tradition – his family's and Rome's.

The Roman administrator: his training, career and versatility
Romans were never people of great sophistication and culture. When they started to build an empire, they had no literature of their own, nothing comparable with Homer, which from early days had been a kind of Old Testament to the Greeks. They were practical men, their ruling class the most gifted and versatile amateurs. You did not find in Rome separate professions of priests, of barristers and judges, of army officers, of politicians and statesmen or, when there was an empire, of provincial – what we should call 'colonial' – administrators. With no professional training, every one of these functions was expected to be within the range of the able young man of breeding. As time advanced and the governing class broadened to include, first, the leading families of the country towns of Italy and, later, talented and ambitious men from all over the empire, administration became more complicated and a measure of specialisation became inevitable; but still the same general versatility was demanded for a successful public career.

The schooling of the son of a prominent family (in Greek – and, when it became available, Latin – literature and rhetoric) was over when he was seventeen. Then, with his father or some other distinguished relative or friend to show him the way, he entered public life. He held a minor magistracy which taught him something about

police work, about the upkeep of public highways, about the mint; he made his début in the courts as a (very poorly trained) barrister, prosecuting (which was risky) or better, enabling his family to do its duty to its dependants, by defending some client who was not educated or prominent enough to defend himself. And he had ten years of military service to do – if he showed quality, as a sub-altern, a military tribune. At thirty he stood for his first important office, the quaestorship, and with a colleague he might (with no education in economics or finance) be in control for a year of the operations of the state treasury, the *aerarium Saturni*. After that he might or might not hold the aedileship (involving responsibility for police work in the city and for the public games) or, if his family was plebeian, the tribunate of the plebs. There were ten tribunes and, with the tribune's veto on public business and his power to

The Pantheon at Rome. The classical stone portico with the vast brick
rotunda, a masterpiece of engineering skill, behind it, was constructed by
Hadrian on the site of an earlier Pantheon erected in 27 BC by M. Agrippa,
as the inscription, which was cut for Hadrian's building, shows.
In AD 608 it became a Christian Church called Santa Maria ad Martyres.
It contains the tombs of Raphael and of the kings of Italy.

legislate through the plebeian assembly, this was an office in which
to attract, according to a man's choice, the favourable attention of
the men in power or of the discontented proletariat who had votes.
Next came the praetorship, at about forty; the Roman acquired
this office, and was expected in a moment to have all the qualifications of a trained judge. Finally, if he was good enough and his
family backing strong enough at the polls, he was elected one of the
two annual consuls. The consul's function each year was to hold a
military levy, normally of two legions, of the young citizens who
had to do military service, and then to march off at the head of
them and to fight. The consul was expected to shine for a year as a
general; and many disasters and the loss of hundreds of thousands
of young lives were the price which Rome paid for this easy
assumption. Armies cannot afford amateurs for generals, particularly when matched against experienced military commanders of
great experience and of the highest calibre, such as Hannibal. A
man might be re-elected consul, normally after a certain lapse of
time.

In the course of his career, a man should have been elected to one
of the prominent priestly colleges; which meant, if he was a pontiff
or an augur, that he and his colleagues were the State's standing
authority on questions of constitutional and religious tradition and
propriety, for law was embedded in religion. Election to a priesthood was election for life.

After the consulship, a man was a consularis, an elder statesman,
one of those who spoke first in any debate of the senate, of which he
had been a member since the start of his public career. This was the
moment when his long and varied experience of public life should
pay the State rich dividends. And, for himself, if he had no consuls
among his ancestors and his family was not noble already, he had
ennobled it. His descendants to the end of time were *nobiles*. For
the Roman nobility was a meritocracy, narrowly circumscribed in
the days of Rome's growth to world dominion, but widening all the
time until at the end it included the administrative genius of the
Mediterranean world.

In the course of this public career from start to finish no post was salaried. Men gave their service to the State.

If the Romans had little indigenous culture, as the Greeks understood culture, they had natural gifts which, in the process of romanisation, they were to impart to others, chief among them an interest in and aptitude for the administration and principles of law. The Twelve Tables, which were formulated in 450 BC and which every Roman schoolboy learnt by heart, were the first manifestation of this genius, Justinian's Digest, Code and Novels in the early sixth century AD the last. Romans had, unlike the Greeks, a fetish for sanitation. And, using Greek genius, where this was available, and making their own very practical contribution, Roman concrete, they wrote a new chapter in the history of architecture and of engineering. Despite the vicissitudes of time, even severe earthquake shocks, the Pantheon in Rome and Santa Sofia in Istanbul stand today as marks of the successive peaks of Roman architectural achievement. And there were, and still are, Roman roads.

Conquest through fear and the foundation of the Western Empire

What motive drove this little city of Rome, fifteen miles up the Tiber, to fight for the expansion of its power, first to the mastery of Italy, then to the mastery of most of the known world? The motive was certainly not economic. At no stage in its imperial expansion was Rome faced with serious over-population, with a great surfeit of Romans who must be settled or spread on conquered land, or with the bogey of empty stomachs which could not be filled except by the acquisition through conquest of productive land which belonged to other people. Nor was there at any stage a powerful commercial class which, operating as a strong pressure-group, drove the government to conquer because of the prospective commercial advantages of conquest. On the contrary, the governing class of the Roman Republic despised businessmen and affected to contemn their sordid profits. No government with its mind set on economic advantage would, in the early period of imperial expansion, have destroyed and put out of use, as Rome did, two of the finest harbours and commercial sites in the Mediterranean, Carthage and Corinth.

Indeed, in the first two stages of the expansion, the conquest of Italy and the acquisition of the Western Empire, it is difficult to find any driving impulse other than that of simple fear, however much that fear may have involved (and, later, have been replaced by) a lust for power. Conquest was first the only alternative to being conquered and made subject – by the Etruscans, by the Gauls, by the Samnites. And with fear there went a harsh and singularly cruel relentlessness. The famous precept given to Aeneas in Virgil's *Aeneid* was to spare those who capitulated, and to crush stiff-necked opposition '*Parcere subiectis et debellare superbos*'. This last was the treatment received by the Samnites, the only people who might well have displaced the Romans in the mastery of Italy, and by the Carthaginians.

Carthage, a commercial power, whose empire consisted of rich trade depots protected by the Carthaginian navy and predominantly mercenary army, was from the sixth century onwards the dominant power in the western Mediterranean, controlling, from its home territory in Tunisia, the islands of Sardinia and Corsica, the western part of Sicily, where vestiges of its occupation are still to be seen at Motya, and the southern coast of Spain. Rome, uninterested in commerce, had been in treaty relationship with Carthage since 509 BC. The two powers, indeed, renewed their alliance in the face of Pyrrhus, their common enemy.

Then, only sixteen years after Pyrrhus landed in Italy and eleven years after he left it, in 264 BC the decisive step was taken. To forestall the occupation of Messina on the far side of the Straits by the Carthaginians in Sicily, Romans crossed the Straits and occupied Messina themselves. The Carthaginians reacted and twenty-three years of war, the first Carthaginian war, followed in which, undeterred by their complete inexperience of the sea, the Romans built one fleet as fast as they lost another, engaging in naval warfare against the best trained fleets of the time and under consular commanders who, with no experience of the sea, were expected to become skilled admirals overnight. Undeterred by loss and disaster, they emerged victorious in 241, evicting the Carthaginians from Sicily which, to prevent the Carthaginians from returning, had clearly to be held as Roman territory. Three years later the danger of their using either Sardinia or Corsica to mount an invasion of Italy was averted also; for, with Carthage weakened by a military revolt at home, Rome seized those islands too.

Carthage was left with its metropolitan territory and with its possessions in Spain. Under the resourceful Barcids they went further than exploiting the great mineral and other wealth of Spain; they consolidated territory south of the Ebro and built up and trained a powerful army. Once more the Romans persuaded themselves, not unreasonably perhaps, that here again was a menace directed against themselves, and were determined to weaken Carthage further by fighting its armies in Spain and by invading Carthage itself. Instead, Hannibal took the initiative and marched through Gaul and over the Alps to invade Italy, hoping to receive support from the Gauls of north Italy and expecting numbers of

Rome's subject allies in Italy to throw off the yoke and join him.

He invaded in 218 and in that and the next two years won a series of resounding victories, his own military genius being aided at every turn by the ineptitude of the Roman generals who faced him. The disaster of Cannae was in 216 – and both in Spain, which the Romans had most courageously invaded and kept open as a second front, and in Italy the war dragged on, the Romans having at last learnt caution. Hannibal's chances of success declined from the moment when, after Cannae, the Romans did not do what the world expected them to do: sue for peace. Happily, few of Rome's Italian allies went over to the invader. Why should an Italian prefer a Carthaginian to a Roman master?

Poorly reinforced by his government at home, Hannibal never had the resources to mount a siege of Rome itself. So the tide slowly turned, and in the end the Romans produced a general of Hannibal's standard, P. Scipio Africanus. He defeated the Carthaginian armies in Spain and by 206 was in control of the peninsula. He landed an army in Africa from Sicily in 204. Hannibal was recalled and defeated at Zama two years later. Carthage sued for peace and, by the terms of the peace, was forbidden to have a navy of more than twelve ships. Spain was a menace no longer; nor, without an effective navy, was Carthage herself.

So Rome found herself in possession of three territories outside Italy – Sicily; Sardinia and Corsica (which were always treated as a single unit) and Spain, which it was convenient to divide into two districts – Further and Nearer Spain. They must be held, to prevent the Carthaginians from stealing back, and they must be administered. They were the first four territorial provinces of the Roman empire. As has been seen, the word province (provincia) went back to the earliest days of Roman history and it meant 'the job which, during his magistracy, a Roman magistrate was given to do'. The provincia of a praetor at Rome each year was jurisdiction. Each of the consuls was normally allotted, as his provincia, a theatre of war, to which he should proceed at the head of his troops and then engage the enemy.

The Romans knew no way of administering their public affairs except by annual magistrates, though, when there were more 'jobs' than there were magistrates, as happened when a large number of independent armies were simultaneously in the field during the second Punic war, they hit on the device of continuing a magistrate's command (*imperium*) after the end of his magistracy, giving him the title of pro-magistrate – propraetor or proconsul.

In normal times, however, they preferred to use magistrates. The government of one of the new provinces was optimistically expected to be predominantly a civilian, not a military, function, a matter of seeing that the peace was kept, taxes collected and law justly administered, a function, indeed, which was closely comparable with that of each of the two praetors in Rome. So the number of annual praetors was raised first to four and then to six, of whom two would remain in Rome and the others would go out for a year each to govern one of the new-style provinces.

At Rome the law which the praetors administered was Roman statute law which, while they could not reform, they could influence by their own interpretation and by the regulations which they issued on assuming office in the form of edicts. A similar framework was devised for each of the new provinces. It was given a charter, (a written constitution, the *lex provinciae*) and each governor on assuming office issued his edict, which in general embraced the content of previous edicts and made innovations, often to take account of change made in Rome, either by legislation or by praetors' edicts, in the Roman legal system.

It was reasonable to expect a province to pay the expense of its protection and administration. So taxes were levied, either of a familiar kind, like the tithes on agricultural produce in Sicily and Sardinia or direct taxes on ownership of land or on heads of the population. For this purpose census operations of some sort or another were necessary, and a financial secretary was required in each province, to help administer the levying of taxes. This again, was a function comparable with that discharged by the quaestors of the treasury at Rome. So the number of quaestors must have been increased, like the number of praetors, and each annual provincial praetor had the assistance of an annual provincial quaestor, whose posting likewise, whether to a post in Italy or in the provinces, was determined by lot.

Despite the expense of maintaining troops in Sardinia, which has never in its history been free from bandits, and in Spain, a far more intractable country than the Romans expected it to be, these new provinces were to benefit the Roman economy to an unexpected degree. Huge shipments of corn, which had been paid as tax in Sicily and Sardinia, and therefore cost no more than the expense of collection and shipping, were brought to Rome or diverted to feed Roman armies in the field. The mines in Spain, at first operated by the Roman government but then farmed out to mining companies, showed huge profits, which the Roman treasury annexed. So in 168 BC direct taxation was abolished in Italy and from then until the Empire of the Caesars Romans in Italy could thank their empire for the fact that they had no taxes to pay.

So the foundation was laid of the system by which the provinces of the Roman Empire were to be administered. As the empire consisted of countries into which the Romans had moved for the simple purpose of keeping Carthage out, there may have been few who envisaged the subsequent extension of the system to other parts of the Mediterranean world.

The eastern Mediterranean: first fumblings in diplomacy

While the first half of the second century BC introduced the Romans to the administration of a small empire in the West, it introduced them in the East to the excitement and turmoil of international diplomacy. They moved into the world of the Greek cities and Leagues (particularly the Achaean League in the Peloponnese, the Aetolian League in northern Greece and the maritime republic of Rhodes) and of the Hellenistic monarchies, of Macedon, Pergamon, Syria and Egypt. They were uneducated in the traditional niceties and conventions of eastern Mediterranean states, whose statesmen made no secret of the fact that they regarded the Romans as simple, uncultured barbarians, with one asset only: their military strength. That Roman manners were brusque and crude was evident; how great was their military power, if matched against one of the strong Hellenistic armies, nobody as yet could tell.

The Romans had curiosity, were full of good will, surprised when this good will was not reciprocated and easily contemptuous of what seemed time-wasting and face-saving obstruction. If other peoples did not accept what to the Romans seemed to be the obvious solutions of their generally trifling problems, the Romans were increasingly impatient.

Problems arose in quick succession and had to be referred back to the senate in Rome for a solution, the solution often being nothing better than the dispatch of a fact-finding commission of senators. Communications were inevitably slow, and decisions were often taken at Rome in the light of information which was already out of date. Greeks and Hellenistic kings, too, were often baffled by the fact that Roman generals and proconsuls with their armies were such powerful, often such arrogant, figures; yet they could never assume responsibility for any important decision. Every question of importance had to be referred back to Rome to the mysterious, omnipotent senate. Already Rome was the centre of the new world.

The Romans were always highly pragmatic and, though it would have shocked them to be told so, they were by the middle of the second century BC a highly unprincipled people. They discovered that, once they had weakened a country, it was theirs to mould or destroy. Rival powers could be split and encouraged to destroy each other. Rome could then choose her moment to intervene and deliver the coup de grâce. *Divide et impera.* Allies could be split, and so could reigning houses. Politicians too; one party could be exacerbated, its rivals bribed and seduced. By undermining self-confidence and encouraging belief in their own invincibility, the Romans gradually drove kings, statesmen, peoples of other countries into one extreme action or the other, either to buy inglorious safety at the price of complete submission (*deditio*)

or to fight, however despairingly, to keep the independence which
by now the Romans were out to destroy. Before long their tech-
niques and their intentions became clear to all. And yet the end-
result, Polybius thought, himself one of the victims, was for the
good of the Mediterranean world at large.

The end of Macedon and Carthage

It was Philip v of Macedon who brought the Romans into the East.
When Hannibal's victory seemed certain after Cannae, he quickly
attached himself to the evident winner, and declared war on Rome.
As he had no navy and no transports, and Rome commanded the
sea, he was, for Hannibal, a worthless ally; and he had his own
enemies nearer home, the greedy Aetolian League in Greece, who,
to the horror of far-sighted statesmen in the Aegean world, made
an alliance with the Romans. For the Romans, whose very survival
was at stake in Italy, the war against Philip was a tiresome side-
operation of which they were glad enough to be free when Aetolia
made peace with Philip in 206. They made peace with him themselves a year later and Philip, assuming in his sanguine way that his
little incursion into western power-politics was now forgiven and
forgotten, turned his attention eastwards and made a singularly
unscrupulous contract with Antiochus of Syria to share the external
possessions of Egypt, where a small boy had just succeeded to the
throne. If Italy had proved a bad investment, there was the Aegean
over which he might strengthen his hold.

So far, however, from being forgiven and forgotten, he had
merely been shelved; and as soon as Carthage was defeated at
Zama, the Roman government turned its attention to his punishment. Roman legions crossed the Adriatic; both the Achaean and
Aetolian Leagues, together with Pergamon and the island of
Rhodes, joined in the kill. After Cynoscephalae in 197 the interesting military question was a question no longer; the legion had
proved itself a more powerful fighting unit than the phalanx.
Philip was forced to withdraw from the three strong posts which he
had garrisoned for the last twenty-seven years in Greece, from

Acrocorinth, Chalcis in Euboea and Demetrias in Thessaly.

The war had solved one problem; the peace at once raised a host of others. Was it safe now for the Romans to retire from Greece; to abandon any surveillance of the defeated Philip, who was allowed to retain his kingdom; to hope that King Antiochus the Great of Syria, who had moved into western Asia Minor and had possessions on the Thracian coast in Europe, would keep his distance; to overlook the fact that the Aetolian League, discontented with the peace treaty, was capable of mischief; to turn a blind eye to the fact that the Achaean League, in the management of its own affairs in the Peloponnese, seemed to the Romans to be aggressively incompetent? Or should the Romans themselves garrison 'the fetters of Greece', the posts from which Philip had been forced to withdraw his troops?

The Romans were (and never again) in an idealistic mood. At the Isthmian Games in 196 their intention was announced: they were going home. They kept their word, and in 194 the last Roman soldier left Greece. Two years later the Aetolians invited Antiochus, who now had Hannibal as an adviser, to cross to Greece and save them – from Rome! Mounting an ill-prepared expedition, Antiochus wintered in Euboea in 192. The Romans crossed and drove him out of Greece; they defeated him at Magnesia in Asia Minor in 189. By the peace treaty he was forced to abandon most of Asia Minor and, like Carthage, he had to reduce his navy to a token force of ten ships. After that it was the turn of the Aetolians. They were given peace on humiliating terms by a treaty which made them Rome's dependent clients.

Still, apart from heavy indemnities, Rome took nothing, and it looked as if she would be content to exercise her influence on eastern affairs from a distance. The substantial prizes, territory in Asia Minor from which Antiochus was forced to withdraw, went to Pergamon and to Rhodes. Both states basked in Roman favour – for a time.

Then Roman suspicion was roused against Perseus, who had succeeded his father Philip as King of Macedon, and the Romans went to war with him. By this time every Greek wanted the Romans out of the eastern Mediterranean. The Greek and Hellenistic states would have liked to return to their traditional power-politics, free from the Roman interloper's interference. There is no doubt that at heart, King Eumenes of Pergamon, Rhodes and the Achaean League hoped for Perseus' victory. Instead, he was defeated at Pydna in Macedonia in 168, and lost his throne.

Still Rome showed no acquisitive ambition in the East. Macedonia was divided into four independent republics, and its valuable mines were closed down. But Rome's eastern allies, despite the scrupulous correctness of their official attitude during the war, were now to be punished for what the Romans rightly thought to have been their true feelings. King Eumenes of Pergamon was cold-shouldered; Rhodes was informed that the territory granted her earlier in Asia Minor was not hers at all; and she was extinguished commercially by the Roman declaration of Delos as a free harbour. The Achaeans were told to provide a thousand hostages, who included Polybius, one of their leading statesmen.

After this, Achaean politics disintegrated in the familiar manner of politics in Greece. The pro-Roman party was unscrupulous, strengthening its own position by laying information to the Romans against its opponents, who grew more and more fanatical. In 149, there was a rising in Macedonia, under a pretender to the throne.

More startling still was the sudden decision of the Romans to exterminate Carthage. Carthage had accepted the humiliation of the peace treaty which followed Zama and, despite incessant provocation by her neighbour the King of Numidia, whose agression the Romans openly supported, the Carthaginian government showed patient restraint. In 150, however, their patience was exhausted. They attacked Numidia and were defeated. In Rome the veteran Cato was spokesman of a new policy of ruthlessness. The time had come for Carthage herself to be destroyed.

The Macedonian pretender was fought and beaten. Carthage was invaded, defeated and its city was utterly destroyed. War was declared against the Achaean League, and Corinth too was sacked and pillaged. Rome's patience, it seemed, was exhausted, and was to be replaced by a hideous new ruthlessness. Her honeymoon with diplomacy was at an end, and imperialism was on the march. Africa (Tunisia) was now, like Sicily, Corsica-Sardinia and the two Spains, to be a Roman province. Its capital was Utica, which had prudently allied itself to Rome before the débâcle. Macedonia, too, with Achaea, was made a province.

Told in these simple terms, the story of Roman expansion in the first half of the second century BC has an appearance of simple inevitability. But what motives impelled them? Even though it was Philip who took the initiative in declaring war on them in the Hannibalic war, he was, on his own, no more serious a menace than Pyrrhus who, when Rome was far weaker, was not a serious menace at all. The Hellenistic kingdoms operated in a sphere of their own, and Rome had nothing to fear from them. But by the tradition of their own history Romans disliked kings, and were incapable of understanding that in the Hellenistic world people were accustomed to kings and did not resent their rule. The Greek states irritated them easily, pretentiously claiming a part in world affairs which their strength and resources did not warrant; also they stupidly enjoyed baiting Roman commanders, making fools of them in public, particularly when these commanders were, as the clever Greeks realised, exceeding the instructions which they had received from their government in Rome. So the Romans made few friends, except for the most despicable Greek statesmen who traded on their influence at Rome to achieve their own personal interests.

With Carthage the case was different. The old terror of Carthage revived, however unreasonably. Carthaginian power in Sicily had once menaced Italy; now it could be claimed that Sicily was Roman and menaced in its turn by metropolitan Carthage, 'a sword pointed at the heart of Rome'. So for the peace of the western world Carthage had to be eliminated.

The conqueror demoralised and the conquered humiliated

In just over sixty years, since 218 BC, Rome had mastered the world, and Polybius' history was written to describe the process, to give the facts and to explain them. Though strengthened, Rome was not altogether improved by the extension of her power.

This was the time when 'conquered Greece first took her fierce conqueror captive, and introduced the arts to the uncouth Latin'. At its best, this conquest did no harm. The Romans were none the worse for being given the opportunity, for the first time in their history, of going to the theatre and seeing plays, at first Greek tragedies and comedies in Latin translation. They were none the worse for basing their educational system on that which prevailed in Greece. There was no great harm in introducing 'the uncouth Latin' to Greek painting, sculpture and architecture. Nor was there any harm at first in exchanging the dank private wash-house for the spacious amenities of elegant public baths, or even in the practice of Greek athletic exercises – running, wrestling, throwing the javelin and trundling the hoop, exercises for which young men stripped naked, to supplement, as long as they did not replace, the manly Roman sports of riding and hunting.

But in destruction and pillage the Romans did worse even than later ages were to do – in wanton destruction by the brutal military, worse even than the Turks, who were to turn the Parthenon into a powder-magazine; in pillage, worse even than the Crusaders, the medieval popes or eighteenth- and nineteenth-century military conquerors and opulent private travellers from western states, whose loot now fills the great museums of western Europe and of America. The Romans had not the excuse that they were preserving masterpieces of art which would otherwise have disintegrated or even have perished. They might at first have expressed the specious view that the best things should be in the best places, the temples and fora of their own capital city, Rome; but such patriotic enthusiasm soon gave way to the greed or mania of the private collector. And rich Romans began to covet a new style of living – splendid country houses (villas), with spacious colonnades to set off the masterpieces of Greek sculpture which they had acquired, often from clever Greek forgers, whose 'copies' were convincingly passed off as originals to these new, wealthy and ignorant Roman clients.

But Romans did not only buy; they also stole. In war, the loot of victory had always been the Roman general's prerogative. Part, by long convention, he distributed to his troops. The lion's share was exhibited in the procession at his triumph at Rome, and then made over by him to the State. Or, if the loot was cash, he spent it on the erection of some public building in Rome, often a temple which he had vowed on the eve of the critical battle which he had won. The building, whether a basilica or a temple, was the State's; for himself and for his descendants, it was enough that it carried the inscription of his name as donor.

But Roman generals and administrators in the first half of the second century BC were suspected of taking advantage of their public position to feather their own nests. After the war with Antiochus public charges were laid even against the great Publius

After a successful campaign against foreign enemies (but not against citizens in civil wars) a general was honoured by the Senate with a triumph. He processed with his troops through the streets of Rome to the temple of Jupiter on the Capitol, accompanied by music and the shouting of his troops (who had licence to shout whatever scurrilities they fancied). The booty captured in the war was carried in carts, pictures

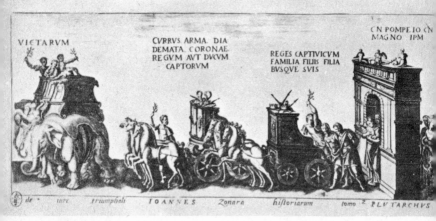

Scipio and his brother. By 149 it was openly recognised that Romans and gentlemen, senators, who by the oldest of Roman traditions received no remuneration for the discharge of public office, were capable of exploiting their official positions abroad to extort money from 'allies', even from the inhabitants of the provinces which they had been appointed to govern. So a permanent extortion court was established at Rome which could be called into session at any moment, and it was open to any Roman 'ally', acting through a patron, normally a member of one of the foremost Roman families, to prosecute at Rome for the recovery of money which he claimed to have been extorted from him illegally by a Roman senator acting in his official capacity.

The period of Rome's imperial conquests was not a happy one from the point of view of the conquered. First-class powers do not enjoy degradation to second-class rank. Still less do they enjoy ceasing to be independent powers at all.

Hellenistic kings, who tended to be easy-going people, had been accustomed to talking to one another as equals, and they had con-

illustrated notable events in the fighting, and conquered
enemy leaders, such as Jugurtha or Vercingetorix, were led in
chains and, when the Roman general mounted the Capitol, taken to
the prison (the *Tullianum*) and strangled. These illustrations,
based on numerous descriptions of triumphs by ancient
writers, were done by Stefano du Pérac in the sixteenth century.

fronted Greek cities and Leagues in the character of patronising
benefactors. Now they received orders from Roman commoners,
who observed none of the traditional diplomatic conventions and
took no trouble to hide the fact that they regarded kings as a class
with complete contempt. They spoke to them as to inferiors.

The appeal of liberty and freedom was the deception which in
history it has so often proved. Where the Romans arrived as
'liberators' – in Spain from the Carthaginians, in Greece from
Macedon and in Asia Minor from Antiochus – they were at first
welcomed by peoples who believed in a simple-minded way that,
once the disinterested act of liberation had been performed, the
Romans would not merely go home in the physical sense but would
also abandon any protective interest in the peoples whom they
freed. They found themselves mistaken. When the Romans came,
they came to stay.

There was something very frightening, very unattractive about
the conquering Roman. His slashing Spanish sword hacked bodies
like meat, disfiguring corpses in a way in which the spear, the
arrow and the thrusting sword did not disfigure them. He con-

quered in virtue of that splendid discipline in the battlefield, which Polybius admired so greatly. But he went further; he looted to order. The general gave the word, and the private secured what he could.

And there was something about the trappings of Roman power which sent a shiver down the foreigner's spine. Not inappropriately did the word 'Rome', spelt in Greek letters, mean 'brute force'. The first honeymoon, when Flamininus announced the freedom of Greece to a hysterical crowd at the Isthmian Games in 196, was soon a memory of the past. There was no mistaking the significance of the symbol of Roman imperialism, the rods and axes which the proconsul's lictors carried. Even in the course of normal administration 'the Roman governor holds assizes. Men attend in answer to summons. They see him on his tall platform, surrounded by his lictors, pronouncing his arrogant sentences. The rods are there to flay their subjects' backs, the axes to cleave their necks. There is a succession of these tyrants, every year a new one.'

Imperial expansion overseas

There is no more effortless means of acquiring property than to inherit the property of others; and once Rome had extinguished the Macedonian monarchy and humbled King Antiochus III of Syria, she proceeded to extend her Eastern Empire in this easy manner. The royal families disintegrated and, by setting son against father and brother against brother and by holding princes as hostages in Rome, the Romans helped on the disintegration. Natural infertility also played its part. So, with no prospective successor of their own blood, kings made Rome heir to their kingdom. By doing this they might hope to buy peace for the remainder of their lifetimes and to save their countries the damage of a civil war between pretenders when they died.

In this way Rome acquired and made provinces of Asia, the earlier Pergamene kingdom, in 133 BC, Cyrene in 74, Cyprus in 58. She could, indeed, have claimed Egypt on similar grounds in the late Republic but preferred to do a financial deal with Ptolemy

Magistrates' attendants (lictors)
carrying rods and axe, symbols of
the magistrate's (or general's) absolute
power of life and death over
non-Romans and (subject to the right
of appeal) over Roman citizens.

Auletes, who had taken possession of the kingdom; which explains why Cleopatra, Auletes' daughter, survived as the last great Hellenistic ruler, to captivate Julius Caesar and, more disastrously, Mark Antony. Bithynia was bequeathed to Rome by its last king Nicomedes, who died in 74 BC, and after eventual success in the severe struggle with Mithridates of Pontus for its acquisition, Rome found herself in effective possession of most of Asia Minor and Syria with, in addition to Asia, provinces of Bithynia-Pontus, Cilicia and Syria. Their acquisition and organisation (in 63) was Pompey's great achievement.

East of Syria lay the kingdoms of Armenia and Parthia. Should they be allowed to arrest the process of eastern imperial expansion? Crassus, who challenged Parthia, was disastrously defeated at Carrhae in 53 BC. Antony campaigned against the Parthians with loud ambition and without success. Was there to be a finality about Pompey's conquests? Or must the Romans go further?

The acquisition of a Hellenistic kingdom brought benefit to Rome, and also responsibility. The royal lands, the property of the late kings, became the absolute property of the Roman people, to sell or to lease for rent; the kingdom itself became a Roman province, an administrative responsibility.

The extension and consolidation of Rome's empire in the West during the late Republic was a very different matter. The mines of Spain produced handsome quantities of precious metal, but there were close on two centuries of intermittent guerilla fighting, often of great severity, before the mountains were cleared and the country mastered, west to the Atlantic coast. Spain was Rome's first continental province, and the last Roman province to be pacified; so Livy wrote at the time of Augustus. Southern Gaul, Provence, on the main road to Spain, was made a province in 121 BC, civilised territory already for the most part, with its ancient Greek cities like Massilia (Marseilles), a very old ally of Rome, and Nice and Antibes on the coast.

The rest of Gaul, up to the Rhine and the English Channel, was

Table 1 Republican provinces

241 BC	Sicily	
238	Sardinia-Corsica	2
198	Nearer and Further Spain	4
146	Africa	
	Macedonia	6
133	Asia	7
121	Transalpine Gaul	8
100?	Cilicia	9
89	Cisalpine Gaul	10
74	Cyrene	11
63	Bithynia-Pontus	
	Syria	13
58	Cyprus (added to Cilicia)	

conquered by Julius Caesar between 58 and 51 BC. Brilliantly and mercilessly accomplished by a man of genius, the conquest was an unprovoked enterprise, aggressive imperialism of the starkest kind. It has been calculated that a third of all the Gauls of military age were killed, and another third captured and sold into slavery. Enormous booty was taken in plunder from Gallic shrines.

The conquest raised further questions and left its imperial legacy. Were the English Channel and the Rhine satisfactory limits? Should Britain now be invaded? Should Rome push further east across the Rhine into the forests and swamps of Germany? Caesar had conducted short explorations in both directions.

The end of republicanism at Rome
An argument of those Romans who were frightened in the second century by the extinction of Carthage, the only opponent whose strength, in their opinion, was sufficient to cause Rome any real

fear, was that, if the aggressive vigour of an expanding power ceases to be, by necessity, outward-looking, that aggressive vigour turns on itself and the result is civil war. In Rome this happened, and the hundred years after the sack of Carthage saw an acceleration of turmoil in Roman internal government, as the old machine of republicanism, which Polybius admired so fervently, was less and less able to deal with the problems of domestic disorder and of imperial conquest and control. For conquest, consolidation and response to the threat of foreign invasion over a huge extension of frontiers, regular, professional armies were needed; annual conscription for a limited number of years of military service of Romans and Italians taken from their civilian employments, to which at the end they would return, was no longer tolerable or, if it had been tolerable, efficient. In 107 BC Marius enrolled volunteers to fight Jugurtha; this act marked the end of the old Roman army and the beginning of the new.

Anyhow, Rome's Italian allies were no longer the convenient milch-cows which, for the supply of military manpower, they had been in the long period of Roman imperial expansion. In 90 BC the Italians revolted, and Rome had no option but to give them the full Roman citizenship. Every free man living south of the Po was henceforth a Roman citizen. As the bulk of Roman citizens was now unable to attend public assemblies and elections in Rome, the traditional city-state form of Roman government was immediately obsolete, though the fact was not appreciated by Roman politicians. Had representative government with parliamentary constituencies been envisaged, a modified republicanism might have continued, but this was something which nobody as yet had the wit to devise. The problem was one to which in the end Roman armies under ambitious self-seeking generals supplied the answer.

Protracted wars at a great distance from Rome could no longer be conducted by a consul who, after a year's command, retired in favour of another annual commander. Regular armies required regular generals, and for great wars they required singularly gifted men like Marius, Sulla, Pompey and Caesar. Such men, through their conquests, achieved a stature and entertained personal ambitions which were incompatible with republicanism. At the end of their campaigns they stormed back to Rome, making demands for themselves and for their armies. The senate, no longer an 'assembly of kings', but a caucus of smaller men than the general by whom they were confronted, replied in the language of republicanism, which was already an archaic language.

The new leaders rose on the shoulders of the new armies – Marius, Sulla and finally Julius Caesar, who in the last months of his life governed Rome and the empire as a dictator with absolute powers. After Caesar's murder in 44 BC, the armed forces of his great-nephew Octavian fought those of Antony, to decide which of the commanders should rule the world. Octavian won the battle of Actium in 31 BC, became Augustus and the empire of the Caesars was established. This, starting as a principate and finishing as an autocracy, was the government of Rome for the last four centuries of its imperial existence.

Administration

Roman magistrates were chosen by popular election, the consuls and praetors by a form of election which was determined by the votes of the rich. The senate in Rome controlled all public policy, both domestic and foreign, and all public administration. Though there were no published reports of its proceedings before Julius Caesar introduced the practice in 59 BC, there was rarely any secrecy about its debates, whose outcome was at once made public. Since peace terms at the end of a war and foreign policy generally were determined by the senate, it was in what were for the future momentous debates (of which we have no record) that the senate in 241 and 238 decided that Rome should assume permanent responsibility first for Sicily, then for Sardinia-Corsica. The senate in fact decided in that moment that there should be a Roman empire. After this the decision whether or not to annex conquered territory (as Macedon was not annexed in 167) or to annex and make a

province of it (as Macedon was made a province in 146) was the
senate's. It was a mark of the arrogance of the new type of war-lord
in the days of the senate's decline that Pompey on his return from
the East in 62 BC expected the senate to rubber-stamp his own
creation of two new eastern provinces, Bithynia-Pontus and Syria,
and his reorganisation of Cilicia without even the formality of a
debate.

On a report from its own officer in the field, usually the announcement of victory and armistice terms by a successful general, the
senate debated the main lines of the settlement and then sent out a
commission of ten of its own members with absolute power, in
association with the general, to make detailed arrangements on the
spot in keeping with the principles of its own resolution. If a permanent province was created, the general and the Ten drew up and
published a provincial charter, a *lex provinciae*, which henceforth
was to be the basic constitution of the province, whose terms
could only be varied by a decision of the senate at Rome, though in
many matters of detail and interpretation it was supplemented by
the edict which each successive governor issued on arrival. In the
case of the extreme western provinces, the two Spains and the
Gauls, which constituted novel territorial units, a variety of tribes
which had never before been united, the Romans were breaking
new ground, even if there was soon a standard constitution which
they introduced with appropriate deviations in individual cases.
The new eastern provinces, on the other hand, had long existed as
political units under their kings and here the Romans, who were
not so foolish as to believe in rigid political ideologies, took over
as much as possible of the existing political organisation, in
particular the system of tax-collection.

If circumstances warranted it, as in Sicily in 131 BC, after the
slave-revolt the senate might scrap the *lex provinciae* and replace it
by another.

Provincial administrators as selected in Rome
At the beginning of each year the senior elected magistrates waited

for the senate to determine – in a debate at which they were present and indeed at which one of the consuls, an interested party, presided – what in their year of office they were to do; in Roman terms, to allocate a *provincia* to each of them, whether directly or, as a general rule, by instructing them to cast lots.

Consuls were thought of always as men of war. Each was generally instructed by the senate to levy a specified number of troops from Roman citizens and Italian allies, and to proceed with them to some theatre of war or disorder, often to replace a consul of the previous year.

Consuls were elected with a view primarily to their being commanders-in-chief of the armed forces. The new regular provinces of the empire were, anyhow in theory, conquered and pacified areas on which a commander-in-chief and a large army would be wasted. It was therefore only on very rare occasions, when there was a military crisis, that the senate selected as the consul's province of the year one of the new established provinces of the empire. Sicily, for example, was made a consular province in 132 BC because of the serious revolt of slaves in the island. Alternatively, a consul might receive one of the settled provinces with the intention that he should use it as a military base from which to conduct a war outside its boundaries and indeed outside the empire's frontiers, as L.Lucullus received Cilicia and perhaps Asia in 74 BC in order to embark on war with Mithridates. Since 123 BC, by a law of C.Gracchus, the consular provinces had to be selected in a senatorial debate before the consuls themselves were elected. This reform had many advantages. It prevented the senate from fobbing off an unpopular consul with an insignificant province. It also suggested to the electors, that, if the consular provinces were likely to involve large and critical military operations, they would be wise to cast their votes for the candidates with the best military records.

Praetors, on the other hand, were predominantly civil administrators, their original function being the administration of the law as supreme judges in Rome, a function which praetors never ceased to perform. When there were two praetors, one administering civil law among Romans, the other dealing with cases in which non-Romans were involved, they cast lots on entering office to determine their respective functions for the year. It was a reasonable decision that the government of a settled province, largely a matter of the just administration of law, was a comparable function and therefore on the creation of the first two and then the second two provinces, the number of praetors was increased first to four and then to six. Normally the praetors were instructed by the senate to cast lots at the start of the year as before to determine their respective duties for the year. So that on assuming office between 198 and 146 BC, a praetor would not know whether he was going to spend the year with his family in Rome, sitting on the Bench, or whether he was going to spend it as a grass-widower in Sardinia, Sicily or in Spain. For women were forbidden to accompany magistrates out of Italy on official duty.

At the start the provinces changed their governors each year.

When Macedonia and Africa were made provinces in 146 BC, the number of praetors should have been increased to eight if the system was to continue. In fact, however, it had already broken down, largely because of the distance between Rome and Spain.

At the end of the year, if not relieved, the governor retained his title to govern, his absolute power (without any appeal from his decisions), which the Romans called *imperium*, but after his magisterial year he held this not as a magistrate but as a pro-magistrate. When his year expired, if he was still in post, he was a pro-magistrate and, whether an ex-consul or an ex-praetor, he was generally called a proconsul. So, as the second century wore on, an increasing number of provincial governors were pro-magistrates and in this way the difficulty created by the inadequate number of praetors was got over.

A result of regulations made by Sulla as dictator (82-79 BC) was that for the future all provincial governors were pro-magistrates from the start. The greater complexity of domestic administration in Rome, in particular the large increase which Sulla made in the number of permanent standing criminal courts, each of which required a praetor as its president, now gave full-time employment during their year of office in Rome for both consuls and praetors, whose number he raised to eight. They were expected – though there was no compulsion on them if they declined – to proceed in the following year to a provincial government.

In the case of the consular provinces this reform of Sulla had consequences which he should have foreseen. For whatever reason, elections were moved back from the end of the year, which since 153 BC had started on 1 January, to July. The consular provinces were generally selected under Gracchus' law in the previous March. Their selection should have indicated anticipation of critical military situations, even the prospect of war. Yet the consuls would not be free to take up their military commands until the end of their consulships, eighteen months after their election and twenty-one months after their provinces had been selected. The ensuing dilemma helped to destroy the Republic, for when a military emergency arose – the war against the pirates, for instance, in 67 or a setback in the third Mithridatic war a year later – an urgent appointment had to be made. Such appointments came to be made not by the senate but by the popular assembly on the proposal of a tribune, since the regular method of senatorial appointment was clearly ineffective. So the way was opened to the new war-lords, Pompey and Julius Caesar.

Governors and their staffs

The visible marks of the provincial administrator's imperium accompanied him when he was engaged on official duties, attendants (lictors) carrying the symbolic rods and axes (*fasces*). If he was preceded by six lictors, each having six rods in his bundle, he was a praetor or an ex-praetor. If there were twelve, he was a consul or ex-consul.

His absolute power (imperium) was restricted to the territory of the province which he was appointed to govern. When he was replaced by a successor, his absolute power ended at the moment when he crossed the boundaries of his province on his way home, though he was accompanied by the trappings of his office, his lictors and fasces until he entered the city of Rome.

As has been seen, each province received from Rome not only a governor but also a financial secretary, one of the quaestors of the year. Sicily received two, one stationed at Lilybaeum in the west, which was the original residence of the governor, the other at Syracuse, which was originally not part of the Roman province and was acquired only in the second Punic war. Very rarely in the late Republic was a governor allowed to select his quaestor, as Caesar chose Antony in 52 BC; normally quaestors like consuls and praetors cast lots to determine their official duties.

A quaestor in the late Republic was about thirty, a praetor ten years older and a consul two or three years older than that. Much obviously depended not only for the two men themselves but also for the province on the good relations of a governor and his quaestor. The governor, if a consul, was at the top of the ladder; if a praetor, he was near the top, perhaps as high as he would ever go. The quaestor's feet were on the bottom rung. A good relationship was something about which Cicero and others spoke lyrically in public: the governor was a second father to his quaestor, a personal relationship was established which would outlive the year or two that they spent together abroad. There were discreditable cases in which this association was nothing better than a partnership in crime.

Apart from the quaestor, the governor was accompanied by a small staff of *legati*, normally senators like himself, men qualified to advise and, if necessary, to deputise for him, whether as judges in court or as commanders on campaign, acting in virtue of his own imperium, which he could confer on them for specific and limited purposes. Normally a consular governor took three legati, the senior of whom might himself be an ex-consul. Such delegation of command was on the increase in the late Republic and the precursor, as will be seen, of the general system of provincial administration in imperial times. In 67 BC, Pompey was given a staff of perhaps twenty-four, certainly fifteen, legati against the pirates, men whom he made admirals of the various flotillas of his fleet in the great 'sweep' by which he rounded the pirates up. Julius Caesar in Gaul had perhaps as many as ten, each of whom acted as a legionary commander under himself as commander-in-chief. Cicero had two military experts, one of them his brother, among his legati when he governed Cilicia in 51-50 BC and, no military man himself, he wisely abandoned the command of his legions to them. For, apart from the great armies which march noisily through the history books, raised for great enterprises and, serving under warlords like Marius, Sulla, Pompey and Caesar, there were small permanent detachments of Roman soldiers, signed on for long-term – perhaps twenty years – service in most provinces, quietly and inconspicuously employed, largely no doubt on police duties.

Legati in the late Republic joined a governor's staff at his personal invitation. They accepted from friendliness and, no doubt, from a general liking for administration, but sometimes, if they were ex-praetors or of lower political standing than that, with an eye on their future careers.

The legati occupied an official position on the governor's staff. This staff was further swollen by a number of young Romans of high rank (*comites*) who wanted to see the world and gather experience which might help them in their later political careers. This might even be a convenient opportunity of doing a little business for the family, if the family happened to own property in the particular province. A governor sometimes took out his sons and nephews, even if they were as young as thirteen or fourteen. He was often embarrassingly importuned by his friends to give places on his staff to their sons.

Under a good governor like Caesar, a cadet acquired valuable experience. Yet it was when serving as a cadet on the staff of his virtuous uncle, the younger Cato, that Marcus Brutus first engaged in a corrupt, illegal, if highly profitable, venture as a money-lender to the city of Salamis in Cyprus.

As so far described, the governor and his staff were all amateurs, however gifted. There were, however, a small number of people with professional qualifications. The governor had his doctor, his priest and a *praeco*, who was a sort of marshal at public ceremonies. And he had his personal secretary, a slave or freedman, his *accensus*. This man has great interest as being the prototype of the important freedman civil servants of the early Empire. He might have experience of the province, like Cicero's accensus in Cilicia, who had already served under an earlier governor. In as far as he controlled the governor's correspondence and, indeed, access to him, his influence was very great, for good or bad. A good accensus was efficient, self-effacing, inconspicuous, a bad accensus sought and found the limelight and, whether justly or not, the governor was criticised for submitting weakly to his influence.

So far, no professional civil servants. The only professional civil servants at Rome were the scribes (*scribae*), some free men, some freedmen, some slaves, in the treasury. They were in regular employment and their relations to the annual quaestors of the treasury were comparable with those of the permanent civil servant to his minister today.

Scribes were not clamped to the benches of the treasury in Rome. Every year they cast lots and a number of them went out to the provinces as professional financial experts, two on the staff of every governor.

Taxation

Taxation and finance are the nub of all administration everywhere at all times, and were to be a major element later in the collapse of the empire.

There were at first two systems of provincial taxation: direct and tithe. Direct taxation (*stipendium*) was based on heads (*per capita*) and on property. For its collection a census had to be made periodically. This was the system of taxation which Rome imposed on her western provinces. As a general rule cities were agents in its collection on behalf of the quaestor and his staff.

In Sicily and in most eastern provinces, however, the Romans inherited a complicated system of taxation based on the tithes of

Roman scribes (*scribae*) making entries on wooden tablets. The *scribae* were permanent officials of the Treasury at Rome and they cast lots each year to determine which of them should accompany proconsuls to the provinces and act as their financial assistants.

crops (*decumae*). This had been devised by Hellenistic kings and had been collected by armies of civil servants such as the Romans did not possess. The Romans, therefore, farmed out the collection of such taxes to private individuals and to commercial companies (*publicani*). In some cases the auction was held in the province; in Sicily, for instance, for the collection of corn tithes.

The sums involved in Asia and some of the eastern provinces were very large indeed and, by a law of C. Gracchus, the auction, to cover a five-year period, was held by the censors in Rome. In Rome there were syndicates with chairmen, boards of directors and shareholders, who bid. These were big businessmen, members of the equestrian class. The company which secured the contract kept agents in the province and, under them, a great staff of smaller fry were tax-collectors, the hated 'publicans'. In bidding at Rome a company assessed the probable yield of the taxes and added a percentage to cover its own expenses and a reasonable profit.

In an honest world the system might have worked well, but in the Roman empire the temptations proved too great. The publicani interested themselves in a number of subsidiary activities. They lent money on a large scale, often to enable a tax-payer to pay his taxes – and then, when he could not pay the interest on the loan, they distrained on his property. They also brought up from cities their bad debts in unpaid local taxes and then proceeded to enforce their payment by the same unprincipled means.

There was, therefore, in a great number of provinces (even in the West, for in Spain, as has been seen, mining rights were farmed out to private companies in a similar manner) a second order which, while no part of official administration, was closely linked to it; for it was obviously the duty of a provincial governor, as the servant of his government in Rome, to ensure that every official assistance was given to the publicani in their honest tax-collection. Regulations in this field were an important section of the edict which the governor issued on taking up post.

It was one of the governor's hardest problems to establish satisfactory relationship with the publicani. They performed a number of services which gave them an almost official status. Their messengers provided a regular postal service between the province and Rome, on which officialdom often depended. And they provided a world-wide banking service. The money, for instance, which they collected in taxes in Asia was banked in Asia. So the headquarters of the company in Rome, instead of making its annual payment in cash to the treasury in Rome, would instead issue notes of credit to the government which could be cashed in its banks in Asia and neighbouring provinces, providing the administration of the province with the cash it required for its official expenditure. The tax-collecting companies, therefore, were inevitably connected closely with the official administration of the empire.

On the other hand, no governor was ignorant of the fact that they often collected more in taxes than was due; indeed, he might find himself, while fully aware of their delinquencies, adjudicating

in a prosecution against them. Also he knew that they were engaged in a number of enterprises which ran counter to the law – the lex provinciae, decrees of the senate and his own edict. He might well be offered a handsome *douceur*, if he was willing to turn a blind eye to such irregularities. There might, on the other hand, be threats: that, if he interfered with them, they would ensure through their business friends in Rome that things were not made easy for him when he got home.

The governor with the quaestor was responsible for official public expenditure in his province. When he was appointed to his governorship, the senate fixed a ceiling on the sum to be expended in the province during the year on public purposes. This, in Roman

language, was *ornare provinciam*. In fixing the sum the senate acted doubtless on the advice of the treasury, which had the provincial accounts of the previous years. So the governor had to be as careful as a modern government department not to exceed its vote. He was compelled to submit his public accounts for scrutiny to the treasury at Rome within ten days of his return and by a law of Julius Caesar passed in 59 he had to publish copies of his accounts in the two chief cities of his province before he left for home. Accounts, of course, are not always easy for the man in the street to understand, and we have the engaging admission of Cicero that neither he nor his quaestor themselves understood their own published accounts. Still, it is hard to think what more a government could have done to keep a severe check on public provincial expenditure. The governor himself, who was paid no stipend, received a private expense allowance, generously assessed, for whose expenditure he was answerable to nobody. From his personal allowance Cicero in a year saved over two million sesterces. Before Caesar clamped down by his severe law of 59 BC, governors had been able to save large sums by distraining on natives of the province for lavish supplies and hospitality when they were travelling.

Duties and temptations of a provincial governor

As the boundaries of Rome's provincial empire expanded, it was obvious policy for the Romans, wherever possible, to establish good relations with the independent states beyond their boundaries. While in most cases there was no written treaty (because treaties involve obligations), there was a friendly understanding between Rome and these 'client kingdoms' or 'client states'. They would give Rome early warning of the danger of invasion or attack, indeed would be Rome's ears to the wider, potentially aggressive, world; Rome would assist them with the prestige of her name and materially by loans of money and of troops, if needed. This was a means, whether deliberate or not, of bringing more and more territory into the Roman ambit. It was never difficult for Rome to find a specious excuse for interference, even for invasion, and in the long history of Rome the client state of today tended to become the Roman province of tomorrow.

The governor of a frontier province, therefore, had one eye on the frontier and on relations with the foreign states beyond it. Since Sulla he had no independence of military manoeuvre; Roman law forbade him to cross the frontier with an army unless he had orders to that effect from the government at home. Before he left Rome he would generally have received instructions from the senate in this matter.

In the province itself the governor's main concerns were public order and security, administration of justice and the collection of taxes. From the first moment of his appointment in Rome he had

started work on the drafting of his provincial edict. The treasury
could supply him with copies of the edicts of his predecessors. The
edict was of particular interest to money-lenders, since it stated the
maximum rate of interest that the courts would recognise – generally 12 per cent, while the rate of interest in Rome was normally far
lower, often as low as 4 per cent. The money-lender had the alternative of lending at the official rate, knowing that he could sue for
payment in the courts, or of lending at a higher rate and risking it.
The publicani, no doubt, at once put their sharpest lawyers on to
discovering loopholes in the clauses of an edict which penalised
their own malpractices.

The governor's edict was awaited with keen anticipation, and so
was the governor himself. He was greeted, particularly in the East,
with flattering obeisance which few, perhaps, accepted, as Cicero
accepted it, at its face value. Horrifying stories were dinned into
his ears of the irregularities of his predecessor who, as a first act,
had to be given his *congé*. The law since Sulla insisted on his leaving
the province within thirty days of his successor's arrival.

The publicani were not alone in putting pressure on a governor
to pervert the justice which it was his duty to administer. He was
lucky if he was not embraced in the tentacles of corruption which
stretched from Rome itself. His mail brought him ingenuous letters
from acquaintances, often very powerful acquaintances in Rome,
written as if they were his closest friends, of a type which the
Romans called *litterae commendaticiae*. Seventy-nine survive
written by Cicero. They bear a common form. Someone, a friend or
connexion of the writer or of one of his powerful friends, has some
interest or other in a business transaction or in some litigation in
the governor's province. He is an admirable person. While the
governor must not, of course, depart from the straight path of
integrity, his act, if the affair ended satisfactorily, would be
noticed at Rome and would not be forgotten.

Prominent Romans visiting or passing through the province
could also prove an embarrassment. There were commissions of
senators bound on official missions. They expected attention. What

attitude should be adopted towards a distinguished exile? More tiresome were Roman senators who had obtained from the senate the special permission which was required before a senator could leave Italy on any but public business, who arrived to pursue some personal interest, perhaps to claim an inheritance. A considerate governor gave them facilities for travel, even allowed them lictors, as if they were on official business. Before 59 BC they had been a heavy expense on the natives, making demands for free transport and accommodation. Caesar's law of 59 put a stop to that.

Communities in the province which had been granted freedom or which remained in treaty-relationship with Rome from a time earlier than the formation of the province (*civitates liberae et foederatae*) lay outside the governor's jurisdiction. For the rest of the province he administered justice in the capital where he had his residence (Syracuse, for instance, in Sicily; Thessalonica in Macedonia) and also on assizes, stopping at each assize-town on his circuit. He sat in the normal manner of a Roman magistrate with a panel of advisers (his *consilium*), which might include members of his own staff (Verres' consilium is said by Cicero to have contained few others) but which consisted in the main of Roman

citizens resident in the district of the assize-town, the local *conventus civium Romanorum*. A number of civil cases he referred in accordance with the provincial charter for trial by native senates or by assessors. Serious criminal trials he reserved for himself, consulting his advisers before he gave judgment; but in no way bound by their opinions. Natives of the province had no appeal against his judgment, but they could appeal to him against a judgment given by the quaestor or by a legate who presided over a trial as his deputy. A Roman citizen who was brought before him on a criminal charge had no formal right of appeal but a governor was reluctant to try a Roman citizen on a criminal charge in the province and normally referred his case for trial to Rome.

There were three offences for which a governor could be brought to trial on his return to Rome: treason (since Sulla's legislation) if he took an army outside the boundaries of his province without senatorial authorisation; *peculatus*, if he pilfered public moneys; extortion (*res repetundae*) if he extorted money from natives illegally. In the case of extortion at first he was liable, if found guilty, to repay the sum which he had extorted. By C. Gracchus' law, if he was found guilty, he was made to repay twice the sum

A relief from a funeral monument at Neumagen, near Trier. It probably illustrates not payment of tribute but payment to a banker or landlord with two assistants (all clean-shaven) by four Gauls, who are bearded and wear rustic Celtic dress.

which was proved against him, by Sulla's law to pay two and a half times the sum. His condemnation led inevitably to his expulsion from the senate and as a general rule he contrived to escape to voluntary exile so as to avoid the enforcement of the judgment of the court, since the payment of the fine was likely to pauperise him. The murder of natives (for instance by accepting a bribe to condemn an innocent man to death) severely aggravated the crime, but it was not until Caesar's legislation of 59 that he could in such shocking circumstances be arraigned on a criminal charge in Rome with liability to the death penalty – in which case his exile would not be voluntary but compulsory, since the Romans, from strong reluctance to enforce the death penalty on a citizen, gave him the chance to leave and live out of Italy so as to avoid its enforcement.

The prudent governor clearly kept the possibility of such charges in mind. The cautious artist in crime perhaps calculated what was a

margin of reasonable safety. Normally a governor expected to be
in post for about a year, assuming that a year after his own
appointment the senate would appoint a successor to him and that
his successor would leave Rome at about the same time of year and
travel at about the same speed as himself; so that his tenure would
be round about twelve months. He could never be certain, however.
His tenure might be extended for a second year, even for a third, as
happened to Verres in Sicily and to Quintus Cicero in Asia. It was
only at the end of the Republic, and then in the military field, that
an experiment was made with finite long-term commands. Pompey's
command against the pirates in 67 was for three years, Caesar's
command in Gaul originally for five. There were great advantages
in such security of tenure. The proconsul was able to plan ahead
for longer than a period of twelve months; also he was normally in
Rome and would be present in the senate when his maximum

legitimate expenditure of public moneys was fixed.

Normally a governor waited for the arrival of his successor and then left for home within the thirty days which, after Sulla, the law allowed, but there seems to have been no obligation on a governor to remain until his successor arrived or indeed until any certain date at all.

If the governor decided to leave his province and come home, he had to leave a deputy behind him, normally the quaestor, who assumed full imperium at the moment when he took over with the title *quaestor pro praetore* (quaestor with the rank of governor). Or the governor might seek to persuade one of his legati to take over from him.

If a governor died or was killed when in post, his quaestor normally assumed at once the rank of acting-governor. C. Cassius, one of Caesar's murderers in 44 BC, did admirably in such circumstances. He was Crassus' quaestor or acting-quaestor when Crassus was killed at Carrhae in 53. He saved what could be saved from the débâcle, got the survivors back to Syria and there, as *quaestor pro praetore*, did everything possible to prepare against a Parthian invasion of Syria until, two years later, a new governor arrived from Rome.

Imperial responsibility of the government at Rome

At Rome, problems of imperial expansion and consolidation were constantly in the government's – that is to say, the senate's – mind. About imperial (provincial) administration the senate did not think imaginatively, but it did think responsibly, being aware of two responsibilities in particular. These were to maintain integrity on the part of proconsuls, by introducing heavy penalties for those who exploited administration as an opportunity to line their own pockets at the expense of the natives and secondly to prevent a proconsul in charge of an army from using it either to engage in campaigns which the senate had not authorised or to interfere, in the proconsul's own interest, in politics at home. A number of laws were passed, therefore, the first in 149 BC, to penalise offenders, in the first case for extortion (*repetundae*) in the second for treason (*maiestas*).

As has been seen, the laws against extortion became successively sterner in that they increased the size of the monetary fine imposed after condemnation, from repayment of the sum pilfered to the payment of two and a half times that sum. In the end Caesar's law, passed in 59 BC, was a very detailed measure with 101 clauses, and it remained operative under the Empire.

Bribery to secure election to office at Rome was a practice which had its repercussions on the integrity of provincial administration, for the security on which money was lent was the prospective profit to be made in the government of a province, for which the tenure of the praetorship or consulship in Rome was a necessary preliminary. As Verres, governor of Sicily from 73 to 71 BC, the perfect exemplar of republican administrative corruption, is reported to have said, a provincial governor's corrupt practices should earn him three fortunes: the third to support him for the rest of his days in comfort, the second to bribe the jury if he was so unfortunate as to be impeached, the first to repay the money which he had spent in bribery at the elections, success in which had given him his lucrative opportunities. So in the late Republic there was a succession of laws against bribery at the elections (*ambitus*), none of them fully effective, until in 52 BC Pompey took the desperate step of interposing an interval of five years between the tenure of magistracy in Rome and the appointment to govern a province, in the hope that money-lenders would be deterred from lending money to candidates by the thought that they could not expect repayment for at least seven or eight years and in the interval were unlikely even to secure interest on the loan.

Laws against treason, which was always a capital offence, with the inevitable consequence of banishment in the case of condemnation, went back to the year 103 BC. The sternest measure – one under which, had it existed earlier, he would himself have been guilty – was passed by Sulla as dictator and was incorporated in the extortion law of Julius Caesar, a law which Caesar transgressed

more flagrantly than anyone in Roman history when he invaded
Italy with his army from Gaul to fight the government in 49 BC,
ten years after it had been passed.

These were all good laws. The trouble was that they could not be
enforced effectively.

First of all, there were great difficulties in mounting a prosecution
for extortion. The wheels had to be set in motion by the natives of
a province themselves. If they were successful, the instigators of the
prosecution were rewarded with Roman citizenship. As against this
uncertain prospect, the collection of witnesses was an arduous
business, and hindrance might be offered by the governor in the
interest of his predecessor who was the object of the prosecution;
the journey to Rome was expensive; in Rome a barrister (a young
senator) had to be found to accept the brief and, even if approach
was made to a family which stood in the relation of a patron to the
province (for instance the Caecilii Metelli in the case of Sicily, a
connexion of which the Sicilians took advantage in prosecuting
Verres), the family might be unwilling to sponsor a prosecution
because of current issues in Roman politics, always a matter of
family and personal relationships. If a barrister was found and a
prosecution launched, there was still the heavy risk of corruption
in the trial itself. Or the accused man, anticipating condemnation,
might slip away from Rome to a province where he had already
salted away his illicit fortune, as Verres did to Marseilles, and the
whole prosecution might prove to have been a forlorn waste of
time and money.

Trials were trials by jury (*quaestiones*) and, despite every kind of
experiment, it proved impossible to find juries which were neither
biassed nor themselves susceptible to bribes. When senators were
empanelled, they were reluctant to condemn a fellow-senator, a man
with whom they were socially on familiar terms. When equites were
empanelled, the standards of right and wrong were all too often
determined by the degree to which the accused man had, as a
governor, shared in or opposed the malpractices of Roman businessmen in his province, particularly the employees of the tax-collecting

syndicates. Integrity in such cases found its reward in condemnation, the most notorious case being that of Rutilius Rufus, who, condemned for maladministration in Asia in 92 BC when equites were jurors, retired to live his days out as a highly popular resident of the province which he had been condemned for oppressing. At the start jurymen were enrolled from senators, then between C. Gracchus and Sulla from equites and finally after 70 BC from a mixture of the two classes; but, while some men were condemned, there were more cases in which with the help of a little bribery the accused man was acquitted.

Police court news, of course, does not make representative history, and it would be a mistake, just because cases of flagrant miscarriage of justice occupy such a large space in our surviving records of republican provincial administration, to forget that there were plenty of responsible governors like Cicero, whose correspondence when governor of Cilicia 51-0 BC is a lasting advertisement of his own integrity in a post which he disliked intensely and regarded as an intolerable interruption of political life in Rome. Better, perhaps, is the case of Cicero's brother Quintus who, unlike his brother, was evidently a highly gifted administrator. He governed Asia after his praetorship for three years, then served as a commissioner under Pompey in the reorganisation of the corn supply in 57-6. After that he commanded a legion with great distinction in Caesar's army in Gaul and, indeed, in the second invasion of Britain and, finally, as a legate on his brother's staff in Cilicia he made – what his brother could never have been – a good commander-in-chief of the legionary army in the province.

The beginnings of Romanisation

Already in the Republic a beginning was made on what will be seen later to be the distinctive features of romanisation. There were, for a start, two of the great arterial roads of the empire, the Via Egnatia and the Via Domitia. The Via Egnatia, set in hand soon after Macedonia was made a province in 146, was to be the main highroad to the East. At Dyrrachium (Durazzo) it picked up the traffic which had come down the Via Appia from Rome to Brundisium or Tarentum and from there had been shipped across the Adriatic; it crossed the mountains to Edessa, Pella and Thessalonica and later was extended to Byzantium. The Via Domitia in southern Gaul from the Rhône to the Pyrenees, started in 121 BC, greatly improved land communication with Spain.

There were Roman and Latin colonies, on the model of such colonies in Italy, the first Latin colony outside Italy being Carteia, near modern Gibraltar. It was established in 171 as a home for over four thousand men, the sons of Roman soldiers who had fought in Spain in the second Punic War and, instead of returning to Italy, had stayed in Spain and married Spanish women. In 118 BC Narbo Martius (Narbonne), the first citizen colony outside Italy, was established in southern Gaul. Then there were the colonies in Africa where soldiers who had fought under Marius against Jugurtha were settled in 103.

To an increasing extent service to Rome by natives of the western provinces was rewarded by Roman citizenship. An inscription records such a grant to Spanish cavalrymen who fought under Pompey's father in the Social War in 89 BC and Pompey himself granted citizenship in a number of cases after the war against Sertorius in Spain in 72, one of the recipients being Cornelius Balbus of Cadiz, who was to rise to the highest eminence as an agent of Julius Caesar in Rome and, after Caesar's death, to hold the consulship.

2 The Second Empire: Augustus and his successors, 27 BC-AD 193

The new system

'For a quick Utopia there is nothing like a little authority.' This was the lesson of the paralysing disorder of the last decades of Republicanism at Rome and of the protracted horror of the civil wars which lasted intermittently from Julius Caesar's invasion of Italy in 49 to the victory at Actium in 31 of his great-nephew and adopted son Octavian. Once peace returned, almost any price was worth paying for its preservation. Rome's future, the empire's and in many ways, the western world's depended on a man of thirty-two, not particularly healthy, not a particularly good general, but an extremely acute politician who was to show himself in the event a great statesman. He started where Julius Caesar stopped. The problems were still the same, but Caesar's fate gave him the advantage over Caesar; it showed him the sort of solution that he must avoid. He had the opportunity. At the head of sixty legions, he had the power.

The state and empire required a single head, but the inherited prejudices of Republicanism prevented the ruling class at Rome from open acknowledgment of that fact. So his powers must be masked, in contrast to Caesar's, which had never been masked at all. He must carry no offensive title; he could not be King or, like Caesar, Dictator. So he was called *Princeps*, 'First Citizen', 'First Man of State'. And he was given a new name, not an arrogant, self-advertising title like Sulla's 'Felix' or Pompey's 'Magnus', but the austere, semi-religious, exalted name of Augustus. His full name became 'Imperator Caesar divi Iuli filius Augustus', for in 42 BC on the evidence of an unanticipated comet which had appeared at the games held in Caesar's honour after his death in July 44, the senate under strong popular pressure decreed that Caesar was a god.

Augustus' first name 'Imperator' (General) emphasised the fact that he had the army behind his back, and in the circumstances of his achievement of power it was a name which he did not hesitate to use. His successors in the Julio-Claudian line dropped it. It was taken again by the Flavian emperors, for by their time there was no point in concealing the military basis of their or indeed of any emperor's power; and after that it was in regular use by emperors.

The new administration

So in Rome after a certain amount of trial and error and with incredible ingenuity a system was devised which, with small adjustments and natural development as the absolute power of the ruler increasingly asserted itself, lasted for more than two centuries. It was a system by which at first in a kind of reconstituted Republic the *Princeps* appeared to rule in association with the senate. There were annual magistrates as before. There were consuls, still two a year at first, but gradually their term of office was shortened from a year to six months (so that there were four consuls a year) and then to shorter periods still. For, as will be seen, the empire was to stand in great need of consulars (ex-consuls). There were still praetors, twelve to fifteen a year, and still twenty annual quaestors. There were still aediles and tribunes. The senate still met, deliberated, carried resolutions. Superficially it was all the same as before. And the provinces were still governed by proconsuls.

Augustus did not preside in the senate but, when present, was to be found sitting between the consuls. He had been given 'tribunician power' in 23 BC and so, without holding the actual office of tribune, he had the tribune's right to summon the senate and to introduce legislation to it; indeed to have his business taken first on the agenda of any meeting. He possessed the tribune's unrestricted right of veto. He may also have been given consular *imperium*, the supreme power of a consul, without being a consul in name.

At the same time he was a proconsul, like any other proconsul, having been given *imperium proconsulare*, but while every other proconsul received a single province to govern, Augustus was given a large number of provinces, with the right to govern them from Rome through *legati Augusti*, viceroys of his own appointment. Moreover, while every other proconsul's imperium was restricted, as it had been in the Republic, to the province which he governed, as long as he was governing it, Augustus' imperium was

Table 2 Distribution of provinces at the end of Augustus'
principate

Those in bold governed by ex-consuls, in italics by Equites, the others
by ex-praetors; the figures show the number of legions stationed in
military provinces.

Under imperial control		Under Senatorial control (public provinces)	
*Dalmatia	2	**Africa**	1
Egypt	2	**Asia**	–
Galatia, from 25 BC	–	Crete-Cyrene	–
Gallia Aquitania	–	Gallia Narbonensis	–
Gallia Lugdunensis	–	Hispania Baetica	–
Gallia Belgica	–	Macedonia-Achaea	–
Germania Inferior	4	Bithynia-Pontus	–
Germania Superior	4	Sicily	–
Hispania Lusitania	–		
Hispania Tarraconensis	3		
Judaea, from AD 6	–		
Moesia	2		
Noricum	–		
*Pannonia	3		
Raetia-Vindelicia	–		
Sardinia-Corsica, from AD 6	–		
Syria	4		

*Pannonia and Dalmatia were made out of Illyricum, which became an imperial province,
having previously been a public province, in 11 BC.

made *maius*. That is to say, he could interfere decisively in the affairs of another proconsul's province, overriding the authority of that proconsul. And there could be an appeal to him even from a province that was not his.

The senate retained nominal control of the peaceful – the public – provinces, most of them already highly civilised, with large numbers of Roman inhabitants: Hispania Baetica, Gallia Narbonensis (Gallia Cisalpina having been incorporated into Italy by Julius Caesar and having ceased to be a province), Sicily, Macedonia-Achaea, Asia, Bithynia-Pontus, Crete and Cyrene, Africa. Their administration remained what it had been under the Republic. The senate appointed governors, normally for a year at a time, ex-consuls to Asia and Africa, ex-praetors to the rest; and Pompey's law of 52 BC (which Julius Caesar had abolished) having been re-introduced by Augustus, it was not until at least five years had elapsed from the holding of the qualifying magistracy that a man was appointed. He received a money 'vote' for his public expenditure, and he was accompanied to his province by legati and a quaestor, all as before. He was under the authority of the senate, whom he normally consulted on any question of policy in his province.

All other provinces were subject to a single proconsul, the Princeps in Rome, who in Augustus' case was formally granted these provinces successively for ten years or for five years at a time; after Augustus there was no such time limit. And, though we have no information on the point, there must have been some kind of a monetary 'vote' to him such as was made to a normal pro-consul, for his provinces were (with the exception of Egypt, which was made a province on Cleopatra's death) those whose administration – including the pay of the troops – must far exceed the income in taxation. The public provinces, on the other hand, should have shown a handsome profit, in particular Asia; and there must have been some system by which profits on the running of these provinces were pumped into the imperial provinces, to balance their deficits on the year's working.

Provinces of the Empire in the second century AD. The dates indicate when the area became a Roman province.

OCEANUS ATLANTICUS

HIBERNIA

SCANDIA

Vallum Antonini
Vallum Hadriani

BRITANNIA AD 43

Camulodunum
Londinium

CHAUCI

BATAVI

LANGOBARDI

CHERUSCI

Burgundiones

GERMANIA INFERIOR

SUGAMBRI

GERMANIA

BELGICA

CHATTI

LUGDUNENSIS

GERMANIA SUPERIOR AD 74

HERMUNDURI

MARCOMANNI

AGRI DECUMATES

GALLIA 27·4 BC
AQUITANIA

RAETIA 15 BC

NORICUM 15 BC

AD 10
PANNONIA

IAZYGAS

TARRACONENSIS

NARBONENSIS 121 BC

ALPES 14 BC

SUPERIOR

INFERIO AD 10

HISPANIA

ILLYRICUM 167 BC

DALMATIA

LUSITANIA 16 BC

197 BC
BAETICA 198 BC

CORSICA

ITALIA

Roma

SARDINIA 238 BC

Neapolis

Brundisium

MARE

MAURETANIA

AD 40

TINGITANA

CAESARIENSIS

Carthago

SICILIA 241 BC

INTE

GAETULIA

AFRICA PROCONSULARIS

146 BC

Lepcis Magna

TRIPOLIS

GARAMANTES

LIB

SARMATIA

DACIA
AD 106-275

MOESIA
SUPERIOR
AD 6 INFERIOR

THRACIA
AD 46

Byzantium

MACEDONIA
146 BC

REGNUM
BOSPORI

PONTUS EUXINUS

CAUCASUS

COLCHIS

IBERIA
ALBANIA

MARE CASPIUM

BITHYNIA
ET PONTUS ▲

GALATIA
25 BC

ARMENIA
AD 114-17

ASIA
133 BC

CAPADOCIA
AD 17

MESOPOTAMIA
AD 115-17

REGNUM
PARTHORUM

ASSYRIA
AD 115-17

Athenae

ACHAEA
27 BC

LYCIA
ET
PAMPHYLIA
AD 43
CYPRUS
58 BC

CILICIA ▲

SYRIA
63 BC

RNUM

JUDAEA
AD 6

Alexandria

ARABIA
PETRAEA
AD 106

ARABIA

DESERTA

CYRENAICA
74 BC

AEGYPTUS
30 BC

NABATAEI

SINUS
ARABICUS

▲ reorganised 63 BC

Y A

Public Provinces (e.g. Asia) : *below* reporting back to Rome ; *right* outward instructions.

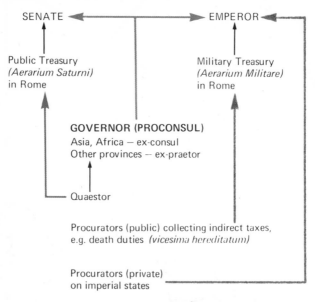

Senate
Public Provinces

Consular (Asia, Africa)	Praetorian	Consular
Governor (Proconsul) ex-consul	Governor (Proconsul) ex-praetor	Governor (*Legatus Augusti propraetore*) ex-consul
Legatus iuridicus (*propraetore*)	*Legatus iuridicus* (*propraetore*)	*Legatus iuridicus*
3 *Legati propraetore*	*Legatus propraetore*	*Legati* (*Legati Augusti legionum*) commanding legions
Quaestor (with 2 *scribae quaestorii*)	Quaestor (with 2 *scribae quaestorii*) (In Sicily, 2 quaestors with 4 *scribae*)	Procurator

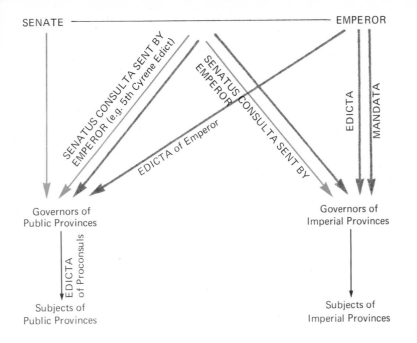

Praetorian	Equestrian (Egypt)	Equestrian (other than Egypt)
Governor (*Legatus Augusti pro praetore*)	Governor (*Praefectus*)	Governor (*Praefectus*, later *Procurator*)
Legatus iuridicus	*Iuridicus Alexandreae* or *Aegypti*	
Legatus (commanding legion, if there was one)	2 *Legati* (equestrian) commanding legions	
Procurator	*Dioicetes* procurators *Idiologus*	
	3 *Epistrategi* (of Upper, Middle and Lower Egypt)	

Emperor

Imperial Provinces

Like any other proconsul, Augustus nominated his legati, each of whom was *legatus Augusti pro praetore*, Augustus' deputy on the spot. There were first his viceroys, ex-consuls in the case of provinces where more than one legion was stationed, ex-praetors in the other major provinces (who were not bound here by the five-year rule which operated in the case of their assuming proconsulships of public provinces). The·title of an imperial viceroy of Syria, for instance, was *legatus Augusti pro praetore provinciae Syriae*.

The legates commanded the armies of their provinces in wars in and beyond the frontiers, but it was not they but the Princeps in Rome who was the commander-in-chief under whose 'auspices' the troops fought. So that after a victory the troops saluted the absent emperor, not the present commander, as the victor and, if a triumph was celebrated in Rome for the success, it was the emperor in person who triumphed. The commander who had won the war for him might be honoured with 'triumphal decorations'.

There were, below the governors, the commanders of the individual legions, again the emperor's personal appointments, each of whom was *legatus legionis* or, formally, *legatus Augusti legionis*. They were normally ex-praetors.

There were certain anomalies. Egypt inspired the fear that an ambitious senator appointed as its governor might repeat Antony's venture, cut the vital corn supply from the province to Rome and challenge the emperor of the day. So far, then, from being allowed to govern Egypt, senators were forbidden even to set foot in the province without the emperor's explicit leave. Instead an equestrian was appointed its governor (*praefectus Aegypti*), and the commanders and officers of its legions were equites too.

In a different way Upper and Lower Germany were also anomalies, tracts on the west bank of the Rhine, south and north of Coblenz (Confluentes) respectively, which had been set up as bases for military expansion across the river into Germany, a project which was in fact abandoned soon after Augustus' death. The two 'governors' of Upper and Lower Germany were, in fact, under Augustus, commanders of two different detachments of the Roman

Army on the Rhine. The civil administration of their territories and the payment of the troops were in the hands of the legate and the financial secretary of Gallia Belgica, one of the three provinces created out of Julius Caesar's conquests.

So by the end of Augustus' principate there was active employment in the empire, in public and imperial provinces together, for nine ex-consuls and thirty-four ex-praetors (eleven governing provinces as proconsuls or legates, twenty-three commanding the legions stationed elsewhere than in Egypt).

This, it seems, exhausted the likely supply of satisfactory senatorial administrators. But there were still provinces which had to be governed: Sardinia-Corsica; the freshly mastered districts between north Italy and the Danube, Raetia-Vindelicia and Noricum, Judaea after AD 6 and, as has been seen, Egypt with its vast wealth and opportunity. There were all the officer-posts in the reorganised auxiliary army. And each of the imperial provinces, like a public province, needed its financial secretary. This last could have been achieved by raising the number of quaestors to forty, as Julius Caesar had done, but in that case the senate would have become unmanageably large, since each ex-quaestor became a member, and a disproportionate number of men would have been frustrated in their careers, achieving no promotion after the quaestorship, since only fifteen of them at the most could have gone further, to hold the praetorship.

So to fill all these posts Augustus created a junior administrative service. The senior administration, as has been seen, was in the hands of senators; the junior service was to be recruited from equites, men with a capital of 400,000 sesterces, while a senator had to possess a million. This was a second step in the process which C. Gracchus had started when he gave the equestrian class the commission of collecting taxes as *publicani* on the state's behalf. Augustus now used them to build an extensive and vital public administrative service. The governors (*praefecti*) of the new minor provinces were equites; and so were the financial officials (procurators) in the imperial provinces, balancing the quaestors in the public provinces. In this last case Augustus may not have failed to reflect that the relation of an equestrian procurator to the imperial legate of a province, a senator, was unlikely to be as close as that of a quaestor to his proconsul; that legates in control of big armies were always potentially dangerous men whose sinister activities a quaestor might have shared but which an equestrian procurator, it was hoped, would lose no time in reporting. Later, from the middle of the first century AD onwards, equites commanded the cohorts and squadrons of the auxiliary army, posts at first held by ex-centurions.

The new army

The army which under the Republic had never been put on a regular footing with fixed terms of service and a guaranteed gratuity or pension had, under the command of rival generals, destroyed the Republic. The emperor's position as commander-in-chief should prevent such a conflict of rival generals for the future. But what kind of army should the new army be? What should be its size? How should it be recruited? What should be its terms of service?

Traditionally the Roman army consisted partly of legions of Roman citizens and partly of specialist units – cavalry, archers and slingers, light-armed skirmishing troops – who were conscripted or who enrolled as volunteers; often they came from allied communities and kingdoms and were commanded by their own compatriots. These were the auxiliaries, largely recruited, because of special skills, from particular areas, Numidians, Gauls and Germans as cavalry, men from the Balearic Isles as slingers, Cretans, Thracians and Syrians as archers. This distinction Augustus retained, with the general provision that the officers of the legions should be Roman citizens, in the main of senatorial rank (the Egyptian legions excepted) and that, with certain exceptions, like the Batavian cohorts which continued to serve under their own native officers, auxiliaries should as far as possible be officered by Romans. The auxiliary army would consist as before of infantry cohorts and of cavalry squadrons (*alae*).

In fixing the size of the new army Augustus made, as the future was to show, an extremely acute calculation. He decided on a legionary army of twenty-eight legions, which was reduced to twenty-five after the loss of three legions in Germany in Varus' disaster of AD 9. The prospective garrisoning of Britain after its conquest in AD 43 called for an increase and in the late first and second centuries AD the size of the army varied between twenty-eight and thirty legions. Thus there were between one hundred and twenty-five thousand and one hundred and fifty thousand legionaries; the auxiliary army was of roughly the same size, but rose in the second century above two hundred thousand.

In addition he created a personal guard, on the model of the cohorts of veterans by which he and Antony had been attended after the battle of Philippi. These were stationed in Italy and, after his death, had barracks on the Esquiline in Rome – nine cohorts, each of five hundred men, under two equestrian praetorian prefects. They were his personal guard in Rome and when he travelled, and in Rome they were available to suppress at the start the kind of rioting which in the late Republic had made a shambles of everyday life in the city. There were also three urban cohorts, under the control of the prefect of the city (a new post), normally a senior consular, who had responsibility among other things for ensuring order at the public games.

To reintroduce from the earlier days of the Republic a system of compulsory military service for Roman citizens, so that the army should be a citizen militia, would have been neither practical nor efficient. The citizen legionaries were to be 'regulars', volunteers or, if volunteers were unavailable in sufficient numbers, men recruited by levy who, in the light of experience, proved to be the better soldiers. If a good recruit presented himself who was not a Roman citizen, he was given the citizenship when he signed on. These men came at first, naturally, from the townships or territory attached to the towns of Italy and the more civilised western provinces, Narbonese Gaul and Spain, where most Roman citizens were to be found; for the legions in the East they came chiefly from Asia Minor.

The auxiliaries, too, consisting of natives or foreigners (*peregrini*), were either volunteers or conscripts, at first recruited largely from client kingdoms on the border of the empire to do local service under their own officers but, with the gradual absorption of the client kingdoms, they were increasingly enrolled by Rome to do service under Roman equestrian officers and liable for transfer from one frontier of the empire to another as exigencies demanded. In fact, specialist troops continued to be recruited from particular quarters of the empire, but other auxiliary units soon came to be replenished by recruiting in the locality where they served. A penalty which the Romans paid for this system in the early days of the empire was to find her troops engaged on the frontiers against Roman-trained auxiliaries who had revolted, as in the Pannonian revolt of AD 6, or against a foreign army – Germans across the Rhine and Musulamii in Africa in the early years of Tiberius – who had been instructed in Roman discipline and fighting methods by a commander who had himself learnt his soldiering in the Roman auxiliary army – Arminius in the first case, Tacfarinas in the second.

The new army was to be recruited on fixed terms of service. Augustus hoped for a term of fifteen years, with five more on the reserve (*sub vexillis*) for legionaries, but a combination of recruiting and financial difficulties enforced a period of twenty years service followed by five in the reserve. Legionaries had fixed pay, 900 sesterces a year, and a guaranteed gratuity of twelve thousand sesterces on discharge. They were forbidden to marry.

This last regulation, in such stark contrast to Augustus' other measures to encourage the procreation of Roman children, was made, presumably, in the expectation that legions would be constantly on the move from one frontier to another. It was first relaxed after more than two centuries by Septimius Severus. Human nature, however, is not controlled by statute law. Legionaries kept women in the civilian quarters which rapidly grew up round their barracks. Their children, born during their period of service, were not Roman citizens unless the women with whom they lived were Roman citizens, which cannot often have been the case.

Auxiliary soldiers served for twenty-five years. They were allowed to marry during that period and after twenty-five years they received Roman citizenship for themselves and the sons who had been born to them or who might be born to them in the future, provided this was from one marriage only. The grant, with names, was inscribed each year in Rome and individuals secured copies, bronze *diplomata*, each with his own name, guaranteed by the seals of witnesses in Rome, which they carried as evidence of their citizenship. Large numbers of such diplomata have been discovered, none earlier than the principate of Claudius; so that it is possible that this automatic grant of citizenship after a fixed term of service was introduced by Claudius and not by Augustus. Some, it seems, took their citizenship and continued in the service, just as some legionaries on discharge signed on again, and it was not until the end of the first century that auxiliaries seem regularly to have taken their discharge at the conclusion of their twenty-five years' service. There is no reason to think that any compensation was paid to their wives if they died or were killed, and we do not know, as we do in the case of the legionaries, what they were paid on service or how large a gratuity they received on discharge.

The payment of gratuities to disbanded armies had provoked recurrent political crises in the Republic. For the future this was admirably regulated, by the arrangements made by Augustus in AD 6. Given the regular length of service and the fixed size of the army, it was easy to work out the maximum sum that could be required each year for the payment of discharge grants. It was then calculated that the income to the state from two new taxes, five per cent death duty and one per cent sales tax, would together produce the necessary sum. So these taxes were earmarked for the *aerarium militare*, a new treasury set up in AD 6, concerned with paying gratuities and nothing else. It was placed in the charge of three ex-praetors, appointed by the emperor and answerable to him.

When a member of the Roman auxiliary army completed twenty-five years service and qualified for discharge, he received Roman citizenship for himself and his sons. The grants were officially posted at Rome, and each beneficiary acquired a sealed bronze diptych (*diploma*) giving his name, unit and date of discharge. This he carried henceforth as evidence of his citizenship. This diploma was discovered at Corbridge and is dated 19 January AD 103. British Museum.

The administration stabilised

With piracy eliminated from the Mediterranean, the navy was a service of secondary importance. There were two permanent home fleets, based on Misenum in the Bay of Naples and Ravenna on the Adriatic, manned by freedmen and slaves, and there were auxiliary flotillas on the borders of the empire, in the Black Sea and on the Danube, in the English Channel and on the Rhine.

There was, however, a Mediterranean life-line by which the great corn ships, vessels carrying up to 350 tons (the equivalent of 7500 sacks) reached Puteoli and Ostia from Egypt and Africa, on which the citizens of Rome depended for their daily bread and, as Republican history had shown, there was no greater cause of demoralisation and panic in the city than fear of a corn shortage. Pompey had been given special control of the corn supply in 57 BC and Augustus assumed responsibility for it in 22 BC, administering it after AD 8 through an equestrian corn commissioner (*praefectus annonae*), who supervised the shipping and the storage in huge granaries at Ostia and at Rome. Special privileges were given to the corn shippers, particularly by Claudius and later emperors. Sixty million modii of corn (just over 400,000 tons) were imported each year, a third from Egypt, a third from Africa and a third from Sicily and the western provinces. The distribution of the monthly free corn ration to between 150,000 and 200,000 registered heads of families domiciled in Rome was placed in the hands of the senate.

These, then, were the emperor's vast responsibilities, on whose successful discharge the safety and well-being of the whole empire depended. He himself depended on the efficiency and loyalty of his subordinates and delegates; in Rome on the swiftly expanding staff of personal freedmen and slaves housed in new blocks of offices on the Palatine who constituted a vast and efficient executive and clerical civil service; on the senators and equites who governed his provinces and commanded his armies.

In the first case he had no option but to employ freedmen and slaves because the notion of working in such a subordinate capacity

...NIC POTEST QVII IMP IIII P P COS
...NITIBVS ET PEDITIBVS QVI MILITANT IN A
...S ALA VOR ET COHORTI BVS DECEM ET VNA QVA
...PPELLANTVR I THRACVM ET I PANNONIOR
...AM DIANA ET GALLORVM EBOSIANA ET HI
...PANORVM VETTONVM C R ET HISPANORVM
ET I VEL CION VM MILLIARIA ET I ALPIN
...RVM ET I MORINORVM ET I CNGERNOC
ET I BAETASIORVM ET I TVNGRORVM MIL
LIARIA ET II THRACVM ET II BRACARAV
GVSTANORVM ET II LINGON VM ET II
DELMATARVM ET S VNT IN BRITANNIA
SVB I NERATIO MARCELLO QVI QVINA ET
NICENA PLVRA VE STIPENDIA MERVE
RVNT QVORVM NOMINA SVB

...RIPTA....
...RIS QVE EORVM C VITATEM DEDIT ET CON
BIVM CVM VXOR BVS QVAS TVNC HABV
SENT CVM EST CIV ITAS I IS DATA AVT SI
QVI CAELIBES ESSENT CVM IIS QVAS POSTE
DVXISSENT DVM TAXAT SINGVLI SINGVLA
A D XIIII K FEBR
M LABERIO MAXIMO II CO
Q GLITIO ATILIO AGRICOLA II C
ALA ET PANNONIORVM TAMPIANAE CVI PRAES
C VALERIVS CELSVS
DECVRIONI
REBVRRO SE VERI F HISPAN
DESCRIPTVM ET RE COGNITVM EX TABV
LA AENEA QVAE FIXA EST ROMAE

At Ostia there were vast granaries for the storage of corn and wholesale depots for the storage of other goods which came in by sea. This splendid building, the Horrea Epagathiana et Epaphroditiana, was erected at the time of Antoninus Pius in the second century AD by two evidently rich and enterprising freedmen, Epagathus and Epaphroditus. It was a warehouse with sixteen large rooms on the ground floor and at least two floors above.

was not at first consistent with a free Roman's dignity. So clever and efficient freedmen, Greeks in particular, did admirable work until, under Claudius, it began to be suspected that, as may happen to civil servants, they were beginning to shape imperial policy; and so adjustments had to be made, as will be seen later.

In the second case everything depended on the skill of the emperor's personal selection. Once Rome had depended on good politicians and statesmen; now its chief need was of good army commanders and good administrators. Here the emperor relied on the reports which he received from senior officers on their subordinates and, among senators, his own virtual control of election to the magistracies in Rome (strengthened by the powers which he later possessed, from Flavian times onwards, of bringing outsiders into the senate by selection) was of great importance. Senators had to adapt themselves to new conditions, to the fact that in holding high military and administrative posts they were no longer virtually independent but were now the emperor's deputies, holding posts and liable to recall at his will, but as the senate rapidly changed its character and the old Roman aristocracy of birth gave way to men of the new world, the Italian municipal and the provincial aristocracy, the situation changed. These last were from the start the kind of men who joined and made careers for themselves in the new equestrian civilian and military services.

Considerable changes were made in the conditions of service in a senatorial career. Governors of public provinces and legates of the emperor alike were now paid a salary, and their wives were allowed to accompany them when they held appointments in the provinces. In the case of wives whose characters were stronger than their husbands', this could make trouble and, if two were in the same province at the same time (Germanicus' wife Agrippina and Piso's wife Plancina in Syria in AD 19), it caused disaster. It made for a different kind of trouble if their morals were not strong at all. But on the whole the change, vigorously opposed by the die-hards in the senate, was a good one.

The general course of the able senator's career would vary only in as far as he showed himself to be predominantly qualified for the tenure of civilian or military posts. He started always by holding a minor magistracy in Rome, and then rose through the quaestorship to the praetorship, after which he was employed in the provinces to command a legion or govern a second-class province. If he achieved the consulship, he qualified for the governorship of a major province and the command of one of the big armies. When in Rome, there were plenty of committees and commissions for him to sit on. His public service was rewarded by public honours, election to a priestly college or the grant of patrician status. And – ultimate distinction, if he was so fortunate – he would become prefect of the city or, some fifteen years after his consulship, pro-consul of Asia or Africa.

For equestrians there was no such regular ascent to the highest offices; the prefecture of the corn supply, the prefecture of the praetorian guard and the prefecture of Egypt. A good emperor's nomination for these posts showed recognition of merit; a bad emperor's nomination sometimes reflected his own incompetence or irresponsibility, as when Nero came to interest himself in the activities of the villainous Ofonius Tigellinus as a horse-breeder and appointed him prefect of the praetorian guard.

A great part of the emperor's strength derived from his immense personal wealth, whose transactions were handled, like the accounts of the public moneys spent in the administration of his provinces, by freedmen and slaves of his secretariat, under his chief financial secretary, the *a rationibus*. This wealth increased steadily by good means and bad, as emperors received legacy after legacy and in due course the impounded property of men who were condemned. Their private estates, managed by personal bailiffs (*procuratores*), mostly freedmen, extended through the length and breadth of the empire. In a world which knew nothing of public loans, the imperial fortune was the only reserve from which, with great emphasis on the emperor's personal generosity, large sums of money could be drawn in the event of sudden calamity – earthquake disaster, the destruction of a city by fire or a serious economic crisis comparable in the modern world with a run on the banks.

A weakness of the emperor's position was that nothing was further from the Republican traditions of the late Republic than the notion of hereditary dynastic succession in a ruling house. Here Augustus was helped by the army's devotion to the memory of Julius Caesar and its determination never to countenance a return to the conditions of service under the Republic. Augustus left no doubt from the start that he intended to establish a dynasty and was perhaps fortunate in the misfortune which he lamented publicly that the young princes of his blood died and he was succeeded by his step-son Tiberius; for Tiberius at his succession was not only the greatest Roman general alive but also probably the man best qualified to be an emperor. However, the system was to run into difficulties. Emperors died without sons, or without good sons, to succeed them. Indeed the fact that the imperial system survived the lives and deaths of Gaius and of Nero shows the immense strength of the foundations which Augustus laid.

History

At the end of the civil wars Augustus had sixty legions on his hands, more than half of which had to be discharged in order to reduce the army to one of twenty-eight legions. The discharged men were settled in twenty-eight military colonies in Italy. Further discharges took place in 14 BC, to military colonies in the provinces, especially Narbonese Gaul and Spain in the West and also Africa, Sicily, Achaea, Asia, Pisidia and Syria, and between 7 and 2 BC of men who returned to their homes and did not need to be settled in colonies. The military treasury not yet being established, Augustus shouldered the whole expense of this operation, mainly from the spoils of the civil war. The cost in all was over a thousand million sesterces.

Table 3 Disposition of the legions in the first two centuries of the empire

This table illustrates the build-up of the Danube army (12 legions in AD 112 as against 7 in AD 20) at the expense of the Rhine army (8 legions in AD 20; 4 in AD 112); also of the army in the East (Egypt excluded), which from 4 legions in AD 20 rose to 7 in 112 and 10 in 215.

It also shows that, apart from sending detachments to wars elsewhere, a number of legions were virtually stationary throughout the period: III Augusta in Africa;

	AD 20	December 68
Hispania Tarraconensis	IV Macedonica, until 39/43 VI Victrix X Gemina, to Pannonia, 63	VI Victrix X Gemina, returned, 68-71, then to Germania Inferior
Germania Superior	II Augusta XIII Gemina, until 45 XIV Gemina, until 43 XVI	IV Macedonica, cashiered in 70 XXI Rapax, destroyed on Danube, 92 XXII Primigenia
Germania Inferior	I V Alaudae XX XXI Rapax	I cashiered in 70 V Alaudae, destroyed in Dacian war, 86 XV Primigenia, cashiered in 70 XVI cashiered in 70
Britain		II Augusta IX Hispana XX Valeria Victrix
Dalmatia	VII XI	XI Claudia p.f. XIV—in transit
Pannonia	VIII Augusta IX Hispana XV Apollinaris	VII Gemina (Galbiana) XIII Gemina, since 45
Moesia	IV Scythica V Macedonica	III Gallica, from Syria in 68 VII Claudia p.f., from Dalmatia, c. 56/7 VIII Augusta, from Pannonia in 45

XXII Primigenia in Germany from the time of its creation by Gaius; II Augusta and XX Valeria Victrix in Britain from the time of the invasion, and VII Gemina, recruited by Galba, in Spain. Two legions VII and XI (both *Claudia pia fidelis* since they had second thoughts about mutinying in AD 42) stayed in the Balkans. The eastern legions, too, remained continuously in the East: Legion XX won its title Valeria Victrix for suppressing Boudicca's revolt in Britain in AD 61.

	AD 20		December 68
Syria	III Gallica VI Ferrata X Fretensis XII Fulminata		IV Scythica, from Moesia, 56/7 VI Ferrata XII Fulminata
		Judaea Jewish War	V Macedonica, in East from 61 X Fretensis XV Apollinaris, in East from 62
Egypt	III Cyrenaica XXII Deiotariana		III Cyrenaica XXII Deiotariana
Africa	III Augusta		III Augusta
	Total: 25		**Total: 30** [*]

5 New Legions

XV Primigenia
XXII Primigenia, both raised by Gaius

[*] I Italica, Nero's new legion, raised in 67, in Lugdunum at end of 68

VII Gemina (Galbiana), raised by Galba in Spain in 68

[*] I Adiutrix, raised in 68 from marines, in Rome at end of 68

	AD 112		AD 215
Hispania Tarraconensis	VII Gemina, since 71		VII Gemina
Germania Superior	VIII Augusta, since 70 XXII Primigenia		VIII Augusta XXII Primigenia
Germania Inferior	I Minervia VI Victrix, since 70		I Minervia XXX Ulpia Victrix
Britain	II Augusta IX Hispana, destroyed ? in 119/20 XX Valeria Victrix		II Augusta XX Valeria Victrix VI Victrix, since 122
		Italia	II Parthica
		Raetia	III Italica
		Noricum	II Italica, since 176
Pannonia Superior	X Gemina, from Germania Inferior, 105 XIV Gem, Mart. Victrix XV Apollinaris, returned from East, 71 XXX Ulpia Victrix		X Gemina XIV Gemina Mart. Victrix
Pannonia Inferior	II Adiutrix, from Britain, 85 ?		I Adiutrix II Adiutrix
Moesia Superior	IV Flavia VII Claudia p.f.		IV Flavia VII Claudia p.f.
Moesia Inferior	I Italica V Macedonica, since 71 XI Claudia p.f.		I Italica XI Claudia p.f.
Dacia	I Adiutrix ? XIII Gemina		V Macedonica XIII Gemina

	AD 112		AD 215
Galatia-Cappadocia	XII Fulminata XVI Flavia		XII Fulminata XV Apollinaris, since 114
Syria	III Gallica, from Moesia in 69 IV Scythica II Traiana?	**Syria Coele**	IV Scythica XVI Flavia
		Syria Phoenice	III Gallica
Judaea	X Fretensis	**Syria Palaestina**	VI Ferrata X Fretensis
		Mesopotamia	I Parthica III Parthia
Arabia	VI Ferrata?		III Cyrenaica

Egypt	III Cyrenaica
	XXII Deiotariana,
	   destroyed in Jewish
	   revolt, 132-4
			II Traiana

Africa	III Augusta		III Augusta
	Total: 30		**Total: 33** eighteen of them legions of Augustus' army

6 New Legions, AD 69–112
II Adiutrix, raised from
   marines at Ravenna, 69
IV Flavia
XVI Flavia, both raised by
      Vespasian in 70
I Minervia, raised by Domitian, in 83?
II Traiana
XXX Ulpia, both raised by
      Trajan in 101?

5 New Legions, AD 113–215
II Italica
III Italica, both raised by Marcus
      Aurelius in 168
I Parthica
II Parthica
III Parthica, all raised by
      Septimius Severus in 197

Reorganisation of the Western Empire

What the Romans had not managed to do in two hundred years must be accomplished: Spain must be reduced to order and peace. Augustus took personal command of operations from 27 to 25 BC. Six legions were engaged and, the task – as he thought – accomplished, he returned to Rome, where the temple of Janus was closed, an indication that the world was at peace. An imprudence; fighting broke out again, as fierce as ever, and a lasting peace was finally enforced by Agrippa in 19. Spain was now organised into three provinces: Baetica, which was senatorial, and the two other imperial, Lusitania (Portugal) and Tarraconensis (the old 'Nearer Spain'). No risks were taken. Three legions were left to keep order in Tarraconensis.

Next Gaul, which Caesar had conquered, but had not had time to organise. The coastal stretch west of the Alps which had been a province since 121 was called Gallia Transalpina or, disparagingly, 'Gaul in trousers', *Gallia Bracata*, in distinction from Cisalpine Gaul, now incorporated in Italy, which was known as 'Toga-clad Gaul', *Gallia Togata*, because since 90 BC many of its inhabitants were Roman citizens. Gaul at large, north of the Alps, was also 'Gaul with long hair', *Gallia Comata*. In Augustus' reorganisation Gallia Transalpina survived as Gallia Narbonensis, taking its name from its capital, Narbo Martius.

Three new provinces were made out of the territory which Caesar had conquered: Aquitania, Lugdunensis, which retained its tribal organisation, 'the Sixty-Four Tribes', and Belgica to the north-east. All were to be second-class imperial provinces, under the administration of ex-praetors. The reorganisation was supervised by Augustus, who spent the years 16 to 13 in Gaul.

Gallia Lugdunensis was an artificial creation. Except in Vercingetorix's great attempt to throw Caesar out of Gaul in 52 BC, the Gallic tribes had never combined, and Augustus hoped to give unity to the new province by the creation of a 'Council of Chiefs' which was to meet annually at Lugdunum (Lyons), the capital, for the formality of electing a priest of Rome and Augustus. Once assembled, the council, it was hoped, would ventilate public feeling and co-operate with the Roman administration. In 12 BC an altar of Rome and Augustus was dedicated with impressive cere-mony by Augustus' step-son Drusus, Rome's first introduction to the West of that ruler-cult which, surviving from the Hellenistic kings in the East, had there sprung into fresh life, as will be seen later.

During the period when Augustus was in Gaul the reduction of the Alps was undertaken by his two step-sons, Tiberius and Drusus, to safeguard north Italy from raiders and to drive through good lines of communication to west, north and east. Noricum and Raetia-Vindelicia were made provinces, at first with legions but later without them and under equestrian governors. In the Cottian Alps the son of a native prince, M. Iulius Cottius, ruled as a dependant of Rome with the title of prefect. Above Monaco a vast trophy was erected in 8 BC, visible from far out at sea, recording that 'under Augustus' command all the Alpine tribes between the Mediterranean and the Adriatic were brought under the suzerainty of Rome'. The names of forty-six different tribes followed. A monument raised by Iulius Cottius gave the names of another eight.

The organisation of Spain and Gaul marked the conclusion of the work which Caesar started with his conquests in Spain and Gaul in 61 and from 58 to 51. But what of Caesar's unaccomplished projects, the conquest of Britain and the conquest of Germany east of the Rhine?

When Augustus left for the North in 27 BC optimists believed that he was bound for one or other of these enterprises and Horace in an ode prayed Fortune to protect him on his expedition against the Britons, 'the last people on earth'. Augustus must have smiled; he had more pressing business on hand. Germany, however, was a different matter. After Gaul was organised and the Alps subdued, he looked for great river frontiers for the northern empire. On the lower Danube the kingdom of Dacia had recently been united under Burebista, but had split again at his death. This was a part of the world that Julius Caesar had been on the point of investigating when he was murdered. Now under Agrippa and, after his death in 12 BC, Tiberius, Pannonia seemed to be mastered and there was the chance of pushing the frontier up to the Danube. Should the Rhine-Danube constitute the frontier, or should the Romans master Germany to the Elbe? The Elbe-Danube had the advantage of being a shorter line, but Germany was a forbidding country to the invader, marshy and thickly forested, without any of the good roads, which had helped Caesar so greatly in his conquest of Gaul. However, proceeding both by land and sea, plentifully assisted by fortune, Drusus reached the Elbe in campaigns between 12 and 9 BC; but then he fell off his horse and died. The hope of conquest, however, was not abandoned; indeed, between 9 BC and AD 4 an altar was built on the west bank of the Rhine at Cologne, now called Ara Ubiorum, which was optimistically intended to win the sympathies of the barbarous Germans and unite them in devotion to Rome, doing what, it was hoped, the altar at Lyons was doing for the sixty-four cantons of Gallia Lugdunensis. In AD 6 a major operation was mounted, an attack from the south-east (under Tiberius) and another from the west on the kingdom of Bohemia, under its king Maroboduus. Twelve legions were engaged.

This was the last moment of optimism. Violent and unanticipated revolt broke out in Pannonia and Illyricum, mastered at the end of three years by Tiberius after desperate fighting. But there was no respite. Immediately in AD 9 came the news that Quinctilius Varus, commander of the Rhine army, husband of a great-niece of Augustus and a sublimely unmilitary general, had been set on in the Teutoberg Forest at a moment when he was introducing native Germans to the charm of Roman law. His three legions were annihilated. There was consternation in Rome, where in the emergency, even slaves were recruited into the legions. Tiberius was given the task of restoring Roman morale and consolidating Roman tenure of the Rhine. The German success was to the credit of an inspired leader, Arminius, a young prince of the Cherusci who had learnt his soldiering as an auxiliary in the Roman army. The Rhine-Danube line was now accepted. Upper and Lower Germany, as has been seen, were two military commands on the west bank of the Rhine, each with four legions. Pannonia now extended to the Danube with three legions, and on the lower Danube there was Moesia with two. Behind this was Illyricum (Dalmatia) with two legions. All were first-class imperial provinces.

Reorganisation of the Eastern Empire

The eastern frontier problem had for its background the terrible defeat of Crassus at Carrhae in 53, Julius Caesar's plans to avenge it by an aggressive war which were frustrated by his death, and the subsequent ineptitudes of Antony, when he revived Caesar's intentions. For the rest of Roman – and early Byzantine – history there were three approaches to the problem. Foolhardy bravado urged the conquest of Armenia (which would involve the assumption by Rome of responsibility for the difficult Caucasus frontier) and of Mesopotamia, with heavy military garrisoning of the conquered territory; moderate imperialism urged that Rome should exercise real mastery over Armenia, insisting that the Armenian king should be a Roman nominee and make full acknowledgment of Roman sovereignty. The first policy and, more likely than not, the second would involve war with Parthia, who regarded the throne of Armenia as the perquisite of a cadet of the Parthian royal family. It was true that, faced by the rivalry of their nobles, few Parthian kings felt great security on their thrones, that Parthia never showed dangerous offensive instincts in the west, being normally fully absorbed by the problems of her vast eastern frontier; but the Parthians were a difficult enemy to fight – first because theirs was a fast-moving, quickly deploying army of cavalry and horse-archers and the Romans were never at any time in their history adept at cavalry fighting; secondly because troops brought from Europe – and for a large-scale war they must be brought – wilted under the intense heat and water-shortage in desert-fighting.

There was a third solution – compromise, a notion dear to the heart of such a statesman as Augustus. Let a suitable Armenian, even a Parthian cadet, rule in Armenia, but let him at the same time acknowledge Roman suzerainty. So, on both sides, honour and prestige would be satisfied; for on both sides it was prestige rather than any economic or strategic advantage that was at issue. Soundings were made. An accommodation was reached when Augustus was in Greece in 21-20 BC. He had already sent back to Parthia the son of the Parthian king, who had conveniently fallen into his hands, on condition that the Roman standards lost at Carrhae were returned in exchange, and when no answering move was made by Phraates, he sent for Tiberius and a strong legionary force from Europe. Phraates, whose own position was insecure in Parthia, lost his nerve and the standards were handed back to representatives of Rome. Tiberius arrived, the king of Armenia was conveniently murdered and Tiberius presided at the coronation of the murdered king's brother Tigranes, who acknowledged the suzerainty of Rome. Ten years later the insecurity of Phraates' throne was shown when he sent all four of his legitimate sons to live, in a style befitting princes, in Rome.

In a world without sensationalist newspapers and war-correspondents the simple means of propaganda were in the emperor's hands. What Rome had anticipated was a smashing military victory over Parthia, not an unsensational diplomatic settlement. Coinage, however, advertised the return of the standards, even 'the capture of Armenia'; and for the reception of the standards the great temple of Mars the Avenger was built in Augustus' new forum in Rome.

In Asia Minor Galatia's existence as a client kingdom had ended in 25 BC with the death of its king Amyntas. It became an imperial province, governed by an ex-praetor, with no legionary troops. In fact from a military point of view there was no eastern frontier which could be quickly alerted in a crisis – merely four legions in Syria and two in Egypt. The strategic weakness of this situation was to be exposed when Nero was emperor.

The Western Empire under the Julio-Claudian emperors
In AD 14 Augustus died, leaving, in the manner of an oriental king,

his own grandiloquent account of his stupendous achievements for inscription on the great mausoleum which he had built, and which survives in Rome. Copies were evidently solicited by certain provinces, and two have been found in Asia Minor, one on the wall of the temple of Rome and Augustus, which later became a mosque, at Ankara (Ancyra) in Galatia, the other, more fragmentary, at Antioch in Pisidia. Augustus' description of his frontier settlements in West and East was not a little disingenuous: 'I pacified Germany up to the Elbe'; 'I could have made Armenia a province, but preferred not to'.

In addition to this, the *Res Gestae*, Augustus left to his successor the 'advice' (*consilium*) of pushing the frontiers no further. In the west this advice was twice disregarded, in neither case unwisely, when Claudius invaded and made a province of Britain in AD 43 and when Trajan conquered Dacia and it became a province in AD 107.

Tacitus, taking his standpoint at the year AD 98 and looking back as far as the days of the Republic, wrote, 'It has taken all this time to master Germany' – and in AD 98 it was no more mastered than it ever had been; much blood had been shed, but the Rhine was still the Roman frontier. Tacitus contrasted the history of Rome in the East. There was nothing in the East for the Romans to fear, nothing comparable with the lasting threat of the Germans.

Tiberius had never received an honorific title to mark the achievements of his brilliant military career, though he deserved several. His brother Drusus, fatally, was given the title Germanicus. It descended in his family, together with the sanguine temperament which they inherited from Antony, whose younger daughter was Drusus' wife. Germanicus, their son, whom Tiberius had been forced by Augustus to adopt, as attractive and impetuous a man as ever lived, was in command of the Rhine armies in AD 14 when Augustus died and Tiberius, who already possessed the major constitutents of imperial power, the tribunician power and the *imperium proconsulare*, was proclaimed Augustus' successor. The succession was inevitable, even if the rancour of high-placed senators and the unforthcoming diffidence of Tiberius himself created an atmosphere of ill-feeling and embarrassment from the start. The situation was not brightened by the news that the armies in Lower Germany and in Pannonia had mutinied. Germanicus was on the spot to deal with the one; the emperor's son Drusus was sent to deal with the other. The troops had a powerful case; something had gone wrong with the arrangements made for regular discharge in AD 6. Partly, perhaps, because of shortage of recruits and the critical anxiety of the days which followed the disaster of Varus, soldiers were not getting their discharge at the proper time. The old soldiers had the grievance; the young soldiers were determined to make capital out of the crisis, to secure even better conditions of service than those on which they joined up – fifteen years under the colours instead of twenty. The emperor in Rome was the enemy (Tiberius, under whom so many of them had served), the emperor and the senate. A very small spark was needed to inflame the troops to proclaim Germanicus emperor.

Concessions were made, and the storm abated. Germanicus then decided to restore his army's morale by invading Germany and in three successive years, 14, 15 and 16, he advanced with his troops into Germany, to the scene of Varus' disaster, where the ground was still covered with bones, and even to the Elbe. He suffered as his father had suffered from the vicissitudes of forest, swamp, flood and on the sea (by which part of his force was transported) storm. If morale was improved, it was at the expense of heavy losses of men and equipment; and at the end of 16 Tiberius had the courage to recall Germanicus, on the convenient opportunity of an important posting to the East. There is no reason to think that Tiberius had ever been asked to approve, or had approved, of Germanicus' German frolic. For the rest of Tiberius' principate useful, unsensational work went on, barrack-building, and road-building, on the west bank of the Rhine.

There were occasional military exercises. Detachments from both Rhine armies were sent to help the legate of Lugdunensis, who had no troops of his own, apart from one urban cohort in charge of the mint at Lyons, to put down the extensive revolt, provoked by the exactions of money-lenders, which broke out in AD 21, led by the Aedui and Treveri under Florus and Sacrovir, both from families which had had Roman citizenship for more than a generation. The revolt was a forlorn enterprise from the start. The rebels had no arms and no training and were mown down by the legionaries from the Rhine army when they arrived.

In 39, the Rhine frontier once more came to life sensationally with the advent of the new Germanicus, Gaius Caligula, Germanicus' erratic son, who succeeded Tiberius as emperor in 37. Adventure was in his blood and he had some large project in mind, whether another invasion of Germany in the footsteps of his father and grandfather, or even the invasion of Britain. Two new legions were raised, xv Primigenia and xxii Primigenia, intended evidently to replace on the Rhine two experienced legions which were needed for Gaius' adventure. The governor of Upper Germany, Gaetulicus, planned to murder him on arrival, but Gaius was forewarned and instead Gaetulicus and his fellow-plotters, one of them M. Aemilius Lepidus, the emperor's brother-in-law, were executed. Then Gaius took the Upper German legions in hand; he exercised them in formidable manoeuvres and in the end, according to surviving accounts, which are evident travesties of the truth, marched the army to the Channel coast and there commanded it to pick up shells and go home.

There were still the two new legions. In AD 41 Claudius had succeeded Gaius and, as Germanicus' younger brother, annexed the title Germanicus. He was a most unmilitary man, with no experience of fighting; and there were a number of strong reasons for which he needed to cut a military figure. For he owed his position to the acclamation of the praetorian guard after Gaius' murder in 41, when at the price of a huge donative they forced the senate to accept their choice – this, an emperor's payment to his troops for the succession, being Claudius' disastrous legacy to the later world. In the first year of his rule he had been faced by a revolt of the two legions in Dalmatia under a forlorn republican commander,

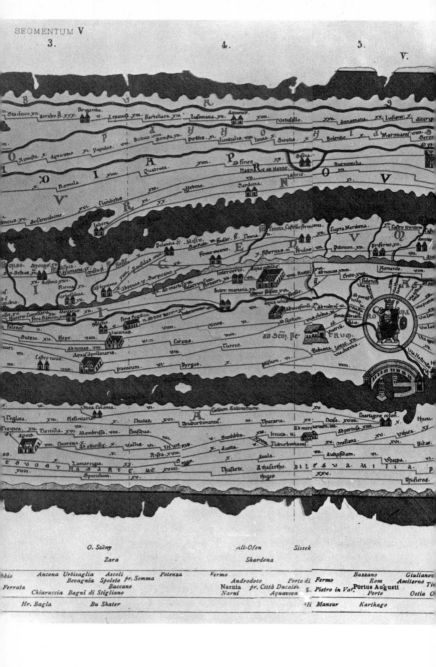

		O. Szöny			Alt-Ofen	Sissek			
		Zara			Skardona				
bbio	Ancona	Urbisaglia	Ascoli	Potenza	Fermo		Fermo	Bazzano	Giulianov
		Bevagnia	Spoleto pr. Somma		Androdoco	Porto di	Rom	Amiterno	Ti
Ferrata			Baccano		Narnia	pr. Città Ducale	S. Pietro in Va?	Portus Augusti	
	Chiaruccia	Bagni di Stigliano			Narni		Aquaviva	Porto	Ostia O
Hr. Bagla		Bu Shater				ali	Mansur	Karthago	

The Peutinger table dates perhaps from the late second century AD; it is a road map of the Roman Empire, copied in the thirteenth century and preserved through Peutinger, a scholar of the sixteenth century. This section shows Rome and Trajan's great harbour at Ostia. The dark bands indicate the sea; so the top section is of the Balkans, the middle section Italy, and the bottom sec⁚ on Africa.

Furius Camillus Scribonianus, whom after twenty-four hours they prudently deserted and so won, rather easily, the proud title, 'Pia Claudia Fidelis'. Claudius decided on the invasion of Britain, for which considerable planning may already have been done. Though Britain was on the other side of Ocean, which circled the civilised world, Ocean at the Straits of Dover was not particularly wide.

The pretext for the invasion was given by the earlier appeal to Rome of Amminius, expelled from Britain by his elderly father, the Belgic king, Cunobelinus, who from his capital in Colchester had pursued a policy of strong independence, simply disregarding the existence of Roman Gaul as a neighbour. Between 40 and 43 he died, a very old man, and was succeeded by two fanatically anti-Roman sons, Togodumnus and Caratacus. Druidism, which the Romans were determined to eliminate in Gaul, had its source in Britain. There might be trading advantages if Britain joined the European community; and there were economic temptations: lead and pearls – pearls which in the event proved disappointingly dark and small. An excellent choice was made of commander of the invasion force, A. Plautius, legate of Pannonia. He was given four legions, II Augusta and XIV Gemina, which was to make a great reputation for itself in the next twenty-five years, both from Upper Germany; XX from Lower Germany and IX Hispana, whose quality he knew well and bro .ght with him from Pannonia.

The invasion got off to a bad start in 43 for, good fighters though they evidently were, the troops were frightened by the sea and some weeks were wasted before, riled by the appearance of Claudius' freedman Narcissus, sent from Rome to harangue them, they embarked. The force landed unopposed at Richborough (Rutupiae) and met little serious opposition south of the Thames, in the course of which fighting Togodumnus was killed. There was a halt until Claudius himself arrived, to be in at the kill. The advance was then resumed and Colchester captured, to be the capital of the new province. The legions fanned out, Vespasian with legion II moving west, the ninth legion north and the other two legions under Plautius north-west. By 47 the Fosse Way, from Lincoln to south

A centurion of legion xx, part of the invasion army to Britain in AD 43, which remained there for the rest of its existence until the fourth century. It has left many records in inscriptions on Hadrian's wall and in the north of Britain. The staff which the centurion carried marked his rank: it was *vitis*, a vine-rod, used to beat soldiers.

Devon, was established as a Roman frontier. There were however, still vassal rulers, Cogidumnus in the west, ruling from his splendid palace at Fishbourne near Chichester which has recently been so successfully excavated, Prasutagus of the Iceni to the north-east and Cartimandua of the Brigantes further north still. The outlook was bright, until Caratacus persuaded the Silures in Wales to fight, and against them there was thirty years of tough struggle. When Prasutagus died, and Boudicca, his widow, made to succeed him, she was told that the independence of the Iceni was at an end. The hideous revolt of 61 followed, at a moment when the governor, Suetonius Paulinus, was campaigning in north Wales. Camulodunum (Colchester), which had been made a Roman colony and whose settlers, retired soldiers, had earned nothing but hatred for themselves, was sacked, London was abandoned and the ninth legion cut to pieces before Suetonius succeeded in restoring order.

There was no more thought of conquering Germany. When Cn. Domitius Corbulo, governor of Lower Germany in 47, engaged in operations against the Chauci, he quickly received instructions from Claudius in Rome to withdraw to the west bank of the river.

The Eastern Empire under the Julio-Claudian emperors
Augustus' diplomatic settlement of the East turned out in the event to be a diplomatic nightmare. Nearly every time an Armenian king died, his death provoked a crisis. The general pattern of events was that the anti-Roman party in Armenia placed its own candidate on the throne, usually with Parthian support. The Romans blustered. Sometimes they sent out a powerful diplomat who came to some kind of accommodation. He returned to Rome, and the arrangement was overthrown. So Gaius Caesar, Augustus' grandson, was sent out in 1 BC, Germanicus in AD 17 and L. Vitellius in 35. Both in Armenia and in Parthia the Romans intrigued to secure the expulsion of unfriendly kings, parties unfriendly to Rome in these countries to secure the expulsion or death of the kings whom Rome supported. Things came to a head under Claudius and Nero, after

an Iberian adventurer murdered his uncle and seized the throne of Armenia, only to be deposed and in due course executed, Vologeses, king of Parthia, having intervened to proclaim his brother Tiridates as Armenian king. These events occupied the years 51 to 54, when at the age of sixteen Nero became emperor. Nero decided to have a war.

The eastern frontier not being well-designed for war, aggressive or defensive, special arrangments had to be made. Ummidius Quadratus, holding the highest-ranking post in the East as governor of Syria, could not be moved. So a second command was created, junior naturally to that of Quadratus, in Cappadocia (a province since AD 17, normally governed by an equestrian), and an excellent soldier, Domitius Corbulo, was appointed to hold it.

The war was the only considerable war in the Empire which was not conducted personally by an emperor or by a prince of the imperial house. It was fought under two different commands, that of Nero's government in Rome which, because of slow communications, was never in touch with the current situation and that of Domitius Corbulo, a wilful man (he was subsequently summoned to Greece and executed by Nero in 67) who evidently had his own ideas, one of which was that the issue could have been settled diplomatically at the start. In the course of the war three legions were drafted from the West: IV Scythica and V Macedonica from Moesia and XV Apollinaris from Pannonia, to reinforce the Syrian army, three of whose legions were seconded to Corbulo. A whole winter was occupied at the start in training and toughening them to a state in which they were fit to engage an enemy; after which, with little fighting, they mastered Armenia, their task being eased by the fact that Vologeses was summoned away to deal with a war on Parthia's eastern frontier. Rome sent out an ineffective king of its own, a Cappadocian, who had soon to be withdrawn. Then, on Quadratus' death, Corbulo was promoted to govern Syria and the Armenian command was taken over by Caesennius Paetus, to whom Corbulo gave support as half-hearted as that which he had once received from Quadratus. The sanguine Paetus was beleaguered by Vologeses, now back from his eastern war, and, through the dilatoriness of Corbulo, forced to surrender. Corbulo then repeated his victory march through Armenia, and the accommodation which he had suggested at the start was accepted. Tiridates surrendered his diadem – the war had now lasted for five years – and in AD 66 arrived in Rome to receive it back from Nero's hands. In a pageant of oriental extravagance after the heart of the emperor, himself the impresario who arranged it all, in Pompey's theatre which was gilded for the occasion, Nero crowned Tiridates King of Armenia.

Nero-worshippers regard the outcome of his Armenian war as a triumph, because Rome and Parthia were subsequently at peace for half a century. This, however, is more likely to be explained by the fact that after the civil war Vespasian reorganised the eastern frontier so that there were three legions stationed on the Euphrates: two Syrian legions, probably at Zeugma and Samosata, and further north one at the important crossing at Melitene. The last was one of the two legions permanently stationed in Galatia-Cappadocia, now made a single first-class imperial province under a consular legate. At last Rome had a military frontier in the East. Parthia and Armenia took notice of the fact.

Judaea represents one of the greatest of all Rome's imperialist failures. There was, perhaps, only one solution with any chance of success: to abandon it to its theocracy as a state in client-relationship with Rome, for with the vast numbers of Jews of the Dispersion (six to seven millions, seven per cent of the entire population of the empire), each of them scrupulously bound to send his offering of two drachmae a year to the temple in Jerusalem, the state would have had an evident interest in maintaining a working relationship with Rome. Instead, when Herod the Great died in 4 BC and Archelaus, having shown his incompetence to reign, was banished to Vienne in Gaul in AD 6, Augustus decided that Judaea should be administered directly as the lowest class of Roman province under an equestrian prefect, who could always call over his shoulder to the governor of Syria for military support if this was needed; and, except for the period from 41 to 44 when Agrippa I, a friend of Gaius and of Claudius, received the kingdom, the Augustan system survived. The country was split internally this way and that. There were the rich, landowners, generally friendly to the Roman administration as the guarantor of their social and economic security for, as in the empire generally, theirs was the class which Rome supported and through whom she ruled. There were the poor, often very poor indeed. There were the Sadducees, from whom the High Priest was appointed, generally synonymous with the rich, and the Pharisees, generally of the lower class, from whom minor priests were appointed. There were extremist nationalists, the Zealots. There were the Assassins (*Sicarii*), of whom property-owners lived in terror. There was a general reluctance to pay tribute, and the presence of alien Roman soldiers gave offence. There were Messianic hopes and illusions. There were Jews and there were Gentiles, fired by a reciprocal hatred here as elsewhere, particularly at Alexandria.

The Romans made concessions to Jewish prejudice. There was a special coinage which did not carry the emperor's head. There was no representation of him on the standards of the troops. But this was not enough, and the province with its unique and testing problems required a governor of the highest administrative gifts, infinite imagination, infinite patience in dealing with what seemed an insufferable people. Instead it received a series of procurators of very poor quality, who were well-intentioned but weak like Pontius Pilate, or else quickly exasperated or corrupt. Not one escaped the hatred of the people whom he ruled. Rebellion was narrowly avoided in AD 40 when Gaius decided, as Antiochus Epiphanes had once decided, to impose ruler-cult on the province, by commanding that a statue of himself should be erected in the Temple at Jerusalem. Just in time he was persuaded to change his mind; rebellion was postponed for twenty-six years until AD 66, when it was sparked off by the annexation of seventeen talents from the Temple treasury by the procurator Gessius Florus. It started well: the twelfth legion, sent by the governor of Syria, was forced to retreat.

There may still have been some hopes of a peaceful settlement, for the young Josephus, no extremist at all, was put in charge of Galilee which would be on the route of the Roman invading army. But, by his own account, the extremists and fanatics prevailed and made it a war *à outrance*. On the Roman side Vespasian was appointed to the command and in early 67 he invaded with v Macedonica and x Fretensis, while his elder son Titus brought up xv Apollinaris from Egypt, where it had been stationed since the end of Corbulo's campaigns. He was successful in guerilla operations and by the summer of 68 Jerusalem was under siege. At which moment civil war broke out in the empire and the war was virtually suspended for a year.

So much for the main development of frontier policy and of military activity in the northern and eastern empire under the Julio-Claudians. South of the Mediterranean, too, there had been changes. Mauretania, made a client kingdom by Augustus, had been annexed by Gaius and after a rising which Suetonius Paulinus helped to suppress, organised as two provinces, Tingitana and Caesariensis, each under an equestrian governor, by Claudius.

Gaius too ended the anomaly by which the legion in Africa, iii Augusta, was under the command of the proconsul of Africa. The unsuitability of this arrangement was demonstrated by the failure of a number of proconsuls in Tiberius' principate to deal with the desert marauder Tacfarinas. Gaius withdrew the command of the legion from the proconsul and transferred it to a legate appointed in the normal way by himself. The legate and legion were stationed in the western district of Numidia which virtually, if not formally, hived off from Africa and became a separate province.

Early in Augustus' principate, legates of Egypt – Cornelius Gallus, who suffered for being too big for his boots, Aelius Gallus and C. Petronius – had made forays into Ethiopia and Arabia, but these adventures were not repeated. Nero, it is true, at some time planned a visit to Egypt. Special baths were built for him, we do not know where, and a detachment of praetorian troops was sent to explore the possibility of an attack on Ethiopia – as if the legate of Egypt could not have sent him far more reliable information. Some time after the Parthian war Nero thought in even more practical terms of a war in the Caucasus, the Caspian Gates. A new legion was raised for the purpose, perhaps in September 67. This was I Italica, recruits for which had to be over six feet tall. He also selected XIV Gemina from Britain, on account of the great reputation which it had won for itself in the suppression of Boudicca's revolt. The plans – whatever they were – were formed presumably before or during Nero's campaign as a singer in Greece in 67. They were effectively quashed by the revolt of Vindex in Gaul in 68. We do not know how far the legions had got on their journey to the East; they were promptly recalled to deal with the crisis nearer home.

The civil war of 69 and the Flavian Emperors
One civil war destroyed the Roman Republic. A succession of civil wars were in their turn to destroy the Empire, the first of them in 69, the 'Year of the Four Emperors', provoked by a reasonable wish to dispense with Nero and after that inflamed by the fears, greed and jealousies of individual armies as much as by the ambitions of their commanders. In all this time the function and duties of frontier armies were forgotten. The Jewish war, as has been seen, was shelved for twelve months. On the Rhine the withdrawal of the troops created the opportunity for a serious rising in which Gauls and Germans joined. The Danube, too, was crossed by invaders, though not in great force. The resources of the empire were cripplingly exhausted. It was, in fact, a demonstration of utter irresponsibility on the part of what purported to be an imperial power, a throw-back to the last and worst days of Republicanism.

In 68 the men who were to be protagonists in the struggle were distributed about the empire, mostly in high administrative posts. M. Salvius Otho, a man of thirty-six, had been governor of Lusitania since 59, well out of sight of Nero, who had annexed and married Otho's wife Poppaea. The septuagenarian Ser. Sulpicius Galba, an austere man of immense military distinction, consul in

33, had been governor of Hispania Tarraconensis since 60. Gallia Lugdunensis was governed by the only northern Gaul of public distinction in the early Empire, Julius Vindex. The commander of the Upper German army was L. Verginius Rufus, an ex-consul aged fifty-four. A. Vitellius, a year younger, consul in 48, was unoccupied in Rome. T. Flavius Vespasianus, fifty-nine, a man of humble origins from Reate and an ex-consul who had accompanied Nero to Greece, commanded the Roman army in the Jewish war.

The civil war was triggered off by Vindex who, with no military backing of his own but with the known support of Galba, wrote letters to the great army commanders urging the deposition of Nero. The Upper German army under Rufus marched against him and, taking the law into its own hands, smashed his scratch force; he committed suicide, and the troops tried unsuccessfully to persuade Verginius Rufus to be emperor. In Rome Nero, who with any strength of mind could have restored order, lost his nerve; the praetorians abandoned him and the senate proclaimed Galba emperor. Galba sent Vitellius to command the army in Lower Germany, inflamed the loyal Gauls by showing favours to the supporters of Vindex and inflamed the praetorian guard by the announcement that he did not propose to pay them a donative. He tried to strengthen his position by adopting as his son Piso Licinianus, a man of thirty, virtuous but undistinguished. Otho, who had accompanied Galba from Spain, took this as a personal affront; he made common cause with the praetorians, who killed Galba and made Otho emperor.

In the meanwhile the German legions, detesting Galba as a supporter of Vindex, proclaimed Vitellius emperor, only to discover that it was not Galba but Otho whom they must depose. The bulk of the German army marched south, for the Alps and Italy, their passage marked by destruction and pillage (the city of Vienne only escaped by making a very heavy payment); and they defeated Otho's force – the praetorians, reinforced by legions from the Danube, the main body of whom did not arrive in time – at the first battle of Bedriacum near Cremona in the Po valley. So

The arch of Titus from which the Via Sacra descends into the Forum at Rome. It was completed and dedicated after Titus' death. On the inner jambs of the arch are reliefs glorifying his triumph in Rome in early summer AD 71 after his capture of Jerusalem. This (on the south side) illustrates the spoils from the temple in Jerusalem: the table of shewbread, the seven-branched candlestick and the silver trumpets.

Vitellius became emperor in Rome, soon to learn that Vespasian had been proclaimed emperor in Alexandria and acclaimed by the troops in Syria, and that his rising had the support of the Danube legions, who were on the march to Italy. This time, at the second battle of Bedriacum, they were victorious. Cremona was burnt to the ground and in the last fighting in Rome, where Vitellius made his stand, the Capitol with the great temple of Juppiter was burnt down. Vespasian's own hands were conveniently unstained by blood, for he had remained in the East and the fighting had been done by officers subordinate to himself, in particular Antonius Primus, a legionary commander in Pannonia. In all this fighting in the course of the year 69 immense damage had been done, estimated by Vespasian at the staggering figure of forty thousand million sesterces.

Harm had been done to other things than the economy. The abandonment of effective power by the senate, demonstrated more than quarter of a century earlier, when the praetorian soldiers had compelled it to accept their own nominee Claudius after Gaius had been murdered, had been abundantly confirmed. In recognising Otho, Vitellius and Vespasian in turn, the senate accepted the candidate of one section of the army or another. The dictatorship of Julius Caesar and the subsequent accession of Augustus had been the first demonstration of the effective power of the soldiery, the proclamation of Claudius was the second. Vespasian's ultimate triumph was the third. There were worse things to come.

At the end, Vespasian apart, only one of the protagonists was alive, Verginius Rufus; in the anarchy of the third century he too would have been dead, for by that time the troops had discovered their power and, when they offered a general the purple, they offered it with the alternative of immediate death.

The conclusion of the civil war was not the end of the melancholy story. When Galba sent Vitellius to command the legions of Lower Germany, he replaced Verginius Rufus in Upper Germany by an ineffective and infirm old man, Hordeonius Flaccus. The bulk and the best of the Rhine army was already in Italy, and to prevent further reinforcement from reaching it Antonius Primus induced a Batavian, Julius Civilis, to create a diversionary movement on the Rhine in Vespasian's interest. The morale of the Roman troops in opposing him was weakened by the suspicion that Flaccus and others of their officers were disloyal to Vitellius and secretly sympathised with Vespasian. Still, with the death of Vitellius and the proclamation of Vespasian the trouble should have been at an end. But Civilis went on fighting and Gauls, who had made common cause with him on the west bank of the Rhine, proclaimed an 'Empire of the Gauls'. The Roman troops made a disgraceful exhibition of themselves, murdering their own officers and in the end many of them, after capitulation, took an oath of loyalty to the Empire of the Gauls.

There were, however, two illustrations of the fact that romanisation had already struck roots. The native inhabitants of Cologne (a Roman colony, called Colonia Agrippinensis since AD 50) were in their origin Ubii, Germans from across the Rhine. When they were forced to surrender by the Gallic insurgents, the Tencteri from across the river suggested that they should mark their emancipation from slavery by massacring all Romans in their city and abandoning the practice by which they closed the city gates at night. The citizens replied that most of the Romans were their own relatives, and that nobody could be expected to murder his relations; also that they felt safer at night with their gates closed. And the Remi, the last tribe to remain loyal to Julius Caesar in the Gallic rising of 52 BC, again rallied resistance to the rebels, summoning a council of Gauls and demonstrating that, now the civil war was over and Rome was in a position to act, the rebellion had not even a shadowy prospect of success. The arrival of Petillius Cerealis with a large army from Italy confirmed their good sense. The rebellion was put down and, in the reorganisation, four of the legions which had disgraced themselves were cashiered, I, XV Primigenia and XVI from Lower Germany and IV Macedonica from the Upper Rhine. The frontier camps were re-garrisoned by legions which were not discredited by previous associations.

The Flavian house, Vespasian and his two sons Titus and Domitian, ruled for twenty-six years until AD 96, all of them such experienced soldiers as no emperor of the Julio-Claudian line except Tiberius had been. The Italian middle class now took control of Roman public life under the first middle-class emperors and at the Court and in leading society in Rome wild licence gave way to sober, even sombre, respectability. In the empire much was achieved. As has already been seen, a firm military frontier was established in face of Armenia. The Jewish war was concluded; first by the capture and destruction of the temple in Jerusalem by Titus in May 70 and finally in 73, when the last fortress of Masada could no longer hold out and its defenders killed themselves. The seven-branched candlestick was carried in Titus' triumph and is depicted vividly on his triumphal arch in Rome; Judaea became a second-class military province with a permanent legionary garrison (legion x Fretensis), and Jews all over the world were registered and taxed – two drachmae a head, the sum which previously every Jew had piously despatched each year to the temple in Jerusalem.

We can read in his son-in-law Tacitus' account a description of the Roman advance northwards in Britain under Agricola between 78 and 84, as far as the isthmus of the Forth and Clyde in Scotland; and recent excavation at Inchtuthill shows that there were plans for holding a permanent frontier even further north. In Germany patient and valuable work was done to cut out the re-entrant angle between the Upper Rhine and Danube by the construction of a *limes*, a road behind an earth rampart, with forts at regular intervals and with extensive rides cut through the forests into enemy country for scouting in face of the danger of surprise attacks. Starting near Rheinbrohl, it followed the line of the Taunus, then was drawn almost due south to Lorch and, after that, east to the Danube at Eining. This greatly shortened and improved communications between the Rhine and the Danube armies. A further reorganisation was made on the Rhine after a military revolt in Upper Germany in 89. From being districts of military occupation (the Roman army on the Rhine), Upper and Lower Germany were converted into normal first-class military provinces with governors who not only commanded their armies but were also responsible for civil administration.

More important, this period saw the beginning of that barbarian pressure on the northern frontiers under whose strain in the centuries to come the frontiers themselves were to break. The Roxolani, horsemen in heavy mail armour, terrifying in their galloping attacks and helpless as tortoises on their backs if they were thrown by their chargers, had crossed the Danube in 69. In 85 Dacians crossed the river and a governor of Moesia was killed. Under the general command of the emperor Domitian, the prefect of the praetorian guard, Cornelius Fuscus, led an attack across the Danube into Dacia; he was killed and a legion, probably V Alaudae, Julius Caesar's famous Gallic regiment whose troops carried a lark on their helmets, was wiped out, a disaster which is perhaps commemorated in the surviving cenotaph at Adamklissi in the Dobrudja. A second invasion in 89 was more successful, and King Decebalus opened negotiations. Peace was made on what later would have been regarded as sensible but at the time were commonly thought to be humiliating terms: the establishment of Dacia as a client kingdom, receiving a subsidy in money from Rome and the dispatch to Dacia of Roman engineers. The settlement was forced on Rome by the build-up of heavy pressure on Pannonia to the West of Dacia from Marcomanni, Quadi, Jazyges and Sarmatians north of the Danube. They crossed the river in 92 and, before they were driven back, another legion, XXI Rapax, had been destroyed.

Trajan's rule
In 96 Domitian was murdered and succeeded by the sexagenarian Nerva who a year later, in something like Galba's earlier dilemma, followed Galba's example but, with greater wisdom, adopted for his son (who on his death in 98 succeeded him) an outstanding and aggressive soldier, Trajan, then governor of Upper Germany. War against Dacia was resumed in two campaigns. In 101 Trajan in-

vaded Dacia, returned south for the winter, when a great bridge
sixty feet wide on twenty piers was built over the Danube, and in
102 he campaigned again with success. Decebalus surrendered;
Sarmizegetusa, his capital, was occupied by a Roman garrison; the
Roman engineers, whose works had so greatly assisted the Dacian
defence, were handed back. Decebalus, now a subject king, planned
his revenge. In 105 he captured the commander of the Roman
garrison by a trick, and then invaded Roman territory south of the
river. The second war, commanded again by Trajan himself, lasted
into 106 and in the end Decebalus committed suicide. Dacia was
made a Roman province, the first considerable enlargement of the
empire since Claudius' conquest of Britain. There were economic
gains, the salt mines and gold mines of Transylvania. Sarmizegetusa
became a Roman colony, Ulpia Traiana, and other cities received

in AD 113 and consisted of the forum proper, the Basilica Ulpia, the column
of Trajan and a library. The surface of the column is covered with reliefs
representing Trajan's conquest of Dacia between AD 101 and 106. In this scene
military standards are seen on the left, Trajan in the centre, and on the right
his soldiers display the heads of slaughtered enemies.

municipal status. Roads were built. Apulum, occupied by XIII
Gemina, was made a garrison town. Probably I Adiutrix also
remained for a few years in the province.

With only five words surviving from Trajan's own published
account of the campaigns and a few scrappy fragments from the
historian Cassius Dio, a detailed history of the two wars is impossible. Yet those wars occasioned the most splendid pictorial
representation that we possess of the Roman army on campaign:
the 155 scenes carved on the column of Trajan which still stands in
his magnificent forum in Rome – a forum which was designed by
the architect of the Danube bridge, Apollodorus of Damascus.
Some scenes can be related with certainty, other only imaginatively,
to recorded episodes in the fighting.

The war disturbed the shape of Roman northern frontier defence.
In 68 there had been seven legions on the Rhine and five on the
Danube. At the end of the Dacian wars the Rhine garrison was
down to four legions and the Danube army up to twelve.

In the East, Arabia Petraea was annexed and made a Roman
province in 106 and entered, like Palmyra to the north, on an era
of great prosperity, as is shown by the surviving monuments of its
rich trading cities, at the end of the long caravan routes from the
Persian Gulf, Petra, Bostra (Nova Traiana, the capital, garrison of
a legion, perhaps VI Ferrata) and Gerasa.

Finally, like Crassus and Julius Caesar before him, and like so
many later rulers in the declining Roman and early Byzantine
empires, Trajan was captivated by the thought of great eastern
conquests, of the extension of the Roman empire to include
Armenia and Mesopotamia, with the Tigris as its eastern frontier.
There was to be war against Chosroes, king of Parthia, son perhaps
of Vologeses, whose offence in provoking the war is uncertain,
perhaps failure to consult Trajan when he placed his nephew on the
Armenian throne. Once he realised his offence, his abject apologies
were disregarded. Trajan came to Antioch in 114, to put himself
at the head of the reinforced Syrian army. Armenia and northern
Mesopotamia were overrun and made provinces. In 116

Palmyra had always been an important caravan post in trade with the East. It was brought into the Roman empire (in the province of Syria) at the end of Trajan's rule and was given the constitution of a Greek city by Hadrian and called Hadriana. When Aurelian defeated Zenobia, it was destroyed. Its architecture, as shown is this temple of Baal, was a conflation of eastern and western styles.

Ctesiphon was captured, and Chosroes fled to the East. Trajan sailed down the Tigris to the Persian Gulf. Then the storm broke, a revolt in his rear with Edessa and Nisibis captured. Still there was time for a display of Roman grandeur. At Ctesiphon Trajan crowned a son of Chosroes king of Parthia. He got back to Antioch in Syria after a disastrously unsuccessful attempt to capture Hatra, a rehearsal for Septimius Severus' later and equally disastrous failure. He was by this time a very sick man, having suffered a stroke, and he died in Cilicia in 117 on his way back to Rome. His successor Hadrian wisely decided to relinquish Armenia and Mesopotamia. Chosroes unseated his upstart son. So in the outcome Trajan's great eastern conquests were a failure.

In the empire itself yet other disasters, for which Trajan had no responsibility, disfigured the end of a rule which, in Dacia, had started with such distinction. In 116, victims of an infectious frenzy, the Jews in Cyrenaica, where the trouble started, Egypt, Cyprus and Palestine set on their gentile neighbours, Romans and non-Romans alike, and there were wild, inhuman massacres with, in all, something like a million victims, a quarter of a million in Cyrenaica, where an insurgent Jew was crowned King of the Jews, and another quarter of a million in Cyprus. The revolts were harshly suppressed and their consequences long-lasting; Cyrenaica never again recovered its prosperity. A decree was passed forbidding Jews ever again to set foot in Cyprus. Between 130 and 134 there was more trouble, this time in Judaea, now the province of Syria Palaestina, where Hadrian had ordered the rebuilding of Jerusalem as a pagan Roman city with the name Aelia Capitolina and with a temple of Juppiter Capitolinus on the site of the old temple. The spirit which had opposed Gaius Caligula was not dead. A Messiah appeared, Bar Kochba, Son of the Star. There was guerilla fighting up and down the country, in the course of which legion XXII Deiotariana, whose home had been in Egypt, was destroyed. Over half a million Jews were killed, and a great number of their enemies.

A second legion, IX Hispana, was lost under Hadrian, either in a

Legionary soldiers with eagle and standard. The silver and gold
eagle (*aquila*) with wings outspread and a thunderbolt held in its
claws, was the ensign of a legion, carried before it on the march
and behind the first of the ten legionary cohorts in battle.
If it was captured, the legion was disbanded. The *signum* was the
standard of a subordinate unit (for instance, a cohort).

British rising or elsewhere. It was the most unfortunate legion in
the Roman army; it had suffered heavily in Boudicca's revolt and
in Agricola's last campaigns; and now it was destroyed.

Hadrian and the Antonine emperors

Hadrian, the most remarkable perhaps of all the emperors after
Augustus, a Spaniard like his predecessor Trajan, was the Roman
Prince of Peace, a peace which, admittedly, might not have been
possible without Trajan's recent display of Roman might. He was
a man with a keen regard for law, a strong natural feeling of
justice and a deep sympathy with the weaker sections of society,
the *humiliores*. He was steeped in Greek culture, a true Philhellene.
And he deliberately devoted the greater part of his rule, twelve out
of the twenty-one years 117-38, to travel (which even for an emperor was not always a particularly comfortable process) particularly in the eastern section of the empire. Between 121 and 125 he
toured Gaul, Germany, Raetia, Noricum, Britain, Spain, Mauretania, Africa, Cyrene. From Cyrene, via the islands and Asia Minor
he travelled to the Euphrates, returning through northern Asia
Minor, the Balkan provinces and Greece. Between 128 and 133 he
visited Africa, Athens, southern Asia Minor, Syria, Phoenicia,
Arabia, Palestine, Egypt and came back by way of Asia Minor to
the Black Sea and Athens. Between 134 and 135 he was in Palestine.
This must have astounded the natives of the provinces. In the
previous century and a half Gaul had endured Gaius' follies in the
winter of 39-40 and Greece listened to Nero singing in 67; otherwise, after Augustus, the provinces had never seen an emperor
except in quick transit to a frontier to conduct a war.

Hadrian visited troops in their barracks and watched their
military exercises. He heard cases in court and dealt with complaints, particularly from the tenants of his own extensive provincial estates, activities of which abundant evidence survives today in
papyri and on inscriptions. Apart from the general correction of
injustice, he had two objects always in mind, the proliferation of
city life and greater use of the agricultural resources of the empire

A section of Hadrian's wall near Housesteads. The wall, between Newcastle-on-Tyne and Solway Firth in northern Britain, was completed in about AD 127 and was 20 feet high and 80 Roman (73 English) miles long. To the north and south were thirty-foot wide ditches. The stone wall was eight Roman feet thick with small forts a mile apart and signal-towers between them. It was admirably sited for its primary purpose of observation.

to increase food production. In the first case old cities were rebuilt and new ones founded in the Balkans, with the object of creating a civilised background to the military defence line on the Danube comparable with the already civilised state of Gaul, the background of the Rhine armies. These cities had the attractive features of fora, basilicas, schools, temples and baths, often as benefactions of his own. In the second case he greatly increased olive production in Africa, encouraging the reclaiming of waste land which had gone out of production, with tax-remissions in the early stages and encouraging prospects of ownership to those who undertook the reclamation. And on his own estates he devised new forms of assured tenancy which came near to ownership.

He left abiding monuments: Hadrian's wall in Britain, the Pantheon in Rome, his most individual villa below Tivoli, the great temple of Zeus in Athens, completed at last after the long centuries.

After Hadrian, Antoninus Pius, his adopted son, whose family came from Nemausus (Nîmes), a man who, given his wish, would have been a farmer. The twenty-three years of his rule (138 to 161) are years without history; the world lived in contented stagnation. His adopted son followed him, Marcus Aurelius, sprung from a Spanish family, the Philosopher Emperor, a slave to the high Stoic concept of Duty. He was unfortunate in that Fortune, whose buffetings and caprices the Stoic was taught to contemn, had hard tests in store for him. From 161 to 169 he ruled in association with L. Verus, whom Antoninus had also adopted, a man of very different character from his own.

Immediately on Marcus' accession there was, once again, the need for serious fighting on the frontiers. In the East it started in the familiar manner, by Parthia placing an Arsacid prince on the Armenian throne. When the Romans made to interfere, they were met by a Parthian army, the governor of Galatia-Cappadocia was killed and the ill-prepared Roman troops scattered. Instead of going to the East himself, Marcus sent L. Verus, who, thanks to the admirable generals on his staff, fought an aggressive war whose results were as startling as those of Trajan. Armenia was taken, and

northern Mesopotamia. Ctesiphon was captured and the Persian king driven to flight. But triumph turned in a moment to disaster when the Roman army was smitten by one of the most terrible plagues in history, which decimated the troops and drove the remnants to retire in 166. Worse still, it followed the survivors home and spread over the whole length of the empire, a disaster so extensive that some historians have seen it as the first cause of the coming disintegration of the Roman empire. However, the Persian empire itself was by this time in an advanced state of decline, and there was no more Parthian aggression.

By this time there were signs of far more serious trouble on the Rhine and Danube fronts where tribes from across the rivers were feeling the pressure behind them of the great movement of Goths from the Vistula in north Germany to the Black Sea. In 167 the Langobardi and Obii, together with Marcomanni and Quadi crossed the Danube, broke through Roman opposition and moved south to cross the Julian Alps into Italy and put Aquileia under siege. Dacia too was invaded. The invaders' success was due partly to the fact that the Danube garrisons were depleted through detachments which they had sent to the eastern war, partly to the devastating effects of the plague. In 170 invaders crossed the Danube and pressed on into Macedonia, even to the neighbourhood of Athens.

Two new legions were raised (II and III Italica), every fit man, gladiators and brigands included, being pressed into service. The siege of Aquileia was raised, and the invaders were driven back across the Alps. With infinite resolution and fortitude the mind of M. Aurelius – alone now, since L. Verus died of sudden apoplexy in 169 – was set not merely on restoring the Danube frontier but on pushing the frontier further north across the river. There is no material for writing the history of the wars – only coins, inscrip-tions and the sculptured reliefs on the column of M. Aurelius in the Piazza Colonna at Rome, companion to the column of Trajan in Trajan's forum. By 171 Marcus' headquarters were at Carnuntum on the Danube and the invaders were being attacked in their own territory north of the river. By 173 (ominous presage of the future) captives were being settled in Roman territory, in Dacia, Pannonia, Moesia, even in Italy, to reinforce populations thinned by the plague. The Quadi, Marcomanni and Sarmatians in their turn submitted. There was an interruption in 175 when the Syrian-born Avidius Cassius, governor of Syria, a man who had contributed powerfully to the success of L. Verus in his eastern wars, rebelled in his province and was proclaimed emperor. A centurion killed him and sent his head to Marcus; but Marcus knew his stern duty, to visit the East in person and to sit in judgment, everywhere tem-pering justice with mercy. He returned to face, with his young son Commodus, a renewal of disorder on the Danube. He was poised for further advances across the river when in spring 180 he died. He had been a stupendously successful ruler.

Commodus, the golden-haired boy, disregarded his father's last advice and the advice of his father's friends, to continue the offen-sive. Instead he patched up a peace and returned to Rome, where

for twelve years he delighted the populace by exhibitions of skilful shooting in wild-beast shows and identified himself more and more openly with the life of professional gladiators until in 192 he was murdered in a palace revolution. Pertinax, a man with an admirable military record, who had played a large part in M. Aurelius' wars, was proclaimed his successor and murdered three months later by the praetorians who then shut themselves in their camp and over the walls held an auction for the empire. Didius Julianus, who had done distinguished military service on the Rhine in his time, bid highest in terms of donatives to the troops and was proclaimed. Which, as will be seen, was more than Septimius Severus on the Danube or Pescennius Niger in Syria could stomach.

Imperial Administration

The governing class

Italians and provincials from the West The men who in direct or indirect subordination to the emperor manned the senior posts in the provincial administrative services were senators and knights.

Under Augustus the senator had to make what was at first a difficult readjustment. Although a provincial governor was in fact subordinate to the senate during the Republic, he had enjoyed the illusion of independence. When he governed a province or commanded a legion as the emperor's legate in the empire, he had no illusion of independence at all. The emperor appointed him, the emperor could at any moment recall him, and his future career depended on the emperor's favour. His independence was sapped in other ways too. When he was out in a province he was being watched and, for all he knew, reported on by agents of the emperor. Once the rebellion of Boudicca had been repressed in Britain in AD 61, Suetonius Paulinus cannot have been ignorant of the fact that his own equestrian procurator Iulius Classicianus, was not only maligning him to the natives but was also urging his recall in the dispatches which he sent to Rome.

More than this, the whole outlook of a senator on his public life and career required basic readjustment. In the Republic spells of provincial administration had been so many interruptions in a career whose interests were primarily political and focused on the city of Rome. With the advent of the Empire life went out of politics and the importance and interest of the magistracies was correspondingly curtailed. Careers were now to be made in the main in the imperial service and outside Rome itself. The position was reversed; it was the tenure of magistracies in Rome which constituted the interruption. The administrator, in fact, replaced the politician. Success in the new world was won not by brilliant oratory or skilful political intrigue, but by less conspicuous qualities, a readiness to face hard work (*labor*), self-effacement (*modestia*) and loyalty (*obsequium*, a word which had to lose its pejorative sense). It was in such terms that Tacitus accounted for the successful public career of his father-in-law, Julius Agricola.

He might have added a fourth quality, a readiness to face danger – not only the periodic danger involved in military service on the frontiers but also the danger of too great success under a malign or jealous emperor. Domitius Corbulo under Nero and Lusius Quietus at Hadrian's accession were not the only distinguished Roman generals whose lives ended with execution or suicide. The more insecure the emperor's tenure of power, the greater the danger for any figure of high public standing. So in the early days of the empire Tiberius found that a number of well qualified ex-consuls declined high provincial posts and some members of senatorial families preferred the greater safety of the equestrian service to the potential danger of a senatorial career.

In the anarchy and near-anarchy of the third century everybody in government service took his life in his hands. When in 238 a party of young assassins arrived in Rome, dispatched by Gordian I, who had just been proclaimed emperor in Africa, and, having secured an audience, killed Vitalianus, prefect of the guard, a man loyal to the ruling emperor Maximinus I, bystanders did not interfere, assuming that the assassins had come from Maximinus, 'who often treated his seemingly closest friends in this way'.

It was harder for the Roman aristocrat than for a 'new man' to stomach the dominance of the Caesars; but in the Julio-Claudian period the descendants of Republican aristocrats soon disappeared. Some retired from politics, others were executed or committed suicide. Natural infertility played its mysterious part; families simply died out.

So that the senate was filled, and the senior posts in the administration were staffed, by a new type: careerists from the upper-class families of the country towns of Italy and from the most civilised provinces of the West, Spain and Narbonese Gaul. It has been calculated that there were already forty-two senators of provincial extraction under Nero. Such provincials were sometimes the descendants of Romans or Italians who had gone out as settlers or who had been established in colonies generations earlier, sometimes the descendants of natives who had been given Roman citizenship. The process of broadening the basis of the government and making it more representative, like the process of widening the field of Roman citizenship, was fundamental to the whole development of Rome. It went back to the time when in the early Republic plebeians were admitted to equality with patricians; and it goes forward to the time when the senate could be thought of first as a parliament of Italy, then as predominantly a parliament of Italy and the West, and finally as a parliament of the whole empire.

Already between AD 37 and 68 at least thirteen men were elected to the consulship who came from the western provinces, five from Spain and eight from Narbonese Gaul, three of the latter from the single city of Vienne. The thirteen include two pairs of brothers – Seneca and Iunius Annaeus Gallio, the man who refused to take any action against St Paul when he was proconsul of Achaea in 51, and D. Valerius Asiaticus, consul for the second time in 46 and dead by Messallina's plotting a year later and his brother. And there are others like Domitius Corbulo whose roots may well have been outside Italy in the West.

Of men who played prominent parts in the civil war of 69, Vitellius' two generals, Fabius Valens and Aulus Caecina, came from Anagni (Anagnia) and Vicenza (Vicetia) respectively. Vespasian came from Rieti (Reate). His second-in-command Mucianus may have been Spanish. The home town of Antonius Primus, who led the invasion army from the Danube into Italy, was Toulouse (Tolosa). Already in AD 48 Claudius had persuaded the senate to agree that men with Roman citizenship from northern Gaul (Lugdunensis), where tribal organisations still survived and municipal life was not as yet developed comparably with Narbonese Gaul, might be considered for admission to the senate and careers as senators. His speech survives, as uncouth in form as it is statesmanlike in content, pointing out that the expansion of the Roman body politic by the admission of outsiders was a key to dynamic political survival which the Romans had discovered and the city-states of Greece, to their great loss, had never discovered at all.

In AD 94 for the first time in Roman history, as far as we know, there was a pair of consuls both of whom had provincial backgrounds, a descendant of Valerius Asiaticus from Vienne and Iulius Quadratus who came from Pergamon.

By the end of the first century north Africa was providing Rome with consuls, the first of them, Q. Pactumeius Fronto, brought into the senate by Vespasian and consul in AD 80. Lusius Quietus who as an ex-consul held an important command in Trajan's Parthian war was a Moor. Only two western provinces lagged behind. Western Gaul produced Iulius Vindex, a descendant of Aquitanian kings, who held the praetorship and was then appointed governor of the province of Gallia Lugdunensis, where his action started the civil war of 69. Perhaps this, together with Civilis' revolt in 69-70, frightened the Romans; anyhow northern Gaul failed after this to produce senators of distinction. Britain failed too. In his speech to the Gauls at Trier in Gallia Belgica in AD 70 Cerealis said, 'It is mostly you yourselves who are in command of our legions and who provide the governors of this and other provinces; you are not debarred in any way from such appointments'. This could have been said with truth at any time in the late first and second century in one of the older western provinces, in Narbonese Gaul or Spain. If Cerealis was generalising from the case of Vindex, the remark was true in north Gaul at the time when it was made; for the future it was not to be true at all.

Provincials from the East. The contribution of orientals (which means, in effect, Greeks) to the government of the empire is a more complicated story. The legions stationed in the East were recruited from the East, predominantly from Asia Minor, and their officers were increasingly men of eastern Mediterranean origins, because such men had better physical stamina for service in an eastern Mediterranean climate. Many of the known tribunes of IV Scythica, a legion which after AD 58 never moved from Syria, came from the eastern Mediterranean and, with one exception, the only legions commanded by orientals before the time of Antoninus Pius were, in addition to IV Scythica, III Gallica and II Traiana, both of them stationed in the East.

Orientals of ability were also employed to fill important equestrian posts in the East. Tiberius Claudius Balbillus, a man who had received Roman citizenship from Claudius, was prefect of Egypt early in Nero's principate. Tiberius Julius Alexander, whose citizenship evidently derived from Tiberius, enjoyed a really startling career. He was an Egyptian Jew by birth, and so must have received Alexandrian citizenship for a start, for in Egypt this was a necessary bridge to Roman citizenship. He was Philo's nephew, but a renegade from Judaism. Claudius strangely made him procurator of Judaea; he then served on Corbulo's staff and in AD 66 was made prefect of Egypt by Nero. In this post he helped to determine the succession to the principate, for it was at Alexandria on 1 July 69 on his initiative that Vespasian was proclaimed emperor. There are plausible reasons for thinking that after this he became prefect of the praetorian guard in Rome.

At central government level, it was in the executive civil service of the emperors that Greeks first made their strong and very unpopular mark. In the early empire the well-known heads of the various branches of the civil service, who are likely to have been as efficient as they were socially notorious. were men like Narcissus and Pallas, 'the descendant of Arcadian kings', under Claudius and Helius under Nero. They offended conservative Roman prejudice on a number of counts because of their personal wealth and social advancement, the *quaestoria ornamenta* of Narcissus, the *praetoria ornamenta* of Pallas (honours which in Roman opinion should be reserved for Romans and gentlemen) and because of their powerful influence in the highest issues of Roman politics – the part played by Pallas, for instance, in engineering Claudius' marriage to his niece Agrippina and, as a consequence, in securing the succession of Nero to the principate. Yet such men were not without a serious sense of public responsibility. When in Greece in 67 Nero paid no attention to dispatches from Rome, Helius went to Greece himself to warn him that, in his own interest, he should lose no time in returning home. Life was good for such men while their power lasted. When misfortune struck, it struck hard.

It would have been a mistake to dispense with the ability of these men, and a solution was found, starting with Domitian and reaching its conclusion. under Hadrian, by demoting them to second place in the imperial bureaux and making them subordinate in every case to Roman knights – for by this time equites were prepared to accept posts in the imperial household under the emperors which a century earlier would have been inconsistent with their dignity.

Admission to the senate and the top administrative posts in the empire was a more ticklish matter. Conservative senatorial prejudices at first resented the admission to the senate even of men from the western provinces; the notion of Greeks for colleagues stuck even more firmly in their throats. With their greater consciousness of imperial responsibility emperors were less prejudiced. Orientals understood their own peoples better, and so might make better administrators in the eastern provinces. They might strengthen the administration, even strengthen the senate; and the emperors who brought orientals into the senate were generally emperors who were

One of the most interesting buildings to have been excavated at Ephesus is this library, evidence of a rich Greek family from Asia Minor which played a prominent part in Roman public life in the first and second centuries AD. After a career in provincial government, Ti. Iulius Celsus of Ephesus was consul in AD 92. The library in his home town was built in his memory by his son.

anxious to co-operate with the senate – Nero in the early years of his rule and in the second century Hadrian, Antoninus Pius and Marcus Aurelius. The Greeks whom they advanced came in the main from Asia Minor and not from mainland Greece, and emperors restricted the field of their selection to men of very great wealth whose families had held the Roman citizenship for a considerable time. They were at first earmarked for a career in eastern provinces. The men of distinction brought into the senate from the East by each of the early emperors are to be counted in single figures – five under Augustus, one or two under Tiberius and Claudius, five or six under Nero. In due course such men were to have distinguished careers, like Ti.Iulius Celsus Polemaeanus of Ephesus, consul in 92 and proconsul of Asia, who was honoured after his death by his son, consul in 110, who erected a magnificent library in his home town, a splendid monument even in its ruins today; and C.Iulius Quadratus of Pergamon, also a man who was probably adlected to the senate by Vespasian. and who governed Syria and held a second consulship in AD 105. Herodes Atticus, who owed his public career to Hadrian, was son of the first senator from mainland Greece. The first senator from Lycia in Asia Minor entered the senate under Trajan.

Already there were eastern senators whose careers were no longer restricted to eastern provinces, for instance C.Caristanius Fronto from Caesarea in Pisidia who was legate of the ninth legion in Britain under Vespasian, probably when Agricola was governor; consul in AD 90, he is the first attested eastern consular. From Hadrian onwards this incursion of easterners into western administration was increasingly common. C.Iulius Severus from Ancyra in Galatia governed lower Germany from AD 143 to 150. C.Iulius Eurycles Herklanus, descendant of a Spartan family which had given trouble to Augustus, served on the staff of the governor of Baetica. By this time a change had taken place in the relationship of East to West which is smugly expressed in the Roman oration of Aelius Aristides at the time of Antoninus Pius. He declared that the old Greek-barbarian dichotomy had vanished; now the dis-

tinction lay between Romans and non-Romans. Rich Greek families were now fired by ambition to see their sons enter the Roman senate, and from this time onwards more than half of the provincial senators whose origins are known to us come from the eastern half of the empire. They include a descendant of the fifth-century BC Spartan Brasidas, and Avidius Cassius who governed Syria and was confident enough to stake a claim to govern the empire in AD 175. Ti.Claudius Pompeianus of Antioch, son-in-law of Marcus Aurelius, consul for the second time in 173, may have been descended from a Roman settler; on the other hand iconographers detect in him, as the figure beside Marcus on the column, distinct semitic features. He gave Commodus better advice in AD 180 on northern frontier policy than Commodus was prepared to

Table 4 The increasing representation of the provinces in the Senate from Vespasian to Alexander Severus

	Number of known senators	Number whose origins are known	(Percentage of those with known origins)	
			Italians	Provincials
Vespasian	386	178(46·1%)	83·2	16·8
Domitian	404	163(40·3)	76·6	23·4
Trajan	428	152(35·5)	65·8	34·2
Hadrian	332	156(47)	56·4	43·6
Antoninus Pius	355	167(47)	57·5	42·5
Marcus Aurelius	342	180(52·6)	54·4	45·6
Commodus	259	114(44)	55·3	44·7
Septimius Severus/ Caracalla	937	479(51)	42·6	57·4
Elagabalus/Alexander Severus	471	238(50)	47·5	52·5

The changing origins of provincial senators in the same period (percentage of those with known origins)

	West	East	Africa	Illyria
Vespasian	70	16·7	10	3·3
Domitian	76·3	15·8	5·3	2·6
Trajan	55·8	34·6	5·8	3·8
Hadrian	45·6	36·8	16·2	1·4
Antoninus Pius	23·9	46·5	26·8	2·8
Marcus Aurelius	9·7	53·7	30·5	6·1
Commodus	7·8	60·8	31·4	—
Septimius Severus/ Caracalla	15	57	26	2
Elagabalus/Alexander Severus	13·6	57·6	26·4	2·4

These figures must be used with great caution. The percentage of senators whose origins are identifiable is never more than about half the number of *known* senators, and known senators themselves are considerably less than half the number of actual senators in any of the emperors' reigns. Another factor of importance is that, as a general rule, inscriptions have survived in greater numbers in the East and in Africa than in the West outside Italy itself. With this important caveat, the figures suggest: **1** a steady decline in the percentage of Italians; **2** a steady rise in the percentage of provincials; **3** a very considerable drop after the early second century in the percentage of senators from the western provinces; **4** a remarkable and steady increase in the percentage of provincials from eastern provinces; **5** a general rise in the percentage of senators from Africa.

take. The later emperor Julian thought Marcus should have made him his successor instead of Commodus; and indeed, when Commodus was dead, he was invited to share the purple both by Pertinax and by Didius Julianus. In 212 the first Egyptian, Aelius Coeranus, entered the senate and was at once made consul.

With Elagabalus the situation changed. The days of co-operation between emperor and senate, except for the rule of Severus Alexander, were over. Equestrian procurators were found in what had previously been senatorial posts and, while Greeks were re-cruited in great numbers to fill the gaps in the decimated senate, they were no longer chosen with an eye to their merits and ability. The effective part of the senate in administration was over.

Orientals now tasted supreme power; but they were not senators with distinguished careers behind them. Elagabalus was a young priest in Syria; his cousin Severus Alexander came from Syria too. He was killed in AD 235. Nine years later Philip, an Arab of obscure origins, prefect of the praetorian guard, arranged the murder of Gordian III and became emperor in time to celebrate the thousandth anniversary of the foundation of Rome in 248 before he met his death a year later.

The central government: imperial responsibility

In the Republic the senate was the body which considered provincial conditions and was responsible for imperial and provincial policy. It is hard to imagine a body whose qualifications were better in point of knowledge and experience. Most senators had been out in the provinces at some time or other in the course of their military careers; most senior senators had experience of provincial govern-ment and finance. Their performance should have been better.

Information reached the senate through the dispatches of proconsuls, like Cicero's dispatch describing his meeting with King Ariobarzanes of Cappadocia, and through reports made by returning governors and generals; the senate was perfectly right, for instance, in 61 BC to oppose Pompey's demand that his eastern settlement should be confirmed formally without any opportunity for questioning or discussion. From 149 to 123 and from 81 BC onwards, when juries in the criminal courts were composed wholly or partially of senators, some members of the senate learnt as jurymen much that was discreditable about current provincial conditions. And from time to time deputations or individuals from the provinces received a hearing in the senate at Rome either directly or through a patron, a senator to whom the deputation made its case and who acted as its mouthpiece in the senate.

From listening to a large number of such deputations an inexperienced person might have assumed that the standard of provincial government was very high. Hard on the heels of a returning governor, delegates from the province would arrive to deliver an official vote of thanks for the benefits which they had received from him. Men of experience knew that more often than not such delegates had been sent with reluctance under strong pressure from the retiring governor himself, who hoped that their panegyric might deflect the prosecution for extortionate government which he could reasonably anticipate. Unless the delegates had left the province for Rome before himself, the retiring governor found himself, in this matter, in the hands of his successor; Cicero received angry letters from Appius Claudius, whom he had replaced in Cilicia in 51 BC because a clause in Cicero's edict discouraged the sending of such delegations, whose expense weighed heavily on communities and individuals. The abuse continued into the Empire and when in AD 62 an overweening and rich Cretan on trial in Rome made the blatant statement that, in the case of Crete, it depended on him whether or not such embassies were sent to Rome, Paetus Thrasea made a spirited protest in the senate and Nero took positive action. For the future provincial delegations of this kind were forbidden.

Often natives of a province wished to send representatives to Rome for the opposite purpose, to urge the prosecution of an ex-governor for extortion. Here again, from no creditable motive, their journey to Rome might be impeded by a proconsul acting in the corrupt interest of his predecessor. If they reached Rome, they might or might not find a patron.

In rare cases complaints from natives against a governor might reach Rome while he was still governing his province, but they are unlikely ever to have been more effective than the report that Verres as pro-consul of Sicily was violating a fundamental principle of Roman law by conducting trials and giving judgment in the absence of the accused man. The consuls were incensed. Vigorous speeches of protest were made in the senate. Verres' father promised to write to his son, and nothing more was done. Whether he received a letter from his father or not, Verres, so far from reforming, found a man guilty when not only was he not present or represented in court, but his prosecutor was not present either.

Proconsuls were the senate's servants and bound to obey the senate's instructions, which were normally transmitted to them through the consuls. Though there is some doubt on the point, it is most improbable that consuls were entitled to issue their own independent instructions to provincial governors.

In the Empire the senate retained in the case of the public provinces the responsibility which it had held for all provinces under the Republic, but the emperor was entitled by his *maius imperium* to issue instructions to governors of public as well as of imperial provinces. Indeed, through the presence in public provinces of his personal agents (procurators), men in charge of his private estates, and of public procurators, men engaged in the collection of earmarked taxes, like death duties, which fed the military treasury, for which he had ultimate responsibility, the emperor was supplied with up-to-date information about conditions in the public provinces. Since the senate had no permanent secretariat other than the scribes of the public treasury in Rome who audited the accounts of retiring proconsuls, the emperor often had a better idea of what was going on in a public province than had the senate itself.

The five surviving edicts from Cyrene illustrate Augustus' interference in that province in 7-6 and in 4 BC. In one case he was – perfectly constitutionally – usurping the senate's responsibility. Evidence given by delegates from the province in Rome convinced him that, through connivance between Romans in the province (prosecutors, witnesses and jurymen), justice had been seriously perverted and innocent natives had been condemned to death. And this was under a system by which in criminal trials in the province juries were enrolled from resident Romans. Augustus issued an edict altering the rules for criminal trials. A defendant in the future was to be given the option of trial before a jury composed half of Romans and half of natives (Greeks), if he chose; and for the future, Romans in the province (except for enfranchised Greeks, acting in the interest of a relative) were forbidden to institute proceedings for murder against a native. In the case of votes of thanks to retiring governors from public provinces, as has been seen, it was the senate which talked and Nero who acted.

Under the empire the senate acquired new and important powers, in that, sitting under the presidency of the consuls, it came to constitute a supreme criminal court, and criminal cases of major importance, which included charges of extortionate provincial government, often represented as a concomitant of treason, were no longer brought before the old *quaestiones* but either before the senate or before the emperor in person. So, as in the first days of the quaestiones, senators sat in judgment on their peers. Left to themselves, their natural inclination was to be lenient and to condone misconduct. Yet when the senate was split into fiercely conflicting parties or was frightened of an emperor, as it was of Tiberius, its decisions were often rabidly severe. After all, senators might reflect, it was always open to the emperor, in virtue of his tribunican power, to modify the harsh terms of a sentence. The emperor often sat in the senate and sometimes spoke himself when such cases were being heard.

Co-operation with the senate, a highly sensitive body, was a field in which the highest tact (*civilitas*) was demanded of an emperor. So in the case of criminal trials in Cyrene Augustus did not issue blunt instructions to the proconsul; he introduced his reform with the words, 'Until the senate debates the matter or I have some better proposal to make, it will, I think, be right and proper for governors of Cyrene to act as follows . . .'.

Tiberius' relations with the senate were never easy, and there was some embarrassment in AD 21 when the Numidian Tacfarinas, who had organised and disciplined his army of Musulamii on principles which he had learnt from service in the Roman auxiliary army, resumed his raiding of the province of Africa after being twice defeated by proconsuls who had been honoured with laurelled statues in Rome for their successes. The legion in Africa was the only legion which was then not under the direct command of the emperor; and proconsuls of Africa were chosen by lot from senior, and therefore elderly, ex-consuls. Tiberius wrote to the senate suggesting that it should vary its procedure and select a competent general as proconsul. It replied, asking him to make the appointment. Not unnaturally, Tiberius remonstrated – and then gave them the choice of two names.

Tiberius did not hesitate, however, in preventing the senate from sending a discredited spendthrift, the brother of the later emperor Galba, out to govern Asia or Africa in AD 36; and with the increase in imperial autocracy the need for extreme delicacy disappeared. Domitian had no difficulty in conveying to Agricola when he returned from Britain that, whether he wanted the proconsulship of Africa or Asia or not, he was not to have it.

Occasionally with every appearance of constitutional propriety (an approving decree of the senate) the emperor assumed direct responsibility for a public province. This was done in AD 15 in the case of Macedonia and Achaea after complaints by the natives themselves about the expense of the administration, which was no doubt reflected in the taxes that they paid. Tiberius attached Macedonia and Achaea to his own military province of Moesia and as a result, though they may in the future have seen less of their governor – indeed perhaps because of that fact – they presumably had the satisfaction of paying lower taxes. The arrangement was reversed by Claudius in AD 44.

Trajan's interest in checking the wasteful extravagance with which cities managed their own finances, embarking on ambitious building projects which were often abandoned half-finished, led him to interfere extensively·in areas for whose control the senate was nominally responsible. In Italy itself and in the public provinces he appointed auditors (*correctores* or *curatores*) to investigate the public finances of particular cities, and it seems that the public expenditure of such cities was henceforth dependent on the curator's approval. Trajan's example was followed by succeeding emperors, and we know the names of about a hundred men who received such appointments in cities in Italy between the time of Trajan and Diocletian, over forty in public provinces in the West and over twenty-five in the East.

There were cases when intemperate and ill-advised expenditure was prevalent in the cities oi aɪ entire province and in such cases Trajan sent the equivalent of a corrector with responsibility for checking the finances of the province as a whole. In fact such a man replaced the proconsul and had greater power in that he was authorised to investigate the affairs of 'free cities' in the province, which were normally outside the governor's control. A certain Maximus was sent in this way to Achaea early in the second century AD, and the younger Pliny was sent to Bithynia in AD 109, to be succeeded there after his death by his friend Cornutus Tertullus. In such appointments the public decencies were observed, and the title of the special commissioner indicated that he was an imperial legate appointed with the approval of the senate.

The appointment of auditors to cities showed the emperor's concern for the subjects of the empire, but it showed too that a great number of cities were incapable of responsible management of their own affairs, and the fact was brought home to them in a humiliating fashion. What started as paternalism was to end as yet another element in growing imperial bureaucracy.

Co-operative government, whether friendly or not, between the senate and the emperors survived until the Severan age, the degree of co-operation depending on the character of the ruling emperor. It was particularly close in the second century when Antoninus Pius and Marcus Aurelius ruled. In the third century, at least after the death of Severus Alexander, the senate as a body and senators as individuals were gradually ousted from responsibility for imperial administration.

Imperial government: the emperor and his advisors. The emperor's responsibility for what went on in the public provinces was secondary. His primary responsibility was for the vast field of policy and administration which was under his direct control: the army, the imperial provinces, foreign relations and diplomacy, the food supply and the general finance of the empire.

In the formulation of policy a good emperor had his own ideas, but he needed the advice and criticism of reliable men of experience and good judgment. A young emperor might lean heavily on other people's advice, sometimes for good, as when the young Nero's administration was largely controlled by Seneca and Burrus, sometimes for bad, as when the young Severus Alexander took orders from his mother.

The emperor invited expert advice both informally and in council, the *consilium principis.* This was in the oldest Roman tradition. Magistrates at Rome had often taken formal advice from friends whom they summoned as counsellors and a provincial governor invited other Romans, whether from his staff or from residents in the district where the assizes were being held, to sit with him on the Bench. So, from Augustus onwards, emperors invited advisers who were technically known as his 'friends' (*amici*) both from among senators and from among equites to sit in council with him.

The question for discussion might be a matter of imperial policy. Hadrian is reported as having consulted his amici on whether or not to abandon Trajan's province of Dacia, just as he had abandoned the new province of Mesopotamia. Antoninus Pius is said to have taken no decision affecting the provinces without consulting his 'friends'. Such meetings were summoned in haste in an emergency – if, for instance, there was catastrophic news from one of the frontiers; it must therefore be assumed that they were held frequently under Domitian. This was the kind of council-meeting which Juvenal pilloried in his fourth satire, a meeting summoned 'when the last of the Flavians was lacerating the half-dead world and the empire was in servitude to a bald-headed Nero' – the question for consideration being the correct treatment of a prodigiously large turbot which Domitian had been given. 'It was a meeting summoned in such haste that you might have thought that a terrifying dispatch had arrived from one of the frontiers.'

Alternatively a council might be summoned to advise the emperor when he sat as a supreme judge, most commonly in cases which came to him on appeal from the army or the provinces. Trials are the better for the presence of trained lawyers, and it is to be assumed that from an early stage jurisconsults were among the 'friends' who were present on such occasions, for the judgments were often of far-reaching importance because they established precedents which might later be appealed to as binding. Large questions of imperial law and principle might be raised and decided. It is to be regretted that on the three occasions on which the younger Pliny attended Trajan's councils the agenda contained no items of more world-shaking importance than a tribune who defied the law by refusing to divorce his wife when she committed adultery with a centurion, alleged forgeries of wills and the question whether Vienne in Gaul should be allowed to hold the Greek games for which it had received a benefaction.

The numbers of men summoned to council will have varied in accordance with the importance of the issues and also the whereabouts of the emperor, whether he was in Rome, on the frontiers or, like Hadrian, on tour. There were evidently a considerable number of 'friends' with Severus Alexander when he was murdered on the Rhine in AD 235, just as 'the cream of the senate' had been with M. Aurelius on the Danube at the time of his death in 180. In Rome there were thirty-six senators, sixteen of them ex-consuls, at one of the trials of recalcitrant Alexandrian Greeks recorded in the papyri of the Acts of the Pagan Martyrs. Juvenal's pastiche mentions eleven counsellors by name. Voting was by ballot.

The Council became a little more formal under Hadrian, when its trained professional jurisconsults received salaries and presumably enjoyed permanent membership.

The two forms of council can never be rigidly distinguished, for many of the invited members, being the emperor's 'friends', will have been the same in either case. In the military anarchy of the third century the short-lived emperors evidently needed advisers and must have consulted the best brains available, usually their own senior officers. With the establishment of the tetrarchy later more settled practices were resumed. Each of the Augusti and each of the Caesars summoned his own council, the senior council, whose decisions were those of the senior Augustus, having universally binding force.

In the early empire the council had never lost a certain informality. The members attended on the emperor's personal invitation as his 'friends'. The decision reached was not theirs, but his, even if the critical man in the street liked to think that the emperor called a council meeting so as to avoid personal responsibility. This, for instance, is Lactantius' account of the preliminaries to the great persecution of the Christians by Diocletian and Galerius in AD 303:

Diocletian decided to consult his Friends. He was a nasty man; when he decided to do good, he consulted nobody, so as to receive all the credit himself. When he was up to mischief and knew that what he proposed was blameworthy, he called in a number of advisers, so that his own misdoings might be laid at their doors, So a few legal and military experts were summoned and, in order of importance, asked to give their opinions. Some who loathed the Christians, thought them enemies of the gods and opponents of public religion, and voted for their extermination. Others disagreed; but when they saw what Galerius wanted, either from fear or from the hope of currying favour, they gave their vote with the rest.

While good counsellors took a certain weight off an emperor's shoulders, they left him still with a dauntingly heavy burden to carry. The catalogue of social scandal and police-court news which from the pens of ancient writers passed for history, conceals the sheer bulk of work which a responsible emperor got through in a single day. In public he was never off duty. Even on his way to the games he was liable to have petitions thrust into his hands; at the games themselves Julius Caesar and Marcus Aurelius spent time in reading official papers which they had brought with them. Emperors like Vespasian and Marcus Aurelius worked late into the night and were up and at work well before daybreak. Indeed it was only before daybreak that the elder Pliny could hope to catch Vespasian free for the discussion of official business.

A vast number of questions were passed up to the emperor for decision by the branches of his personal service, each with a freedman at its head until the end of the first century AD and after that an *eques*. The heavy responsibilities of the head of the finance department, the *a rationibus*, are self-evident. The *ab epistulis* was responsible for the dispatch (and often the drafting) of the emperor's official letters, the receipt of all dispatches from provincial and army commanders and from officials (procurators) handling the supply of corn from Africa and Egypt; he also dealt with promotions within the equestrian military service.

The *a libellis* was at the head of the Office of Petitions, and his office eventually absorbed that of the *a cognitionibus*, the emperor's chief adviser in matters of civil law. Petitions were either handed to the emperor in person or transmitted through a provincial governor. They were returned with the emperor's rescript. We possess the texts of a number of *libelli* from the late second and the third centuries from tenants on imperial estates in north Africa and in Asia Minor. They complained of the behaviour of soldiers and public officials who distrained on their services and their possessions, sometimes with the information that they had already appealed without success to the governor of their province. The emperor's rescripts, as we have them, were accommodating, but there is little reason to think that they were effective in suppressing injustice.

The duties of the *a libellis* were relentless indeed, if we judge by the high-flown language of Seneca's *consolatio* to Polybius under Claudius:

Great eminence is what? Pure slavery. You are never your own master. Thousands of petitioners must be given a hearing, thousands of petitions must be arranged in order. Innumerable issues from all over the world must be disposed, so as to be submitted in due order to the attention of our great ruler. You can never break down and cry. If you are to listen to numbers of tearful petitioners and dry the eyes of those who are in danger and seek the compassion of our most gentle prince, you must keep your own eyes dry.

The offices of the imperial bureaux, with all their important records, were in Rome and it is clear that the efficiency of administration must have suffered severely when the emperor was out of Rome for long periods of time. This was evident early on, in the last ten years of the principate of Tiberius, when he was on Capri. From the late first century onwards emperors were often, and in the third century almost continuously, out of Rome and on the frontiers. The most important departmental chiefs accompanied them; administration would have broken down completely if they had not. The father of Claudius Etruscus was on the German front with Gaius in AD 39; Hadrian's *ab epistulis* Suetonius was probably with him in Britain in AD 122. Indeed, until the time of Caracalla the *ab epistulis* and the *a libellis* seem regularly to have accompanied the emperor when he was out in the provinces. But they cannot have been accompanied by the whole of their office staff; they cannot have carried all their files around with them. So the efficiency of the imperial bureaux must have suffered until, in the course of the third century, it broke down altogether.

Problems of the central government
The administration of every section of the empire, large or small, depended on the quality of the individual administrator and, except for those parts which the senate nominally controlled, the

selection of these men was the emperor's responsibility – in the case of the highest posts, his direct responsibility. In making his selection he depended on reports and must have taken advice. Though there were no formal selection-boards, it is clear that in the course of the first century of the empire a careful assessment was made of a man's quality and promise at the very start of his senatorial career, when he held one of the minor magistracies in Rome; he was identified as potentially a soldier, a man to be groomed with a view to his finishing his career as governor of one of the great military provinces or, on the other hand, a man qualified for a predominantly civilian career. Mistakes were made, of course, and these are reflected in the careers of men which at some point or other were suddenly cut short. On the other hand, successful careers have left their records, sometimes in the literary sources, more often in inscriptions, particularly epitaphs. It was no accident that Agricola received three postings to Britain: first as military tribune in AD 61, then as commander of legion xx nine years later and finally as governor and commander of the army of four legions in Britain eight years after that. When the younger Pliny did his military service as a young man in Syria, notice was taken of the fact that he was good with figures and this discovery determined the whole of his future career: prefect of the military treasury, prefect of the public

This inscription on bronze dated 189 BC is the earliest surviving Roman   147
inscription from Spain. It records an act of L. Aemulius Paullus, then
governor of Further Spain. The small village of Lascuta, a dependency of
the neighbouring Hasta, had evidently (unlike Hasta) given assistance to
Paullus in his campaigning. The inscription marked its reward: freedom
and independence at the pleasure of Rome.

treasury in Rome and finally special commissioner to investigate
the disordered finances of Bithynia.

An emperor's next problem, one which was intimately personal
and which could only be shared with his most intimate and trust-
worthy friends, was a problem of personal security: how far could
he trust the loyalty of each of the commanders of the great frontier
armies? He had, and used, spies, either as has been seen, his own –
particularly equestrian – officials who were openly employed by
him or, from Hadrian's time onwards, his secret service, the
frumentarii as they were called at first, later the *agentes in rebus*.

Apart from unpredictable emergencies, emperors must always
have been concerned about long-term frontier problems and
anxious to discuss such problems with their friends. The adventures
of Gaius on the Rhine and the invasion of Britain by Claudius were
not personal whims, spontaneously executed. They must have been
discussed, the pros weighed against the cons and extensive prepara-
tions made beforehand. Similar discussions must have affected
Hadrian's decision to abandon Trajan's eastern conquests,
Commodus' decision not to continue fighting in the North after
Marcus Aurelius' death and, in the third century, the decision of
Aurelian to withdraw the Roman population and Roman troops
from Dacia.

Lowering like thunderclouds, there were the grave problems of
imperial economics. One such problem was never out of mind: the
necessity of ensuring that the citizen of the capital received his
daily bread. This was a reason for Augustus' acceptance of the *cura
annonae*. In the first two centuries of the empire emperors were
generally resident in Rome and knew that morale in the capital was
largely determined by the assurance of food. 'It is easy for an
ordinary man to forget,' Tiberius said, 'that every day the life of the
people of Rome is dependent on the winds and the waves. This is
something that an emperor can never afford to forget.' A consti-
tuent of the panic when Gaius was killed was the rumour that the
public granaries were empty. The emperor's tight control of
Egypt, Vespasian's hold on the province in AD 69, illustrate the

148

For Trajan's column, see page 117.
This scene from the column shows
the transport of wine by river for
the troops during the Dacian wars.

same story. Acute shortage of corn in Rome (through his own control of the available supplies) caused the downfall of the praetorian prefect Cleander under Commodus in 189 or soon after. Zenobia's control of Egypt and the corn supply was a reason why Aurelian was forced to campaign against her. We are told of a panic in Rome from the same cause, terror of a lack of corn, in AD 359. Hence the attention of emperors from Claudius onwards to the guilds of corn-shippers, and the favours granted them.

But there were imperial economic problems of far greater gravity.

First of all, parallel to the steady decline during the present century of the economic predominance of Britain as an exporter of manufactured goods to many of the countries which were once her colonies, the economic importance of Italy at the centre of the Roman empire was declining all the time. In the second century BC Campania had exported wine to southern Gaul; by the end of the first century AD the vineyards of Burgundy, the Moselle and the Rhine were producing better wines, wines which in the Rhineland, where soldiers were big drinkers, and in Gaul generally, on account of the smaller expense of transport, cost less than imported Italian wine. Indeed in the second century AD the city of Rome itself imported wine as well as oil in large quantities from Spain, as can be seen today from the most startling of all the world's rubbish dumps, Monte Testaccio in Rome, where the fragments of over forty million amphorae are evidence, by an expert calculation, of the import of half a billion gallons of cheap Spanish wine. Moreover artifacts which had once been exported to every part of the world from Italy came to be manufactured extensively in the provinces themselves; in pottery, for instance, an Arretine ware which was coarser and cheaper but just as serviceable as the original Italian product. Gaul became one of the main centres of production, and by the end of the first century Italian export of Arretine had sunk to insignificance. New centres for cheaper and, except for Aquileia, better glass than was manufactured in Italy sprang up, particularly on the Rhine.

In an attempt to arrest the decline of the wine-export (and perhaps with some thought of increasing home-grown corn) Domitian's
government faced the problem and tried to solve it by measures
strikingly similar to those taken by the French government in the
1930s in the interest of wine-production in Algeria. An edict was
issued instructing wine-growers in the provinces to grub up half
their vineyards; in Italy no new vineyards were to be planted. However, the edict was evidently ineffective.

There was a danger that, as the senate came to be recruited increasingly from provincials, its outlook would be correspondingly
imperial and that, in economics, the parochial interests of Italy
would be forgotten. As early as Julius Caesar, money-lenders had
not been allowed to operate with more than a third of their capital
and, to encourage a healthy interest in Italian agriculture, had been
compelled to invest the other two-thirds in real estate. So Trajan

Trade map of the Empire showing
principal products and imports.

AMBER

SARMATIA

CORN

HONEY HIDES

MARE CASPIUM

Olbia

FLAX Panticapaeum

Chersonesus

Taurunum

TIMBER

GOLD HORSES

Tomi

RON CORN FISH

SALT

TIMBER

Trapezus

Artaxata

PONTUS EUXINUS

HORSES

Thessalonica

Byzantium Chalcedon

Nicaea Nicomedia Ancyra

WINE

HONEY

Cyzicus

WINE OIL

HORSES

SILK from China

Antium

Mytilene

MARBLE

TIMBER

PARCHMENT

Hatra

METALS

BITUMEN

Chalcis

POTTERY

Athenae

Ephesus

WOOL

CARPETS

Antiochia

Aegina

MARBLE

Miletus

TEXTILES

Dura-Europos Ctesiphon

Delos

OIL

GLASS

Palmyra

Rhodos

COPPER

Byblus

Spasinu Charax

TIMBER

Damascus

INTERNUM

Tyrus Sidon

PURPLE DYE

Caesarea

PURPLE DYE

Gaza

TEXTILES

LEATHER GOODS

Apollonia

Alexandria

Petra

ASPHALT

Ptolemais

SILPHIUM

GLASS

LINEN

TEXTILES

FRANKINCENSE

PAPYRUS

WILD BEASTS

IVORY

Myus Hormus

CORN

PORPHYRY

Berenice

ARABIA DESERTA

Leuce Come

Paper and precious stones from India (Ctesiphon, Bostra, Gerasa, Petra and Dura were all important trade centres)

Ivory imported from central Africa. The route ran either by way of the Sahara or the ports of the Red Sea.

Frankincense, perfumes and spices from south Arabia

IMP·TITO·CAESAR·DIVI·VES
PM·TR·P·VIIII·IMP·XV·COS·VII·DE
ET·CAESARI·DIVI·VESPASIANI·F·DOM
IVVENTVTIS·ET·OMNIVM·
CN·IVLIO·AGRICOLA
MVNICIPIVM·VERVLA

followed, as it would be followed today, by a published programme of retrenchment and vastly increased taxation.

Budgeting in a rough and ready way there must always have been, but there is only one case in which we know of exact budgeting. When Augustus established the military treasury in AD 6 to pay gratuities to discharged soldiers, the prospective annual outlay was calculated and the proceeds of two new taxes, the five per cent death duty paid by Roman citizens and the one per cent purchase tax were allotted to this treasury, on a calculation that its account would be self-balancing. Later, the highly unpopular purchase tax was reduced and eventually abolished, the income from the province of Cappadocia being paid in to the military treasury as a substitute. Vespasian instituted three new separate public accounts, the *fiscus Iudaicus*, which received the tax of two drachmae a year which he imposed on all Jews, and the *fiscus Alexandrinus* and *fiscus Asiaticus* which evidently dealt with moneys of some category or other coming in from Egypt and Asia respectively.

In general there was no variation in standard rates of taxation, with reductions in some years and increases in others, as happens in a modern state. Since the upkeep of the army and the expense of warfare made the biggest call on imperial finances, a reduction in taxation might have been expected in times of peace and a greatly increased standard of taxation in periods of protracted war, as under Domitian, Trajan, Marcus Aurelius and Septimius Severus. Instead a series of ill-regulated distraints were made on property-owners in times of emergency, often unjust and always the cause of great resentment.

SIANI·F·VESPASIANO·AVG
G·VIII·CENSORI·PATRI·PATRIAE
TIANO·COS·VI·DESIG·VII·PRINCIPI
OLLEGIORVM·SACERDOTI
EGATO·AVG·PRO·PR
IVM·BASILICA·ORNATA

ruled that senators must invest a third of their whole capital (not merely a third of the million sesterces which constituted their qualification to be senators) in Italian land – a portion which Marcus Aurelius subsequently reduced to a quarter – and so acquire a personal interest in the agricultural problems of the peninsula. How effectively these regulations were enforced, we cannot say.

Graver by far were the large budgetary and currency problems which, given the same conditions today, would call for the services of armies of highly trained economists, statisticians and 'planners'. In this field the relationship of the transactions of the public treasury of the state (*aerarium Saturni*) to the expenditure of public, semi-public and private moneys by the emperor through his *fiscus*, on which so much ink has been spilt, is a technical matter and has little bearing on the problems themselves.

Regular, and periodically more detailed, surveys of the whole finances of the empire were conducted by the emperors through their trained personal staffs on the basis of census returns and balance-sheets which came in from the separate provinces. Augustus had such an up-to-date survey ready to hand when he fell ill in 23 BC; and one was available and ready for publication at his death, together with the names of those freedmen and slaves who were alone with himself in understanding and being able to explain the figures. A special survey was set in hand by Vespasian after the civil war of AD 69, as a result of which he announced that the empire was, on paper anyhow, in debt to the stupendous figure of forty thousand million sesterces. The announcement was not

Crises arose from time to time on account of there not being sufficient currency in circulation, as a result of hoarding by an excessively cautious emperor like Tiberius or in disturbed and uncertain times by individuals, of insufficient issues of new coinage (an imperial responsibility) and of the regular drain of gold coin out of the empire in exchange for the silks, perfumes and other luxury imports to the empire from the East: at the time of Vespasian a hundred million sesterces a year disappeared in this way.

In general, however, in the first two centuries of the Empire, prices were remarkably stable. This can be inferred from the fact that soldiers' pay was unchanged from Augustus to Domitian, who raised it by a third. After this it remained unchanged for a hundred years until towards the end of the second century when, quite suddenly, the currency system of the empire started its rapid and catastrophic collapse. Commodus raised the soldiers' pay by a quarter, Septimius Severus in the course of a few years by another third, his son Caracalla by another half. In a quarter of a century it jumped from 1200 to 3000 sesterces a year.

Caracalla's extension of Roman citizenship to all free inhabitants of the Roman empire in AD 212 was a fine gesture, a splendid climax to the oldest and strongest tradition which is one of the notable explanations of Roman greatness. Yet, except for propaganda purposes, there is likely to have been little emotion about the act. It was a desperate effort to increase the revenues of the Roman imperial accounts; for on the death of a Roman citizen five per cent death duties were charged on his estate.

In the third century, as will be seen, currency and orderly taxation collapsed together.

Administration in the field

The governor's Residence was in the capital city of a province. There he had his staff and his registry, which contained copies of Roman public criminal law in as far as it affected the provinces, the charter given to the province at its foundation and subsequent senatorial decrees and imperial edicts and rescripts. In public provinces, as in the Republic, there would be copies of the edicts of previous governors.

The governor held court in the capital. He also went on circuit with his *legatus iuridicus*, judging cases in the regular assize towns. Normally he judged criminal cases himself, sitting with a *consilium* of advisers, Roman citizens whom he invited to join him, partly from his own suite of *comites* and partly from residents, who were listed in the assize district, the local *conventus civium Romanorum*. In certain provinces in the East – Bithynia, Asia, Crete and Cyrene – there appears to have been trial by jury in criminal cases, jurors being selected from Romans or from Romans and Greeks, who possessed a certain property qualification. Civil cases were generally tried in native courts.

The governor could condemn to death, exile or hard labour (for instance, to the mines). In the case of offences against Roman public law (e.g. murder, forgery, kidnapping, adultery, breaches of the peace) he could probably condemn even Roman citizens without appeal, but in other cases a Roman citizen – like St Paul – could appeal against corporal or capital punishment with the right of having his case transferred for trial to Rome. Pliny in Bithynia executed natives for Christianity, but referred Roman citizens who had been accused to Rome. After Hadrian, when a distinction was made in the case of natives between the type of punishment that could be inflicted on members of the upper class (*honestiores*) and members of the lower class (*humiliores*), the former acquired the same rights of appeal as were possessed by Roman citizens. While a governor could pass a sentence of exile, he could not 'exile to a named island' without imperial confirmation and he could not in any circumstances 'deport to an island', a sentence which involved complete loss of civic rights; this sentence was only passed by the emperor, the urban prefect, or the prefect of the praetorian guard.

Outside formal jurisdiction, he had the responsibility for the frontiers, if his was a frontier province, and for internal security, the keeping of law and order. So we have vivid pictures from Philo of Avillius Flaccus, prefect of Egypt, desperately at sea when confronted by a pogrom in Alexandria in AD 38 and, in the *Acts*, of Gallio, governor of Achaea thirteen years later, deciding that it was wiser not to take official notice of the conflict which arose from the delation of St Paul, for which there was no legal warrant, by the Jews in Corinth. It was the governor's responsibility, too, to do everything possible to ensure the prompt payment of taxes and, clearly to give all possible advice and assistance to local authorities.

He was on his own, except for the advice which he might invite from his legates and his *comites* and in an age when communications were slow, he was out of touch with his government (the senate or the emperor, as the case might be). He had the responsibility, therefore, of deciding whether an issue confronting him was one which he was competent to settle on his own responsibility or whether it was one on which he should seek advice from Rome. One of the edicts from Cyrene illustrates what a passage from the Digest shows to have been a not uncommon dilemma: men condemned in the courts announced that they had information of the highest importance concerning a conspiracy against the emperor's life. Should attention be paid to them or not? The proconsul of Cyrene sent three such men in chains to Rome; there they admitted to Augustus that their whole story was a fabrication. In his edict, Augustus stated firmly that the proconsul had acted correctly and was not open to criticism. In his patient answers to the younger Pliny Trajan suggested more than once that Pliny might perhaps be a little braver sometimes in taking a decision on his own initiative.

'How far from easy it is to be good', Cicero once wrote in a moment of exasperation, in reference to his own experience as a provincial governor. For the exercise of integrity met with immediate hostility in circles nearest to himself. He had to suppress graft and favouritism in his own staff and, declining invitations to share in the profits, he had to step heavily on the corrupt practices of private agents and tax collectors. One dodge, for instance, in cases where corn was compulsorily purchased for the troops and officials in a province, was to instruct a farmer to deliver his portion in some distant part of the province and, when he complained about the expense of such transport, to confront him with the alternative of paying a sum of money far higher than the value of the corn itself – on the specious pretence that in the district where delivery was required the price of corn was abnormally high. Distraints made on communities and individuals for the supply of animals in connection with the public post (the *cursus publicus*), demands made by officials and soldiers for free board and lodging, distraints made in the third and fourth centuries of the empire for goods and services in lieu of taxes, all involved flagrant injustices. Claudius once wrote of the public post, 'I tried to relieve towns in Italy and the provinces of the burden of providing transport, and I believed that I had found ample safeguards; yet wicked men found ways of getting round them', and many a well-intentioned governor must have had the same experience.

There is an interesting story of two officials in conflict which could be parallelled in the history of other empires. In AD 58, the Upper German legions were commanded by an imaginative man who appreciated the great economic benefits that could result – and, indeed, have since resulted – from the construction of a canal to connect the Saône (Arar) and the Moselle. He wanted work for his troops, and so proposed the enterprise to the governor of Gallia Belgica, who turned it down smartly, refusing to have soldiers in his province. Why, we may ask, did the commander of the army in Upper Germany let the matter drop? Why did he not put his proposal up to the emperor? Or did he – and was it lost in the files of the imperial civil service in Rome?

As in all empires, there were good governors and bad. There were men like Verres in Sicily in the late Republic, and Marius Priscus in Africa at the end of the first century AD, who did not shrink even from condemning innocent men to death, as long as the bribe was sufficiently heavy. On the other hand we can follow the administration of two governors of unquestionable integrity, Cicero and the younger Pliny, from their letters, and we have the biography of Agricola, a far more gifted administrator than either.

For such a man – and there were many – the checking of corruption among his juniors and among tax-collectors was only the negative side of administration. More important by far was its constructive side, developing the standard of living, 'romanising' the native peoples for whose well-being the governor was temporarily responsible. Here the opportunities were far greater in western than in eastern provinces, opportunities in particular for the institution of city life and the development of municipal pride from its beginnings, the erection of handsome public buildings – temples, arcades, *piazze*, public baths. In particular there was the building and staffing of new schools, mainly for boys of good family, like the college for the sons of chiefs which was already flourishing at Autun (Augustodunum) in Gaul in AD 21. For here, an imaginative governor realised, was the material out of which the future government of the empire could be moulded. If the boys were not Roman citizens already, they soon might be; they might themselves one day command legions and govern provinces.

The Provinces: inhabitants

In all provinces there were Romans; also there were people who were not Romans at all. Romans were of four sorts. They might be birds of passage, men who came out from Rome and in due course returned to Rome, members of the administration from the governor and his staff and the big army officers at the top to the lowest tax-collector (a procurator or one of the hated 'publicans' of the New Testament) or a rent-collector on an imperial estate at the bottom; and, if there were troops in the province, they too were part of the establishment. There were also Roman and Italian businessmen who came and went, members of business firms, equivalents of the modern commercial traveller. Thirdly, there were settlers or the descendants of settlers, men who had come out from Italy themselves or whose ancestors had come out perhaps generations earlier, willingly or under compulsion, to seek a living in a new country. Fourthly, there were the natives who had acquired Roman citizenship.

Others were not Romans at all, the natives and families who had immigrated, just as Romans immigrated, to make a new home and set up in trade and business, from some other quarter of the empire.

Romans first and, at the top, the administration – paid men under the Caesars, doing a job, subject to Roman government regulations, which had been framed with the object of frightening them into behaving with integrity. An official administrator, for instance, was forbidden either to marry a native woman – anybody with experience of colonial administration understands well what pressure might be brought to bear on him in such an event – or to acquire property or do business in a province in which he held an official post.

The popularity of officials depended not only on their own character but also on the functions which they discharged. In no society in history have tax-collectors been popular men. And the officials in charge of imperial estates were the objects of vociferous protest in the third and fourth centuries to the emperors by whom they were employed; it was alleged that, instead of standing up for the peasants, they connived, on remunerative terms, in the pillaging and exactions of the soldiery and the tax-collectors.

The second sort of Roman was the often courageous and adventurous businessman, out to advance trade with the flag, often before it. He saw the prospect of big profits in the opening of new markets for Roman exports and, particularly in the days of imperial expansion, he took his life in his hands. Such men were endangered by Jugurtha at Cirta and at Vaga; they were massacred by Mithridates' troops in Asia in 88 BC; they were slaughtered at Noviodunum in the territory of the Aedui in Gaul in 52 BC, in Pannonia in the rebellion of AD 6, across the Danube in AD 19, in the province of Gallia Lugdunensis in the rising of AD 21. Numbers of them would have perished at Utica in 46 BC in the civil war had Cato not behaved as imaginatively as he did.

Settlers, or their ancestors, were of various kinds. There were stragglers, Roman and Italian soldiers, who after a campaign stayed and settled down in a province instead of going home; thus many of Pompey's troops may have remained in the East in 62 BC. Others, discharged soldiers in the main, had been settled, given homes and land, in old towns taken over and enlarged or in new towns specially built (*coloniae*) as part of a government enterprise after a war. This was the origin of the Marian colonies, Uchi Maius, Thuburnica etc., founded in 103 BC in Africa and of the very numerous colonies of ex-soldiers established by Julius Caesar and by Augustus in Narbonese Gaul and in Spain. If the colony was the enlargement of an existing native community, the natives crept under the Roman umbrella and acquired citizenship themselves. Sometimes a non-Roman town was given municipal status, in which event its inhabitants acquired Roman citizenship, like Volubilis in Mauretania from the moment when Claudius made Mauretania a Roman province, in reward for its good services to the Romans in the fighting when the Romans took it over. Also there were Latin colonies whose citizens had Latin citizenship; in the case of those who held the local magistracies, they were automatically granted full Roman citizenship. All colonies and *municipia* were given charters in accordance with which they regulated their own affairs, with annual magistrates, town-counsellors (*decuriones*) and priests.

Like its prototype, the colony established in Italy in the early days of Roman expansion, the provincial military colony had other purposes than that of providing a new home and new opportunities to its settlers. It was intended to show the flag, to disseminate the Roman type of life and at the same time to bare its teeth if natives in its neighbourhood were restive or disloyal. Its first settlers could be alerted in an emergency; if need arose, they required no instruction in the way to fight. Some of these colonies settled down to a future of success and prosperity, like Timgad (Thamugadi), Trajan's settlement in AD 100 for discharged legionaries on the southern frontier of Africa among nomadic tribesmen, an admirably chosen spot, strategic, fertile and with great commercial opportunities. It survived until the Berbers destroyed it in AD 535;

yet in its ruins it is today a superb example of a city built (like Aosta in Italy) on the model of a Roman camp. Such military colonies sometimes had their growing pains, like Colchester (Camulodunum) among the Trinobantes in Britain, whose first military settlers, forgetful of their own vulnerability – for Authority in establishing the township neglected to give it walls – pillaged and insulted the natives for ten years until in AD 61 the patience of the the natives was exhausted. They sacked the place and burnt it down.

Apart from the administrators, the businessmen, the inhabitants of the colonies, there were sporadic Romans all over the empire. There were, for instance, farmers who acquired land in southern Gaul because the prospects seemed to them better there than in Italy. There were Romans who lived in Greece from preference, like retired English who have settled down in Switzerland or in the south of France. And there were exiles, men who had no option but to live outside Italy.

All the time natives were turning into Roman citizens: every magistrate in a Latin colony at the conclusion of his magistracy; every soldier in the Roman auxiliary army when he completed his term of service (something like five thousand men a year). And there were innumerable grants of individual citizenship in return for services, made by the emperor on his own initiative or in response to a personal request, like the younger Pliny's request to Trajan to give Roman citizenship to his doctor, the Egyptian Harpocras.

There were the natives (*peregrini*) who were, technically, Rome's allies (*socii*). Certain communities were allies in fact; these, within provinces, were *civitates liberae* or *liberae ac foederatae*, generally communities which had taken Rome's part at a time when their country, the subsequent province, was conquered by the Romans and whose independence within a province was afterwards respected. They were in a province but not wholly of it; the governor could not interfere in their local administration and jurisdiction. They were, however, liable to taxation, unless in very rare cases they received a special grant of *immunitas*. Such communities apart, all natives, whether belonging to cities or organised cantonally as in Gallia Lugdunensis, were subject to the Roman governor's administration. Though most natives aspired to Roman citizenship, its acquisition by individuals might embarrass the community to which the individual belonged, and one of the edicts of Augustus to Cyrene made it clear that Roman citizenship did not automatically absolve such men from their normal civic duties, the payment of local taxes or their performance of public service.

Romans complaisantly judged all other peoples by a single standard, their own exalted opinion of themselves, and, judged by this standard, all other peoples fell short. Africans were over-sexed, Egyptians tiresomely litigious, Syrians rogues. Greeks and Asiatics were effete. Judged by the current norm, a short Roman, Gauls were disparaged on account of their great size. Also, because they crumpled easily in great heat, they were often described as soft, an epithet which nobody would have applied to them in their own country. Illyrian and Danubian peoples, who were destined in its last stage to take over and run the Roman Empire, were judged to be good fighters but very simple-minded.

Native peoples of the empire, of course, were not to be found only in their own provinces. Great numbers of them emigrated, just as Romans emigrated, from their homelands to another part of the empire as sailors, traders, businessmen. There was a constant flow of natives of the eastern Mediterranean to the West, and this is how religions, in particular, spread; Isis-worship for instance, to nearly every western port and even inland to such important commercial cities as Beneventum (Benevento) in south Italy. Jews, too, and Christians. The victims of the hideous persecution of Christians at Lyons in AD 177 were chiefly Greek.

Greece and Rome

At the news of the battle of Trasimene in 217 BC peace was hurriedly negotiated to end the war of Philip v of Macedon and the Achaean League against the Aetolian League in Greece, and at the peace conference a speaker gave warning: 'If you allow the clouds now

A plan of Trajan's African colony of Timgad, laid out with the orderly precision of a Roman camp. **1** the theatre; **2** the Forum; **3** the public library; **4** the main street cutting through the centre, like the *decumanus maximus* of a camp; **5** and **6** Christian churches.

gathering in the West to settle on Greece, I am afraid that will be the end of our own diversions, making war or peace with one another. The time will come when we shall go down on our knees and pray to the gods to restore us such independent power of settling our own disputes.'

He was a far-sighted man. Within twenty years Greece had come into the ambit of Roman domination.

There was an ambivalence in the Roman attitude to the Greeks. For Greeks of the contemporary world, century after century, they entertained an undiminishing contempt. Greeks were facile, undependable. They were clever talkers and quick thinkers and therefore suspect to Romans whose thought was as ponderous as their speech. Greeks wasted days in public debate, sitting down for the purpose in their stone theatres, and this was a reason why the Romans themselves refused to have permanent stone theatres in Rome until the end of the Republic. There was no longer anything tough or effective about the Greeks as fighters. This was the popular Roman opinion of Greeks, trumpeted in his public utterances as loudly by the humane Cicero as by any Roman philistine.

On the other hand there was classical Greek culture, Greek literature, in particular Homer and the tragedians, and Greek art which the Romans had nothing to match. In the Republic, therefore, and until after Virgil when Romans had their own Homer, literary education at Rome was education in Greek literature. In educated homes the Roman child learnt Greek and was bilingual from an early age. The sons of the rich completed their education in oratory and philosophy in Athens or Rhodes. As a result many Roman proconsuls in eastern provinces were able to speak in public in fluent Greek.

In the course of the first century AD members of the governing class, increasingly of western provincial origin, spoke Greek less and less well. In fact Vespasian was advised to make sure that governors sent to the East could speak and understand Greek, and the example was given of one who could not.

Travelling in Sicily, Greece and Asia Minor, Romans admired

the surviving monuments of Greek antiquity. Indeed, what they admired, they coveted. What men like Verres coveted, they took.

The material impact on Rome of contact with contemporary Greek life in Sicily and South Italy in the third century BC and in Greece and the East in the second century was immediate and lasting. Romans were at once confronted by the realisation of their own barbarous shortcomings. They had no theatre, no rich country houses. Though, like rich Greeks, they enjoyed hunting, they were unaccustomed to the seductive charms of elegant public baths or to the physical exercises and sports which Greeks practised in the palaestra and the gymnasium. So, under Greek influence, a great change came over Roman social life. The rich built themselves extravagant country villas. Dank and sordid bath-houses gave way to extensive, well-lighted public baths and the old and young alike took to exercising themselves in the Greek manner, at Rome in the Campus Martius, before they bathed. The moralists scowled from Cato in the second century BC onwards, and declared that this must inevitably weaken the tough native Roman fibre. The seductive extravagance of private life was a Greek infection the more sententiously condemned by the critics as it was more and more enjoyed by Romans at large. So, in Horace's words, captive Greece captured its tough conqueror.

Throughout history the Greeks regarded the Romans with a mixture of incomprehension, fear, envy and contempt.

Incomprehension, particularly of its government which represented none of the simple constitutional forms; it was neither monarchy, aristocracy nor democracy, but a curious mixture of the three, with the senate occupying a controlling position under the Republic which was difficult for a foreigner to understand. The proconsuls whom the Greeks saw in action behaved like kings; yet, it appeared, they were not independent at all, but servants of this mysterious senate. So Polybius, an admirer of the Romans and particularly of their constitution, was at great pains to explain its working in the history which he wrote particularly for a Greek reading public, and other Greeks who wrote histories of Rome for Greek consumption laboured the same point.

Greeks found an immediate difficulty in understanding Roman names. They themselves were accustomed to the idea of a man having one name and a patronymic, A the son of B. Romans, on the other hand, had two names, often three. The first distinguished Roman general to leave his mark on Greece in the early second century BC was Titus Quinctius Flamininus. The Greeks did the obvious thing and called him Titus, and it was their general habit to refer to a Roman by his *praenomen*. Even Polybius, who knew well enough that a Roman hardly ever used the *praenomen* in speaking to or of another Roman, did the same. It must often have been as hard for Romans in antiquity, faced with references to a man by his first name alone, as it is for historians today confronted with surviving inscriptions and dedications in Greek, to know who the man was. Had the second or the third name been used, there would have been no such difficulty.

As for the Latin language, the Greeks – who in so many respects were the counterpart in antiquity of the French in modern times – found it unattractive and difficult and saw little reason at first for learning it. What reason could there be for learning a foreign language other than to read its literature? And the Romans had no literature that was worth reading. That Latin was a difficult language for a Greek to learn we know from Plutarch's description of his own experience. The situation was to change considerably in the second century AD when increasing numbers of Greeks became senators or entered the Roman administration in other ways. For them, difficult or not, the language had to be learnt.

With admirable good sense the Romans made no attempt to impose Latin as a single language for the empire. The eastern Mediterranean countries spoke Greek as they had spoken it in the days of their independence, and the administration was generally conducted in Greek. At Rome, after the time of Claudius, the emperor had a special Greek secretary, *ab epistulis Graecis*. Decrees of the senate, edicts of the emperors, were translated into Greek either before dispatch from Rome to the East or else in the province itself before publication. Greek could be spoken in the courts instead of Latin, if there was an interpreter. Only in the Roman army in the East was there insistence on Latin as an official language.

Finally, there were the Romans themselves, for whom the Greeks felt a mixture of envy and disparagement. Roman values were material values; their civilisation was a material civilisation. In the absence of comparable material wealth, the cultured Greek fell back on the traditional scale of Greek values, which were cultured and spiritual. The impression made by many Romans and in particular by stories of the extravagant social life in the city of Rome, was the impression made by the New World and by some of its citizens on the older peoples of Europe today. The Greeks shrugged their shoulders at the Romans and, with no great malice, laughed at them, This attitude is admirably illustrated in the writings of that cultured wit Lucian of Sarmosata on the Euphrates in the second century AD, who was an Anatole France before his time.

Matching the movement of Roman and Italian traders into the East, particularly in the second century BC, there was a strong influx of Greeks into the western world, sometimes as slaves (especially after capture by pirates in the Republic), sometimes as free individuals, for there were employments for which they were better qualified than Romans; in particular teaching and medicine. Most grammar-school and rhetoric masters in the West were Greek and practically every doctor was Greek, the medical profession being one for which the Roman was generally considered to be too heavy-handed.

With the establishment of the executive departments in the imperial administration in Rome, a number of Greeks, as has been seen, became very powerful and very rich, like Narcissus and Pallas under Claudius. In the first century AD the father of Claudius Etruscus, whose name we do not know, had a remarkable career of

From Vespasian's time there were professors, 'teachers by imperial appointment', in Rome, and the scheme was extended to the provinces by Trajan and his successors. There were professors of grammar (literature) and rhetoric, both Latin and Greek. This, it is suggested, is the head of a professor of Greek literature.

this kind. He arrived in Rome from Smyrna, a slave to whom Tiberius gave his freedom. He held important posts in the imperial bureaucracy under no less than ten emperors, starting with Tiberius and ending with Domitian. At one point he was chief financial secretary, *a rationibus*. He rose to be a knight and married a senator's sister.

Roman administration in the East. While in the West the Romans had to create an entirely new system of administration, in the East in the case of the former Hellenistic kingdoms they re-tained established systems, particularly of taxation which, as has been seen, involved the extensive employment of tax-farming companies. Another element in Hellenistic government was the officially-sponsored ruler-cult.

As the astonished senate discovered in Rome in 167 BC, when the king of Bithynia fell on his face as he entered the senate house, exclaiming, 'Greetings, saviour gods', easterners addressed their rulers in other than simple manly Roman terms.

Integrity, always a desirable attribute, was more than ever desirable in a Roman administrator in the eastern empire. The flattering offerings might be large, like the four-horse chariots and religious shrines which Cicero declined in Cilicia in 50 BC. Or they might be trifling presents, like those taken by Iulius Bassus, pro-consul of Bithynia shortly after AD 100, who was charged with extortion on his return to Rome and defended by the younger Pliny.

Roman governors in the East had to be careful not to dismiss out of hand as sycophancy what in the tradition of the East was simple politeness – *safarish* – and their consciences, if they had consciences, were strained to distinguish between the gracious acceptance of a present and the dangerous and corrupt acceptance of a bribe.

The Roman administrator, indeed, was often confronted by a difficult dilemma from the fact that the Greek or easterner, courteously and generously offering him a present, did not think

Wild-beast fighting (animals fighting each other or pitted against armed men – *bestiarii*) took place in the Colosseum at Rome and in amphitheatres and theatres in provincial towns. It is frequently represented on reliefs and mosaics, the latter particularly in north Africa. There were also exhibitions of performing animals. In this relief from Sofia wild beasts are shown fighting in the arena and on the altar are performing animals.

in the western manner in terms of bribes. It is a dilemma which has confronted many western administrators in empires of the modern world, notably the British in India and the Far East. To reject such a present might be correct by the standards of western ethics; by eastern standards it could constitute extreme discourtesy.

Of all eastern provinces Asia presented the greatest temptations. It was 'a wealthy province with ready-made opportunities for a dishonest administrator', as Tacitus wrote of Agricola's blameless quaestorship there in AD 64.

The more conscientious the governor, the more likely he was to be offered a handsome price for silence, for keeping his eyes shut, for abandoning enquiries which might expose an ugly story of corruption; for corruption was rife in the politics of eastern cities. When Pliny governed Bithynia from AD 109 to 111, he quickly discovered at Prusa (Bursa) and in other cities that public money had often found its way into private pockets, even into the pockets of the municipal aristocracy. Contracts for public buildings offered particularly good scope for embezzlement. Not every governor was as conscientious as Pliny in pursuing his enquiries to the point where the culprit was discovered and forced to make repayment.

The movement of ideas, of culture and religions in the Empire was consistently from East to West. Gladiatorial fighting was the only large interest which started in the West and spread eastwards. It was beginning to spread already in the second century BC, and in the Roman Empire gladiatorial fighting was every bit as popular in the Greek East as it was in the West.

Romanisation in the West. The western section of the empire embraced the Danube provinces in the north and the provinces of Mauretania, Numidia and Africa in the south. Here Latin was the official language. Cyrene, which bordered on Africa to the east, was an eastern province, with Greek as its official language.

In the West the Roman empire has left its abiding mark. Rumanian as much as French and Spanish is basically a Latin language. Here the Romans were everywhere engaged in spreading

a culture on which their own culture was dependent. Artistically, indeed, their hand was the hand of death. Slavish devotees of Greek art, they had no appreciation at all of the native art which they discovered, an art which is so splendidly represented by the surviving *bronzetti* from Sardinia. No rich Roman collected such things as, in his ignorant way, he bought at a fancy price a poor copy of some piece of fifth- or fourth-century BC Greek sculpture and believed, as his friends believed, that he had acquired an original masterpiece.

Westerners were barbarians in Roman eyes, just as much as the Romans themselves were barbarians in the eyes of the Greeks. In the West the Romans conceived it as their high-minded duty to exterminate barbarism and replace it by civilisation, meaning by 'civilisation' life in the Roman manner, in particular city life by contrast with tribal life. This conversion, in their eyes, marked the march of progress then as to modern eyes it is conceived as marking the march of progress in Africa today.

They were faced by recalcitrant opposition to the change, by natives who preferred to remain barbarous but free. Such an attitude was stigmatised by Caesar and no doubt by many others as

This mosaic was discovered in Britain
in the Roman villa of Lullingstone
in Kent. It portrays Europa on the bull
(Juppiter transformed).

'arrogance'. In the East the Romans never succeeded in freeing
themselves from a certain inferiority complex. In the West they
were arrogance itself.

It was in the West, of course, that the Romans did their great
work of empire-building, spreading the Graeco-Roman type of
education in the schools which they built, the best of them enthus-
iasts for the work which they were doing; like Agricola in Britain
from AD 78 to 84, 'who preferred the natural wit of the Briton to
the trained intelligence of the Gaul', and who was delighted 'when
Britons who had once refused to learn Latin at all were on fire to
speak it with graceful elegance'. He recognised the sad fact that
romanisation did not stop at the improving level of education.
Other less creditable tastes followed on education's heels: Roman
baths, Roman-type dinner parties. It was easy to label these
developments too as 'civilisation'. In fact, they undermined the
free spirit of the natives and were 'slavery'.

A cynical Greek might have said in language more outspoken
than Horace's that Rome conquered the East in order to be civilised.
In the West the Romans conceived it as their function to civilise
others, to tame the savage. Where the savage practised human
sacrifice, as the Druids did in Britain and in Gaul, the sooner he
was tamed, the better. As for the rest, romantics like Tacitus built
up the image of the noble savage, free and unexposed to such
diseases of civilised life as hot baths and conjugal promiscuity.
This in the *Germania*. A German would probably have retorted
that the features of Roman civilisation to which he objected were
not these; they were the taxes.

Foreshadowings of a divided empire. The western and the eastern
empires were from the start two empires, loosely dovetailed.

The view has been held that the Roman decision to embark on
the second Macedonian war in 200 BC, by which Rome committed
herself irretrievably to an interest in the eastern Mediterranean was
a fatal one, and that Europe would have had a happier and a better
future if Rome had contented herself with a western European

empire; that her imperial energy, thus restricted, would have been more galvanic, her empire would have had greater coherence and perhaps in the end, when the barbarians attacked, greater power of resistance; that, left to itself, the East would have developed more constructively on its own non-Roman lines. It can be retorted that in the second century BC when the fate of the eastern Mediterranean was decided, this is not what the Greek Polybius thought. He counted the gain, in particular the achievement of world peace under a power strong enough to enforce that peace, the unification of the Mediterranean and the opening up of the whole Mediterranean world to travel. These gains seemed to him to outweigh the loss, which was the loss of political independence on the part of a number of smaller political units which had not in fact, been making a great success of governing themselves.

It was Cleopatra whose influence emphasised glaringly the division of East and West. When Julius Caesar fell into her clutches,

174

(a) Gold coin struck by Vespasian in AD 73. On the obverse is the the very distinctive head of Vespasian with legend IMP(erator) CAES(ar) VESP(asianus) AVG(ustus) CENS(or) – this being the year when he held the censorship with Titus. The reverse (b) shows the Temple of Vesta, whose statue is between the two central columns. (c) Gold coin struck at Rome in the name of Titus in AD 72/3 recording the capture of Jerusalem. The obverse shows the head of Titus, bearded, laureate, with the legend T(itus) CAES(ar) IMP(erator) VES(pasianus) PONT(ifex) TR(ibunicia) POT(estate); on the reverse (d) a Jewess draped and veiled sits under a palm tree dejected; left of the palm stands a prince, spear in hand, representing Titus.

his enemies spread the story that he would move the capital of the world to Alexandria, and Rome would sink to the status of a second-class city. What was feared then was realised a few years later when Antony and Cleopatra ruled from Alexandria. The unity of the empire was forgotten and Octavian's war against them was more than a campaign; it was a crusade, the first of all the crusades of the West against the East. As, with slight embellishment, he recorded in the *Res Gestae*: 'Of its own free impulse Italy took an oath of loyalty to me and called on me to take command in the war which I won at Actium. The provinces of Gaul, Spain, Africa, Sicily and Sardinia took the same oath.' All the western empire, in fact.

After the death of Septimius Severus in 211 AD we are told, it is hard to know with what truth, that the division of the empire into two, a western and eastern empire, was proposed at an imperial council, to solve the problem raised by the intense hatred of Caracalla for his brother Geta. The Propontis, 'divinely appointed for the purpose', should be the boundary. Caracalla's frontier defences at Byzantium would scowl across the water at those of his brother at Calchedon. The western empire would embrace the whole of Europe (Greece included), Mauretania, Africa and Numidia; the eastern empire, with its capital at Antioch or Alexandria, would include Asia Minor, Syria, Egypt and Cyrene. Julia Domna protested, and Geta's murder was a simpler solution of the problem.

Later, Caracalla was more imaginative still. At Ilium he was Achilles; in Macedonia and in the East Alexander, with his mind set on a fusion of East and West such as Alexander had attempted, the creation of a single world-power. An army consisting of Parthian cavalry and Roman infantrymen would be invincible. There should be a customs union, silks and spices from the East being exchanged in great quantities against metal goods from the West. As a first step, his daughter should marry the Parthian king's son. However, he changed his mind and decided to fight the Parthians instead.

In the end the division of the empire into East and West was made by Diocletian from strategic and administrative necessity. Territorially, it was not a division on the simple lines proposed for Caracalla and Geta, since the eastern Augustus had some responsibility for the Danube front and eventually, after Diocletian's experiment with Nicopolis (Izmit), had its capital in Europe. Modern Turkey has reversed the process, moving its capital from Istanbul to Ankara, from Europe into Asia.

Even so, the abiding influences of the West on the Byzantine empire were more than a veneer. There was still Roman law, codified by Justinian in the sixth century AD and to their enemies like the Persians the Byzantines were still 'the Romans'.

Propaganda and loyalty

In the absence of hoardings or franked envelopes the Roman government advertised on coins, whose issue in peaceful times was entirely controlled by the emperor. By their legends and by the subjects depicted, the coins advertised peace, harmony, imperial achievement, carrying whatever slogan suited the moment best. You turned the coin over, and there was the portrait of the emperor, the source of all these good things.

The first and most obvious feature of the Roman empire until the coming of the dark days from the third century onwards was its unassailable strength and power. In the East this was described sometimes as the Roman Fortune, the climax of a process whose early stages Polybius had admired, in which, like a powerful steam-roller, Rome had flattened and destroyed all obstacles to her growing power. So when the Jews of Judaea, exacerbated by the iniquities of Gessius Florus, their governor, were set on rebellion in AD 66, Agrippa II, in trying to dissuade them, simply described the immensity of Roman power and achievement. When all the enormous resources of this vast power were brought to concentrate on suppressing the pygmy strength of the Jews, what possible chance could there be of the rebellion's success?

The finest, perhaps, of all the temples in Rome was Vespasian's temple of Peace; and the Roman Peace, the *Pax Romana*, or the Augustan Peace, the *Pax Augusta*, was the Roman achievement which was trumpeted most loudly. The establishment of the empire had brought the end of war. The frontiers were defended against barbarian inroads by the Roman frontier armies. Behind this protective barrier the inhabitants of the empire could live in the untroubled enjoyment of peace.

It was unreasonable to expect that the greatest of all human blessings, Peace, should be given to the world as a free gift. Its continuance depended on the frontier armies; and soldiers, like other people, had to be paid. So taxation was to be viewed not as arbitrary imposition but as the individual's reasonable subscription to the upkeep of the armed forces, without whose protection he would not be enjoying the freedom from anxiety and molestation which was the foundation of his everyday life. This, from Cicero onwards, was the government's retort to those who objected to paying their taxes.

There was since Aristotle – and it has continued up to Toynbee – a propensity to look at states (in Toynbee's case, civilisations) in biological terms and to see their span of life as necessarily limited, growth leading to an acme of success which is followed, in its turn, by decline. Even in Republican times, Roman writers were almost pathologically fascinated by plotting the decline of Roman civic virtue and from the early Empire onwards there were writers who traced the periods of Roman growth through youth and maturity into decline. The retort to such demoralised thinking was the exultation of the notion of eternal Rome, *Roma Aeterna*, a notion trumpeted more and more loudly by the propagandists as the signs of disintegration became more and more manifest in the late second century and after.

The instrument for the encouragement of loyalty to the empire was the imperial cult, an inheritance from the Hellenistic world; for when cities and leagues in the Greek-speaking East were left with no more kings to whom to pay cult, they naturally replaced them as objects of worship by their conqueror and supplanter,

Rome. From the early second century BC, temples and altars were erected to Rome as a goddess and sacrifices were offered in Rome's honour. The desire of natives to associate with such cult the names of individual governors, who were to them the visible embodiment of Roman authority, flattered bad Republican governors and embarrassed good ones. In due course the association of Augustus – 'Augustus' signifying the imperial house – was natural and easy; the cult of Rome became the cult of Rome and Augustus, and there were festival days, the emperor's birthday and his accession day in chief, in the course of which offerings were made at the altar. If an emperor was officially consecrated after death by senatorial decree in Rome, a temple could be erected to his divinity. In the East, the imperial cult was to be found both at provincial and at city level, generally spontaneous and often expressed with an extravagance which went far beyond what was officially approved. To such extravagant manifestations authority generally turned a blind eye. At his accession an emperor might expect to receive offers of statues, altars, even temples, from many parts of the eastern Mediterranean world. Attempts to enforce the cult upon unwilling subjects, such as the Jews, were as mistaken and disastrous when made by Gaius as when made by Antiochus Epiphanes earlier.

The value of the imperial cult in inducing a feeling of imperial loyalty was self-evident, and it was transplanted to the western provinces where, as has been seen, altars of Rome and Augustus were dedicated at Lyons (Lugdunum) in 12 BC by Drusus and later at Cologne (then Ara Ubiorum). Its spread was also encouraged in the cities of Italy and the western provinces.

It gave a splendid opportunity to those who sought the vanity of social prominence, to natives who were appointed priests of the cult for provinces, leagues of cities or individual cities – in the provinces of Asia and Bithynia with the proud title of Asiarch and Bithyniarch respectively. Rich men in the provinces and cities competed for such honours, and the priestly office was no light charge on their pockets, for they were expected to give games and gladiatorial shows on a magnificent scale. The Asiarch, for example, kept his own gladiatorial school. They enjoyed the glory of all this and had the pride of feeling that they were a part of imperial Rome. Provincial priests, indeed, had a considerable secular importance, for they presided over the council of prominent natives which assembled for the festivals and on other occasions also and debated matters of provincial interest. A good governor might be helped by this council's advice; a corrupt governor might later be forced to appreciate its power, for it sometimes made the first moves which led eventually to his trial in Rome for extortion or even for treasonable practices.

In the cities of Italy and of the western provinces the cult performed yet another social function. Its observances were placed in the hands of freedmen called *Augustales* or *Seviri Augustales*. Except in Julius Caesar's colonies and in the individual cases of men to whom the emperor had given the golden ring, freedmen were debarred from an active part in local government in that they could not be city-councillors; but freedmen were often rich, generous and vain. Their presidency in celebrations of the imperial cult and at the shows and games, given at their own expense, which went with it, satisfied their ambitions and gave them a pleasing sense of importance.

The Roman empire had its eloquent admirers: the Achaean statesman Polybius writing after the destruction of Carthage, and Strabo, a Greek from Pontus, an author of the Augustan period. Viewing the empire at two successive stages in its expansion, both regarded Roman conquests as the result of a natural superiority on the part of the Romans themselves, disciplined as they were in their constitution and masters of the art of war, and of the folly and weakness of the peoples whom they conquered. Both praised the end-result, the gift to the world, after all the hard fighting, of peace. And finally, there is the great panegyric of Rome delivered in Rome in AD 143 by the Greek sophist Aelius Aristides, 'the greatest literary expression of what the Golden Age could mean to the world of Hadrian and the Antonines'. Protected by the 'ring of iron', an admirably disciplined army, recruited from the cities of the empire under a system which gave universal satisfaction, the Roman world lived at peace, its cities grew, travel was easy and trade flourished. India and Arabia poured their products into Rome in whose markets 'anything you did not see did not exist'. The emperor was a supremely wise judge, settling with expertise issues brought to him at Rome from every quarter in the empire. Best of all, the paths to Roman citizenship were barred to none; the word 'Roman' indicated a common nationality. So Aristides claimed.

Public panegyrics naturally skate over uncomfortable facts, and Agrippa addressing the Jews in 66 and Cerealis speaking at Trier four years later admitted that not every Roman governor was a blameless man. Agrippa's matter-of-fact line was that it was necessary in life to take the rough with the smooth; a bad governor was in due course superseded, and not all governors were bad. Cerealis philosophised. Nature herself, he said, was not without her flaws; there were floods, tempests and plagues. He even admitted, speaking two years after Nero's death, that not every Roman emperor was a paragon, and went on to point out what was generally true: that, while those who lived in close proximity to a tyrannical emperor suffered from his peccadillos, administration in the distant provinces continued under its own impulse, little affected by what was happening in the capital.

That what we should call good and just administration of the provinces ended in the Severan age is not to be doubted. What is difficult to know is how good and just the general standard of administration was before that. It is commonly assumed that there was a great improvement in standards under the emperors, but this is not altogether certain. The malpractices of bad governors of provinces, when detected and exposed in the courts, were little different from what they had been in the Republic; senators at Rome were as anxious to show leniency in judging fellow-senators as they ever had been. Yet administrators in public and imperial provinces alike now received salaries, and this should have reduced the temptation to pilfer. And, as far as the imperial provinces are concerned, we have no means of knowing how often a bad governor was summarily recalled to Rome and told by the emperor that his public career was at an end. There are plenty of known cases in which bad administrators were not recalled.

Weakness, a loss of nerve, or fear of the emperor in Rome may perhaps have been as frequent a cause of bad administration as greed and a corrupt desire for enrichment, and so have given the lie to one of Cerealis' claims. In the Republic, as has been seen, a pro-consul had all the time to be looking back over his shoulder to Rome, for he was often under pressure from Rome, frequently from powerful figures, to connive in their corrupt business dealings in his province. In the empire he might be subject to a different kind of blackmail. When the Jews shouted to Pilate, 'If thou let this man go, thou art not Caesar's friend', they played on his weakness. The shameful conduct of Avillius Flaccus as prefect of Egypt when, instead of trying to suppress the pogrom in Alexandria in AD 38, he acted in such a way as to encourage it, is to be explained by his knowledge that he was already dangerously out of favour with the emperor Gaius, a fanatical enemy of the Jews; and so his first – unavailing – concern was for his own skin.

Opposition to Rome

Nobody in the world's history has enjoyed paying his taxes; and it is a fair assumption that any of Rome's provincial subjects in any part of the empire at any time, if asked to what feature of Roman rule he most objected, would have said that it was the payment of taxes. The stock official answer – that taxation was the price of peace, because its receipts were channelled for the payment of the defence services – can have satisfied few people; for taxes obviously supported other things too, vast imperial buildings and the often notorious extravagances of the imperial court in Rome. Subjects complained, often with reason, of the tax-assessments and of the manner in which tax-payment was enforced. The Pannonian revolt of AD 6 was partly due to exasperation on this account; as its leader told Tiberius, 'To protect your flocks, you send out not shepherds and sheep-dogs, but wolves'. When there were complaints about the rapacity of customs-officers (employees of private companies which had leased the collection of customs at the frontiers and at many further points within the empire), Nero in a euphoric mood suggested a remedy: customs themselves should be abolished. Senators with greater concern for public finance dissuaded him; but reforms in the system were made. The tariffs were officially posted where the customs were collected, and the unwarranted distraints of the collectors were at an end.

Money-lending by Romans to natives provoked hardships and was the cause of much discontent. This was often a side-line on the part of tax-collectors who lent money to defaulting tax-payers (administrative officers were forbidden to lend money in the provinces) and there were also rich Romans, Pompey in the late Republic, Seneca in the early empire, who had large sums out on loan in the provinces. The officially countenanced rates of interest, twelve per cent at least, were considerably higher in the provinces than at Rome; and unscrupulous money-lenders charged higher rates still, with heavy interest on arrears of payment and in the end destrained on the borrower's property. Severe unrest on the part of the Allobroges in Narbonese Gaul in the late Republic and the revolt of Florus and Sacrovir in Gaul in AD 21 were due to the fact that Gauls were closely entangled in the meshes of Roman money-lenders; and there was a belief – we cannot tell how well founded – that Boudicca's revolt in Britain was partly caused by the action of Seneca in Rome, who suddenly called in large sums which he had out on loan in the province.

The most violent denunciations of the Roman empire came naturally from states and tribes on its borders who faced the threat of absorption into that empire and they may well in fact have used the language which Roman historians, trained in oratory and the use of hyperbole, have put into their mouths. Perseus, the last king of Macedon in the second century BC, Mithridates a century later and Calgacus, the Caledonian chief opposing Agricola in the late first century AD, fulminated against the arrogance, aggressiveness and insatiable greed of the Romans and played on

Roman remains at Sabratha, one of the three cities of the African Tripolis, on the coast fifty miles west of Oea (modern Tripoli). It became a Roman colony and there is evidence that the city had a trading depot at Ostia. Extensive excavations since the First World War have revealed in particular a magnificent theatre.

the contrast of Liberty, the possession of those who lived outside the empire, and Servitude, the condition of those who lived inside. 'We are the last bastion of Freedom', Calgacus told the still unconquered Scots.

Liberty was something which was chased like a will-o'-the-wisp by individuals and societies throughout antiquity, always elusive, vanishing as soon as it was grasped. So within the empire it was a figment about which discontented people dreamed dreams. But once the resistance of a subject people was broken, there was little impulse to contract out of the empire, to revolt in the hope of recovering independence. Vindex's revolt in Gaul in AD 68, as its coinage shows, was no revolt for independence, and the 'Empire of the Gauls' which Civilis' rising promoted was an emotional outburst which never had its feet on the ground. Even in the third century, Postumus' independent Gallic empire used devices like *Roma Aeterna* on its coinage. It thought it could do Rome's job in staving off the German invaders better than at that moment Rome seemed able to do it herself.

Only the Jews at times of extreme provocation would have liked an independent Israel, a theocratic state itself, unoffended by the emblems of pagan domination and able diplomatically to ensure the untroubled exercise of their own cult practices by all other Jews – the Diaspora – in the Empire. But this was not at all the Jewish attitude at the time when the Roman government treated them, as in the early empire it treated them, as a favoured people; Julius Caesar, after all, had owed his survival in Alexandria in 48-7 BC to Jews and neither he nor his immediate successors forgot the fact. It was, indeed, one of the great tragedies of the Roman empire that, from being a contented element in the empire, the Jews became first discontented and then rebellious. Ruler-cult, which in the Hellenistic and Roman imperial worlds alike was a focus of patriotism and an expression of contentment, to the Jews was blasphemy. This was the misfortune of monotheists in a polytheistic world, first of the Jews, later of the Christians. For the Jews the problem produced bloodshed on a horrifying scale and was

The Pont du Gard, bridging the valley of the Gardon, 22 kilometres from Nimes (Nemusus), which it served, is one of the finest and highest surviving Roman aqueducts. It is generally believed (without certain evidence) to have been built by M. Agrippa under Augustus. A remarkable piece of engineering, its beauty is enhanced by the unequal spans, which are due to the use of rocks in the river-bed as basis to the piers.

never solved. In the case of the Christians it produced bloodshed but in the end was solved, when polytheism itself, in the person of Constantine, decided to turn monotheistic.

The Roman imperial achievement

What, in fact, had Rome done for the world which she conquered and governed? What were the blessings for which every inhabitant of the empire could feel thankful?

Rome had introduced a new concept of empire. By Greek notions, most eloquently expressed by Thucydides, an imperial power

pursued self-interest to the maximum extent possible within the
terms of its own superiority. By Roman ideas, on the other hand,
the interests of rulers and ruled did not merely dovetail or overlap;
they were identical. Within that empire it was better to be a Roman
than not to be a Roman; so Roman citizenship was a prize to be
won and a matter of pride once it had been won. Witness the
dialogue of St Paul, a citizen of Tarsus, and the Roman army
officer: 'With a great price won I this citizenship'; 'I am a Roman
by birth'. And so, as the governing class was recruited from an ever
widening field, the empire was in effect to the fullest degree
self-governing.

Europe west and south of the Rhine and Danube, Asia Minor,
Syria, Egypt, North Africa with Britain from the other side of
Ocean and, for a time, Dacia were one world, with admirable roads
and good sea communications, generally unmolested by brigands
or pirates. Trade moved far and fast; so did religions and ideas.
The genius of the world was a single genius. Great architecture and
engineering works were not concentrated in the capital but scattered all over the Roman world: the aqueducts of Segovia in Spain
and of the Pont du Gard in southern France; the theatres of
Aspendus in Turkey and of Sabratha in Tripolitania; the amphitheatres of Nîmes in southern France and of El Djem in Tunisia;
the architecture, with its eastern influences, of Palmyra and Baalbek;
the bridge of Alcantara in Spain built by Julius Lacer early in the
second century AD, 'which should survive over all the centuries of
the world's existence', as so far it has succeeded in doing. These and
hundreds more.

It was an empire with few language problems, where knowledge
of two languages would carry a man anywhere, and where Latin
was the common language of the West. When in AD 16 the German
freedom-fighter Arminius taunted his brother Flavus, who served
in the Roman army, they talked in Latin. Here is the origin of
French and Italian, perhaps the two most beautiful languages in
the world. There was no oppression of native tongues and indeed
they continued to be spoken, particularly in country districts (in

Arles (Arelate) on the Rhone was established as a Roman
colony by Julius Caesar and, with the eclipse of Marseilles
(Massilia), was the most important commercial city in
southern Gaul. Its most striking Roman remains are a theatre
and an amphitheatre, illustrated here, probably 2nd century
AD, for gladiatorial and wild beast fighting.

Judaea, an Aramaic-speaking society, the Roman officer was at
first surprised that St Paul spoke Greek); with the collapsing empire these native tongues were to emerge with great vigour, Celtic,
Berber, Syriac and the rest, languages of the lower classes and
therefore powerful in the spread of Christianity.

There was one law for the whole empire, humane, imaginative,
all the time pondered over, corrected and adapted to meet changing
circumstances, for law had always seemed to the Romans to be the
basis of civilised life. It was, with architecture and engineering, the
field of the greatest Roman genius. There were great jurisconsults
at all times, from Scaevola (at whose feet Cicero sat) to Gaius,
Paulus and Ulpian at the end of the second century AD and the
beginning of the third. And the law was subject to successive codification, up to the great codification of Justinian which survives.
Respect for law was accompanied by a humanising of life. Brutal
practices like the ritual murders of Druidism and emasculation in
the cult of Cybele were suppressed.

Education on Roman (which meant on Greek) lines spread to
every part of the empire. Quintilian, who in the first century AD
wrote what is still one of the great books on education, was a
Spaniard. In the fourth century Ausonius, a Gaul educated at
Bordeaux (Burdigala), was tutor to the young prince Gratian.

Civilised life was city life, and there were few more widespread or
vigorous sentiments, the whole empire over, than municipal pride.
The well-to-do competed for municipal office and for the rest of
their lives enjoyed the social prominence and even the responsibilities of city-fathers (*curiales*, members of the local senates), one of
the most considerable of their responsibilities being to act as inter-
mediaries to the Roman administration in tax-collection. Indivi-
dually they were generous, as rich freedmen were generous; and so
were the natives who had gone out into the world, perhaps into
Roman administration, and had achieved success – even, like
Septimius Severus, become emperors. They gave fine public buildings to their cities, just as great Roman generals of the Republic
had devoted the spoils of victory to the building of temples or

basilicas in Rome. The inscriptions on the buildings carried the donors' names. And men who showed generosity to their cities or who reflected credit on their home towns by the public distinction which they won, were honoured by the erection of portrait statues as, particularly in Italy, they have been honoured since. Step into the *piazza* of Arpino today, and you are confronted by the statues of Gaio Mario and of Marco Tullio.

Benefactions took other forms also – magnificent gladiatorial fights and wild beast shows at one extreme and, at the other, endowments (of which we have evidence, in Africa) for childrens' allowances to poor parents on the model of the schemes which from Nerva onwards, emperors had launched in Italy.

Cities themselves were anxious to add to their own splendour and reputation by the erection of public buildings from public funds – often, as Pliny found in Bithynia, with disastrous consequences. A combination of incompetent architects, fraudulent contractors and misleading estimates had its sad consequence: a building aban-

doned when it was half-finished or completed in such a state that it
immediately collapsed. All too often caution was forgotten in a
city's anxiety to outshine its neighbours. The modern world has its
depressing parallels.

Cities whose economic opportunities brought them prosperity
grew and flourished to a point where they could almost, but not
quite, challenge the magnificence of Rome itself. Alexandria and
Carthage (monument to Julius Caesar's wisdom) competed for the
position of second city in the empire. Antioch, noted for its luxur-
ious and dissipated living, was 'the fair crown of the Orient' and
still the greatest city in the East when the Persians burnt it down in
the sixth century AD. In the fourth century, Ammianus Marcellinus

listed the great cities in order of magnificence. Rome, naturally, came first, followed by Constantinople, formerly Byzantium, which, recreated by Constantine after it had been pillaged and destroyed by Septimius Severus, had come rapidly into prominence as the second capital. After that, in order, Carthage, Antioch, Alexandria, Trier, Milan, Capua, Aquileia, Arles, Seville, Cordova, Tarragona, Braga (Bracara in Spain), Athens, Catana, Syracuse, Toulouse, Narbonne, Bordeaux. Some of the greatest cities of the early empire had dropped out; Lyons, for instance, which Septimius Severus gutted in AD 197, and Marseilles. Ammianus Marcellinus listed forty-one cities of eminence in Gaul alone.

There was one thing wrong with the civilisation which in the Roman empire was so well disseminated: it was almost entirely dead. There were three areas of exception: religion, which was perhaps the most dynamic feature of imperial civilisation; portrait sculpture, which achieved its greatest triumph in the second and third centuries AD and architecture, where the discovery of the vault ended the tedious centuries-old dominance of the conventional building of Greek temple type. The architect's exploitation of his new opportunities are to be seen in Hadrian's villa, in the baths of Caracalla and in the basilica of Maxentius and Constantine in the Forum at Rome. Otherwise, both intellectually (unless an exception is made of the third-century Plotinus) and materially life was static, without the excitement of novelty or adventure. There had been great excitement once in the growth of the empire, in the conquest of new worlds, when the empire was expanding; but by the second century AD the expansion had stopped. Education followed its old grooves. Native art had been killed dead, ousted by the fashion-ability of copies, however bad, of old Greek masterpieces. There was no scientific experiment. There were still, and for centuries there would continue to be, interesting and graceful works of literature but, if an exception is made of St Augustine's *Civitas Dei* in the early fifth century, there was to be no more great writing. Development of mechanisation and labour-saving devices had received no stimulus in the days when cheap labour (slaves) was in abundant supply. Tiberius put a man to death for inventing un-breakable glass, after making sure that nobody shared his secret, because the invention would destroy the glass-industry in its familiar form. Later, Vespasian refused to make use of an engineer's invention for transporting heavy stone columns at greatly reduced expense on the ground that it would reduce the demand for labour and put men out of work. Indeed, in almost all respects Roman civilisation was living on its steadily declining supply of fat.

Part 2 Decline

3 The Third Empire: Septimius Severus

The shameful news of the murder of Pertinax and the purchase of the praetorian guard by Didius Julianus in AD 193 provoked better men to stake their claims: Pescennius Niger, acclaimed by the army in Syria, and Septimius Severus, an African of Lepcis Magna, the governor of Pannonia. Septimius marched on Rome and Julianus killed himself. The senate received flattering promises and the praetorians were cashiered, replaced now and for the future by men on promotion from the legions. Septimius lost no time in marching east where, after breaking through Niger's defences at the Bosphorus and on the Taurus, he won yet another battle of the Issus. He returned to defeat D. Clodius Albinus, governor of Britain, who had occupied Gaul and had been proclaimed emperor, a man whom Septimius had suspected earlier and to whom, because of his suspicions, he had offered the title of Caesar. The fighting took the normal toll of civil wars; Antioch was sacked and lost its position as capital of Syria to Laodicea; Byzantium with its splendid walls was razed to the ground; Lugdunum (Lyons) was burnt down. After which Septimius fought a successful eastern war, sacking the Parthian capital Ctesiphon and, like Trajan before him, making a Roman province of Mesopotamia, with two out of his three new legions as garrison; he also visited Egypt. Then in 208 he set off with his Syrian wife Julia Domna, and his two quarrelsome sons Caracalla and Geta, to fight the barbarous Britons in their marshes. He died at Eburacum (York) in 211.

Severus having adopted the dead M. Aurelius for his father, Caracalla had renamed himself M. Aurelius Antoninus. He disposed of his brother Geta and, after winning great popularity with the troops in campaigning on the Danube, he set out on the usual Parthian war and was murdered near Carrhae, with the connivance of another African, the prefect of the praetorian guard, M. Opellius Macrinus, the first equestrian to be proclaimed emperor. Macrinus was a lawyer, not a soldier, and was disliked by his troops who quickly deserted him in favour of the thirteen-year-old priest of the *baal* at Emesa in Syria, called (like his god) Elagabalus. He was a cousin of Caracalla, his grandmother and Julia Domna being sisters. His mother declared him an illegitimate son of Caracalla; so he too took the name M. Aurelius Antoninus. After four years of orgiastic eccentricity largely concerned with the cult of his black stone in Rome, his grandmother realised that he was better dead (the praetorian guard was there to dispose of him), and he was replaced by his first cousin, who was also, on *his* mother's declaration, an illegitimate son of Caracalla. This was a boy of fourteen, Severus Alexander (M. Aurelius Severus Alexander) who, under his powerful mother's thumb, ruled as emperor for thirteen years, until killed by troops on the Rhine in 235. So the Severan house ruled forty years, with the short interruption of Macrinus' bid for power.

Alexander being dead, the troops proclaimed as emperor an un-educated soldier, who was a giant of a man. This was Maximinus, in origin a Thracian peasant, the commander of the Pannonian recruits. The act had its forlorn repercussions, strangely, on Africa, whose proconsul Gordian, a man of seventy-nine, was proclaimed emperor, only to perish with his son Gordian II when opposed by the sole substantial military force in Africa, legion III Augusta, whose commander was loyal to Maximinus. The news shocked the senate in Rome which naturally preferred a proconsul to a Thracian peasant; so they boldly proclaimed two emperors, Balbinus and the septuagenarian Pupienus. The Roman populace insisted on the association with them of Gordian's grandson, Gordian III, a boy of twelve. Maximinus reasonably scoffed at the notion of such opposition, marched on Italy and was held up at Aquileia, which he could not take. His troops lost heart and killed him in 238. The praetorians then killed Pupienus and Balbinus, who had enjoyed exactly ninety-nine days of power. This left the twelve-year-old Gordian III who ruled with competent advisers, particularly the prefect of the praetorian guard, whose daughter he married. Then Mesopotamia was invaded by the vigorous new power of Persia, which had established itself over Parthia. Gordian went east to restore the situation. His father-in-law died and was replaced by Philip who in 244 contrived his murder. So Rome had an Arab for its emperor.

Table 5 Dates of rule, titles, names and ages of emperors

Date of rule	Title	Full name	Age when emperor
27 BC–AD 14	Augustus	Imp(erator) Caesar divi Iuli f(ilius) Aug.	35–75
AD 14–37	Tiberius	Tiberius Caesar divi Augusti f. Aug.	54–77
37–41	Gaius	C. Caesar Aug. Germanicus	24–8
41–54	Claudius	Tiberius Claudius Caesar Aug. Germanicus	49–63
54–68	Nero	Nero Claudius divi Claudi f. Caesar Aug. Germanicus	16–30
68–9	Galba	Ser. Galba Imp. Caesar Aug.	71–2
69	Otho	Imp. M. Otho Caesar Aug.	36
	Vitellius	Imp. A. Vitellius	53–4
69–79	Vespasian	Imp. Caesar Vespasianus Aug.	59–69
79–81	Titus	Imp. T. Caesar divi Vespasiani f. Vespasianus Aug.	39–41
81–96	Domitian	Imp. Caesar divi Vespasiani f. Domitianus Aug.	29–44
96–8	Nerva	Imp. Nerva Caesar Aug.	60–2
97–117	Trajan	Imp. Caesar divi Nervae f. Nerva Traianus Germanicus etc.	41–62
117–38	Hadrian	Imp. Caesar divi Traiani Parthici f. Traianus Hadrianus Aug.	42–63
138–61	Antoninus Pius	Imp. Caesar divi Hadriani f. Aelius Hadrianus Antoninus Aug. Pius	51–74
161–80	Marcus Aurelius	Imp. Caesar M. Aurelius Antoninus Aug.	39–58

Date of rule	Title	Full name	Age when emperor
AD 161-9	L. Verus	Imp. Caesar L. Aurelius Verus Aug.	33-42
180-92	Commodus	Imp. Caesar M. Aurelius Commodus Antoninus Aug.	18-31
193	Pertinax	Imp. Caesar P. Helvius Pertinax Aug.	66
	Didius Iulianus	Imp Caesar M. Didius Severus Iulianus Aug.	60
193-211	Septimius Severus	Imp. Caesar L. Septimius Severus Pius Pertinax Aug.	45-64
211-17	Caracalla	Imp. Caesar M. Aurelius Antoninus Pius Felix Aug.	24-31
217-8	Macrinus	Imp. Caesar M. Opellius Severus Macrinus Aug.	53
218-22	Elagabalus	Imp. Caesar M. Aurelius Antoninus Aug.	13-17
222-35	Severus Alexander	Imp. Caesar M. Aurelius Severus Alexander Aug.	14-27
235-8	Maximinus	Imp. Caesar C. Iulius Verus Maximinus Aug.	?62-5
238	Gordian I	Imp. Caesar M. Antonius Gordianus Sempronianus Romanus Africanus Aug.	79
	Gordian II	Imp. Caesar M. Antonius Gordianus Sempronianus Romanus Africanus Aug.	46
	Balbinus	Imp. Caesar D. Caelius Calvinus Balbinus Aug.	60
	Pupienus	Imp. Caesar M. Clodius Pupienus Maximus Aug.	74
238-44	Gordian III	Imp. Caesar M. Antonius Gordianus Aug.	12-18

Date of rule	Title	Full name	Age when emperor
AD 244-9	Philip the Arab	Imp. Caesar M. Iulius Philippus Aug.	?40-5
249-51	Decius	Imp. Caesar C. Messius Quintus Traianus Decius Aug.	49-51
251-3	Trebonianus Gallus	Imp. Caesar C. Vibius Trebonianus Gallus Aug.	44-6
251-3	Volusianus (son of Trebonianus)	Imp. Caesar C. Vibius Afinius Gallus Veldumnianus Volusianus Aug.	21-3
253	Aemilianus	Imp. Caesar M. Aemilius Aemilianus Aug.	?47
253-59/60	Valerian	Imp. Caesar P. Licinius Valerianus Aug.	60-7
253-68	Gallienus (son of Valerian)	Imp. Caesar P. Licinius Egnatius Gallienus Aug.	35-50
268-70	Claudius II Gothicus	Imp. Caesar M. Aurelius Claudius Aug.	54-6
270	Quintillus (brother of Claudius)	Imp. Caesar M. Aurelius Claudius Quintillus Aug.	?
270-5	Aurelian	Imp. Caesar L. Domitius Aurelianus Aug.	56-61
275-6	Tacitus	Imp. Caesar M. Claudius Tacitus Aug.	75
276	Florian (brother of Tacitus)	Imp. Caesar M. Annius Florianus Aug.	?
276-82	Probus	Imp. Caesar M. Aurelius Probus Aug.	44-50
282-3	Carus	Imp. Caesar M. Aurelius Carus Aug.	?
283-4	Carinus (son of Carus)	Imp. Caesar M. Aurelius Carinus Aug.	?
	Numerianus (son of Carus)	Imp. Caesar M. Aurelius Numerianus Aug.	?

Philip, determined not to repeat the mistake of Maximinus, lost no time in journeying to Rome and ingratiating himself with the senate. Now the serious invasions of barbarians over the Danube were resumed. Philip in the end, after celebrating the thousandth anniversary of the foundation of Rome in 248, sent Decius to the front with consequences whose inevitability the honest Decius is said to have anticipated. His troops, the army of Illyricum, proclaimed him emperor. So, as their commander, he fought Philip and in 249, after five years of rule, Philip was killed. Decius as emperor initiated the first violent persecution of the Christians and in 251 was killed fighting barbarian invaders in the Dobrudja. Two short-lived emperors followed, Trebonianus Gallus and the Moor, Aemilianus, and then in the middle of all the chaos, there was an opportunity for a measure of reconstruction.

The Rhine legions proclaimed Valerian, a man of great distinction, emperor and at his request, the senate appointed his son Gallienus a second Augustus in 253. There followed the first division of the empire. Valerian went east to confront the menace of the Persians, who had invaded Syria and captured Antioch. He was caught between two fires through the penetration of raiding Goths into central Asia Minor, and in the end was captured by Shapur I of Persia in 260 and ended his life in the humiliation of captivity. Gallienus, meanwhile, was tied down by the barbarian invasions of the West and after 260, a year of catastrophes unequalled in Roman history, with five different rebellions in various parts of the empire, he was killed by a conspiracy of his staff in 268, having made a tremendous mark on government.

After the short rules of Claudius, an agent in the murder of Gallienus, and his brother Quintillus, Aurelian, a simple man and a good soldier, who headed a military rising in Illyricum, became emperor in 270. He campaigned in the East against Zenobia, the widow of the Palmyrene sheik Odenathus who, without his widow's later ambitions to establish an independent empire, had held the East firm after Valerian's disaster. Returning west, he put an end to the rebellion of Gaul which had lasted for fourteen years. In

275, he went east again, to recover Mesopotamia, and was murdered near Byzantium through a conspiracy initiated by his personal secretary. The senate to whom, shocked by the murder, the army appealed, made Tacitus emperor, a man of seventy-five, who set out for the north on campaign and died. Then came Florian, a half-brother of Tacitus who was killed and succeeded by Probus, who won great successes in the west, but then was killed by his own soldiers in Pannonia, and succeeded by the prefect of the guard, Carus. Carus' two sons were Carinus and Numerianus. When Numerianus was killed by his troops in the east, a more likely story than that he was struck by lightning, and the prefect of the guard presided over the army's return march through Asia Minor, with Numerianus, supposedly suffering from an eye disease, carried in a closed litter, all was well until at Nicomedia (Izmit), Numerianus was discovered to be a stinking corpse. The prefect had presumably planned the discovery at a place and time suitable to his own ambitions. Instead, a council of officers was summoned and raised to the purple a one-time Illyrian shepherd-boy Diocles, now called Diocletian. He ran his sword through the prefect of the guard; Carinus, who had been left in Europe, was murdered by one of his officers and the stage was set for a recovery, however dismal, in the fortunes of Rome.

The provenance of the emperors illustrated the fact that romanisation was now empire-wide. As has been seen, Septimius Severus was African, Maximinus a Thracian; Philip was the son of an Arab sheik and Aemilianus was a Moor. Then for a hundred years after the middle of the third century, emperors were in almost every case natives of the Balkans. Between Septimius Severus and Numerianus there were twenty-seven emperors, but this number does not include all the upstarts who snatched for a moment at the purple. Of the twenty-seven, seventeen were killed, all but one by the troops; two committed suicide; three were killed fighting and one, Valerian, died as a prisoner in enemy hands. Only four died natural deaths.

Breaching of the northern frontiers

The hideous story of the military anarchy of the third century is either the better or the worse for the fact that we know comparatively little of its details. The reputable histories have vanished. The pretentious biographies of the various emperors are almost wholly untrustworthy, having been composed at the end of the fourth century by an unreliable and highly imaginative writer of fiction. Inscriptions are our safest guides, together with coins and particularly coin-hordes, for coin-hordes are evidence that at the date when they were buried, roughly ascertainable by the dates of the latest coins in them, people were on the run.

This was the century when the imperial defences were breached and the barbarians poured in – Free Dacians, Carpi, Goths, Burgundians, Marcomanni, Juthungi – chiefly over the Danube into the Balkans, even into Italy or across the Euxine into Asia Minor. In 253, 256 and 267 they were in Asia Minor; in 267 burning down the temple of Artemis at Ephesus. Athens fell in 268. In 253 the Alemanni were in the neighbourhood of Rome; in 269 and 270 North Italy was being ravaged. There seemed no limit to the number of such invaders. They were huge, energetic men, vulnerable only in as far as they were badly organised, badly equipped, fighting bare-headed without helmets.

There was terror not in the north only but also in the east, since the Parthians, who had never been an aggressive power, were mastered at the time of Severus Alexander by a revived Achaemenid Persia, the dynasty of the Sassanid kings. In 230 Syria and Cappadocia were overrun and in 242 Shapur I invaded Syria and Antioch was under siege. In 253 the Persians became masters of (Parthian) Armenia. The caravan city of Dura-Europos was destroyed and disappeared – until American archaeologists recovered it from the desert. The Persians took Antioch and Tarsus; better still, in 260 they captured the Roman emperor Valerian.

Two of the three outlying provinces of the empire – Britain, Dacia and Mesopotamia – were increasingly vulnerable. Commodus having abandoned Marcus Aurelius' brave intention to absorb the

Jazyges, who occupied the vast re-entrant between the northern frontier of Dacia and the Danube at Aquincum (Budapest), Roman Dacia was open to attack from three flanks. In 270, Aurelian took the brave, if inevitable, decision that it must be evacuated; a retreat that was not masked when two provinces with the name of Dacia were created south of the Danube. Mesopotamia's position, never secure, was more delicate still when the Persians were to the north of it in Armenia as well as to the south-east. It was under constant invasion and it is hard to know why it too was not abandoned.

The Balkan provinces took the brunt of the attack in the north and huge tracts south of the Danube were devastated areas, abandoned by their Roman inhabitants. Increasingly, the barbarians themselves were settled there as a price of peace, in the hope that they would farm the waste lands and, on the river itself, would

On Trajan's column, see page 117.
Here Roman soldiers are shown
defending a stronghold in the Dacian
wars against barbarian attack.

205

guard the frontiers which they had once invaded. In larger and
larger numbers they were drafted into Roman service as soldiers,
officered by their compatriots, men whose loyalty was never certain, though some did good service; princes who became the
emperor's advisers. Here was the last chapter in the long story of
romanisation: the incorporation of aliens.

Others of the invaders returned home, having impoverished the
lands they had ravaged by the loot which they carried away.
Worse still, they continued to be a drain on the empire's resources,
having extorted a heavy subsidy as the price of their return: the
kind of payment which was thought so ignominious when Domitian
first made it to the Dacians. They might even return to the attack,
as at the time of Philip, if the subsidies were not regularly paid. At
the beginning of the third century, the annual payment in such
subsidies was equivalent to the pay of the entire Roman army. As
the century advanced, it grew greater and greater, a drain all the
time on Rome's diminishing supplies of silver and gold.

The barbarian invaders were not the only scourge; there was also
the plague. A century after it had been brought to Europe by
L. Verus' army, it returned and raged for twenty years from 250,
sapping the fighting strength of Valerian's army in the east and
striking at every level of Roman social life. It killed the son of
Decius, and it killed the emperor Claudius II. It helped, with all the
other disasters, to reduce the population of the empire, according
to some calculations by nearly a third, from seventy to fifty millions.

Behind the frontiers, there were other marks of disintegration; a
great increase in highwaymen and robbers, many of them deserters
from the armies, men who lived by violence and plunder.

Collapse of the economy

Trading suffered and the currency collapsed, as a token coinage
replaced a system under which a gold or silver coin had traditionally
been worth the weight of its metal content. The gold *aureus*, worth
twenty-five silver *denarii*, was reduced to a third of its original
weight by the middle of the third century; the denarius had been

replaced under Caracalla by a new *Antoninianus* valued at two denarii, but weighing only one and a half. This was steadily adulterated, until in the second half of the third century it had lost 98 per cent of its silver content and was no more than a base coin with a silver wash. Yet officially, coins passed at their face value. In practice, of course, they did not. Bankers were reluctant to touch them, there was a galloping inflation in prices and increasingly a return to the barter economy of a primitive society. It has been calculated that prices in Egypt had risen towards the end of the third century from fourteen to twenty times their original level.

Civilians suffered, forced by officialdom to accept current coinage at its face value and, in addition, forced increasingly to supply goods, particularly food, in kind (*annona*) and to perform compulsory services (the hated *angareiai*). They were at the mercy of government collectors (*procuratores*) and of soldiers who demanded not what was legitimate but what they could extort. An inscription of AD 238 from Thrace records the hardships of a community with natural warm baths and a popular market in the neighbourhood; government officials and soldiers descended like locusts, demanding free accommodation and free food.

In the long centuries of peace the cities of the empire had not needed walls. Now even at a distance from the frontier cities were unwise if they did not look to their defences. Aquileia could not have defied Maximinus Thraex but for its powerful walls. Rome retains today a large part of the great wall, 12 miles long and 25 feet high, whose construction started under Aurelian and was finished under Probus. This is the wall from behind which in the sixth century Belisarius defied the Goths.

There continued all over the world to be great cities with notable buildings and vigorous municipal life; for instance, the numerous cities of Gaul which Ausonius and Ammianus Marcellinus listed in the late fourth century and in the East, despite countless destructions, Antioch was 'of great importance, the first city in the East in respect of wealth, size, beauty and prosperity of every sort' when the Persians looted its gold, silver and marbles and then burnt it down in AD 540, and Procopius 'became dizzy when he wrote of such a calamity'. Yet generally, the city life which had been the glory of Greco-Roman civilisation and which Rome had spread and encouraged as the most powerful agent of romanisation, was now at the start of its catastrophic decline. Cities were sacked by barbarians and not rebuilt. Others suffered because of their positions on the great main roads, on the line of march of the Roman armies and consequently victims of harsh and intolerable requisitions or, worse, helpless sources of plunder. Membership of the municipal ruling class (the *decuriones*), once a source of pride and an inspiration to generosity, now became a harsh penalty, from which there was no escape. They were responsible for the collection of taxes and if there was a short-fall – for instance because land liable to taxation had gone out of cultivation – they had to meet the deficit from their own pockets, the burden falling most heavily on a new penalised élite, the Top Ten (Decem Primi or Dekaprotoi). So people moved from the towns into the country and a new social unit came into existence and spread rapidly – in Britain, for instance, which enjoyed great economic prosperity in the third and fourth centuries, and in Gaul – the villa-system, based on a large farm with its considerable buildings and means of food-production, with its own independent villa-industries, fulling cloth, making tiles and bricks. There were blacksmiths and there might be potters. Consequently, except for a few things like glass and metal goods, the importance of the towns diminished in the general economy. There were also villages on the great estates, private and imperial, especially in Syria and in North Africa, inhabited by *coloni*, tenants who paid the landlord part of their produce and were liable for certain services to him; others were attached to towns, and a main recruiting-ground for soldiers. And on the southern frontier, the *limes*, in Africa, there were fortified settlements of peasants and military settlers, with the double responsibility for farming land and protecting the frontier.

The whole structure of military defence in the north required re-organisation. The 'ring of iron', the legions on the frontiers, constituted an ineffective sort of Maginot Line. Once it was breached, invaders poured through the gap. What was required was a defence in depth, mobile forces some way behind the frontiers which could be moved quickly to deal with the danger, wherever it threatened. This had perhaps been in the mind of Septimius Severus when he stationed one of his new legions at Albano near Rome. The new bases of the mobile army were at Milan, Verona and Aquileia in north Italy and on the Save at Sirmium. The infantry units were increasingly detachments from more legions than one (*vexillationes*), not legions themselves, and a powerful new cavalry force, the Equites Dalmatae, was created by Gallienus, whose commander was, in the military sphere, second only to the emperor. It was probably from the tenure of this post that Claudius and Aurelian became emperors. And there were new units of auxiliaries, highly trained specialists with armour of a new type, Moorish cavalry and javelin-throwers, oriental archers and heavy-armed cavalry, often men who employed barbarian tactics themselves.

Roman defensive strength was not increased by the mutual jealousy and hostility of the different armies, which had already done havoc enough in the civil wars of 69 and 193: the Rhine armies, the Danube armies and the armies of the East. One of the reasons why the troops turned on Alexander Severus and killed him at Mainz in 235 was his supposed partiality for the legions from the East. The Danube army resented the fact that Gallienus, by his presence in Gaul, showed that he regarded the invasions of Gaul as more serious than those across the Danube. And there were the breakaway empires which, while not at first setting themselves in overt hostility to the Roman government, thought that on their own ground they could do that government's job better. The revolt of Gaul under Postumus, governor of one of the Germanies, in 260 lasted fourteen years and was joined by Britain and Spain. Trier was its capital, with a senate and consuls on Roman lines. At its height it was joined by the cavalry commander Aureolus at Milan, whose troops proclaimed him emperor.

In the East, there was the Palmyrene empire of the hereditary

The walls of Rome, most of which still stand, were started by Aurelian and finished by Probus. Severely damaged when the city was attacked by Totila, they were restored by Belisarius and much work was done on them later by the Renaissance popes. They are about 12 feet thick, of concrete faced with brick and were originally 25 feet high. This section is at the Porta Tiburtina (the entrance of the road from Tivoli).

The large country villa as a centre of industry and
habitation became widespread in the western provinces as
cities were increasingly abandoned in the third and fourth
centuries AD. Here is a country villa at Coulonvilliers
in France, invisible on the ground but detected, like
so many important ancient sites, by aerial photography.

sheik Odenathus, who did on his own what the Roman government was incapable of doing: he quickly avenged the capture of the
emperor Valerian by invading Persia and attacking its capital
Ctesiphon in 262. His coins proclaimed him *Dux Romanorum,
Corrector Totius Orbis*. Gallienus, who was fully occupied in the
West, could have nothing but gratitude for him, until he was murdered in 267 and his widow Zenobia, dissatisfied with control of
the whole area between the Taurus and the Arabian Gulf, spread
her tentacles wider, aiming to annex Asia Minor and, by taking
Egypt, to control the corn supply of Rome. So in 271, Aurelian
campaigned against her. Palmyra was sacked, and Zenobia walked
as captive in a Roman triumph.

In such conditions of anarchy and disturbance, superstition and
magic flourished from the highest ranks in society to the lowest.
No ruler in history can have been more superstitious than Septimius
Severus, who married Julia Domna for her horoscope. When
Diocletian marked his imperial proclamation by running a sword
through the praetorian commander Aper who, as he suspected, had
murdered Numerianus, was he not fulfilling the earlier prediction
given him at the time when he was a shepherd-boy that he would
kill a boar (*aper*) and become emperor of Rome? In private life
horoscopes were cast phrenetically and no magical device was
unexplored for the purpose of incapacitating or disposing of a rival
whether in love or as charioteer in the Games. And in the despair
and questioning of the times people looked for scapegoats. Why
had settled peace turned into chaos and disaster? Whose fault was
it, whose 'devils' were at the root of the trouble?

The Christians, who refused to subscribe to the most fundamental tenet of imperial loyalty, belief in the emperor's divinity,
were an easy target, an object of general hate. In Cappadocia at the
time of Maximinus, there was a spontaneous local persecution of
Christians who were held responsible for the occurrence of an un-
usually bad earthquake.

At government level, proceedings had been taken against the
Christian clergy by Maximinus, but the first great persecution took

place in 250 under Decius, when every member of the empire was compelled to register and acquire a certificate as evidence of having made an offering to a pagan god; yet many Christians defiantly confessed the faith (the *confessores*) and somehow or other escaped. Seven years later, in an effort to turn popular attention away from contemporary disasters Valerian forbade meetings of Christians and ordered the execution of the Christian clergy. The senate approved warmly of such traditionalist sentiment. Happily for the Christians, Gallienus in 261 reversed this as he reversed all other features of his father's policy.

Absolutism and bureaucracy

Under the system which Augustus so ingeniously devised, imperial government had been in the hands of the emperors, the senate and its members, equites and soldiers, and the system of the Augustan principate had survived with surprisingly little alteration down to Marcus Aurelius. The century after Marcus' death witnessed start-

ling changes. The Princeps turned into a divinely appointed auto-
crat wearing the trappings of an oriental king; the effective power
of the senate and its members waned; a powerful equestrian and
military bureaucracy came into existence.

The emperor was *nobilissimus*. His power was absolute, for it was
now accepted that he was not subject to the laws, and his own
rulings (*constitutiones*) were recognised as having the full force of
law. While Tiberius had once stated that he was lord (*dominus*) to
nobody but his slaves, the emperor was now conventionally
dominus noster in the language of dedications. From Commodus
onwards he included '*pius Felix*' in his titles and also '*Invictus*', the
epithet of the oriental sun-god. The word 'sacred' (*sacer*) had
become the equivalent of 'imperial'; the emperor issued *sacrae
constitutiones*; his palace was *sacrum palatium*. He wore military
uniform in Rome and dressed in purple or triumphal robes. From
the time of Gallienus he fulfilled what Julius Caesar's enemies had
once declared to be Caesar's ambition: he wore the diadem, itself
radiate like the sun. At his receptions an exaggerated punctilio was
observed; men kneeled before him, in the oriental practice of
proskynesis, which Alexander the Great had once vainly attempted
to persuade his Macedonian marshals to adopt. He ruled by the
grace of his favoured god or gods, and his life was in their hands,
as Aurelian once assured soldiers who had floundered in an attempt
to kill him. Aurelian sought by the building of a great temple in
Rome and in other ways to encourage the cult of the Sun God
(that *baal*, Elagabalus at Emesa, which had given Rome its boy-
priest to be emperor), a cult which might appeal also to the wor-
shippers of Apollo and of Mithras. The Sun was *dominus imperii
Romani*, Lord of the Roman Empire, the emperor's personal
protector.

Imperial rule should be dynastic. So Septimius Severus adopted
the dead Marcus Aurelius as his father and by this fiction the
Antonine house ruled until the death of Severus Alexander. After
that, if an emperor had a son, the son was proclaimed Caesar and
sometimes a co-Augustus – an elevation which was in fact as good

as the signature of his death warrant. For the chaotic history of the third century showed that the gods who supposedly had emperors in their keeping failed disastrously to preserve their charges from conspiracy and murder. In particular, Decius and Valerian who, in the cause of paganism, persecuted the Christian church, both came to sticky ends.

Soldiers proclaimed emperors (it is remarkable that in an army at any time the appropriate purple cloak seems to have been available) and, except in AD 238 and 275, the senate accepted the new emperor without hesitation and, according to his wishes, consecrated or declined to consecrate his predecessor. Its membership was in the emperor's hands; its Italian members sank to a third and the bulk of senators came from Africa, Asia Minor and Syria. They were fantastically rich men. Senators were *viri clarissimi*, more and more of a city council, less and less involved directly in the administration of the empire. This was in part because of the need for greater professionalism; in part it was the final expression of a fear which went back through Septimius Severus to Augustus. For this reason Augustus had refused to allow senators to govern or to command legions in Egypt. For this reason Septimius Severus gave the commands of his three new legions to equites and made an eques, not a senator, governor of Mesopotamia. For this reason Domitian had put an end to double legionary camps and Septimius Severus had split up provinces – for instance Britain and Syria, which had supported his rivals – so that no province should have a garrison of more than two legions.

A few provinces still received senators as their governors: Asia and Africa, of course, and also Britain, Hispania Tarraconensis, Moesia Inferior and Coele Syria. Otherwise, from Gallienus onwards, an equestrian 'acting governor' – *procurator vice praesidis* – was appointed, soon to be called, quite simply, '*praeses*'; for it was not until now that the Latin language, the language of a great imperial power, devised a simple term which meant 'a provincial governor'. The sole rule of Gallienus after AD 260 also saw the exclusion of senators from military commands. Young senators were no more appointed to commissions as tribunes in the legions; older senators no longer commanded legions, the place of a senatorial legate being taken by an equestrian *praefectus legionis*.

Military service was now, as never before, a *carrière ouverte aux talents*. The simple ranker, in Europe largely recruited in the Balkans, could rise to the top – even, like Maximinus or Diocletian, become emperor – if he had the talents which the conditions of the new world demanded: not culture, education, or even great literacy, but courage, efficiency, harsh common sense, ruthlessness. The legionary received the gold ring (once the badge of equestrian status) when he joined up. If he rose to be a first-centurion, then he became an equestrian and ahead of him lay the possibility of high commission in the army or employment in procuratorial posts in the new administrative bureaucracy, service which was called *militia*, so that in the end army service required a qualifying epithet and was called *militia armata*. The eques of high promise was promoted to the body of *protectores lateris divini*, high officers whose corps was a kind of Staff College. They were Illyrians largely, and had great careers ahead. In the exclusively military sphere the new commander of cavalry, as has been seen, ranked highest; in the politico-military sphere the prefects of the praetorian guard, the two *viri eminentissimi*, were soldiers and lawyers in one for, leaving jurisdiction within a hundred miles of Rome to the senatorial prefect of the city, they were supreme judges in cases in Italy outside that limit and final judges of appeal as representatives of, then in place of, the emperor, in all other criminal cases which were referred to Rome from the provinces. They alone, with the prefect of the city, could 'deport to an island'. How the two sides of the prefect's activities were co-ordinated, is hard to know. The great jurists at the turn of the second and third centuries, men like Ulpian, were prefects of the praetorian guard; their fate and the fate of Macrinus, who became emperor, shows how little regard the soldiery had for a commander who happened to be a good lawyer. Since Severus Alexander the prefects were automatically members of the senate, *viri clarissimi* and *eminentissimi* in one. Already the prefects had their deputies, *vicarii*, men of increasing power.

They took over other civilian functions, in particular responsibility for the corn supply (*annona*), and here we can see how a division of bureaucratic functions made for confusion and an accentuation of hardships endured throughout the empire by the common man. Requisitions for the army – the *annona militaris* – were enforced on the authority of the prefect of the guard; taxation generally was the responsibility now of the *rationalis*, the chief financial officer of the state, a *vir perfectissimus* like the treasurer of the imperial purse, the *procurator* (later *magister*) *rei privatae*, the enemy behind the scenes for every tenant on the imperial estates.

Not every soldier who joined up had a career of glittering success ahead. Gone were the days of the early empire, when military service offered the prospect of long years of garrison duty relieved by road-building and barrack-building, with comparatively little fighting or danger. Service now involved continuous and dangerous warfare, in which casualties must have been high. Emperors, therefore, conscious also of the fact that their own survival depended on the armies' favour, added every attraction that they could to military service. Since Septimius Severus legionaries were allowed to marry. Their pay was startlingly increased between the time of Commodus and Caracalla, and they were in frequent receipt of largesse in the form of handsome gold medallions. 'Enrich the soldiery and pay attention to nobody else': this was Septimius Severus' advice on his death-bed to his two sons.

Though battered everywhere, civilised life was anything but dead. The end of the second century and the beginning of the third was the period of the great jurisconsults, Papinian, Paulus and Ulpian, all easterners, who made their powerful contribution to one of Rome's greatest achievements, the body of civil law. Elementary education was more widespread in the third century than ever before. With Philostratus as her secretary, Julia Domna presided over a *salon* of literary men and philosophers; her niece, the mother of Severus Alexander, was sufficiently interested in Christianity to send for Origen to preach her a sermon. Zenobia's interest in Greek literature brought the rhetorician Longinus to her court. Plotinus was teaching and writing in Rome under Gallienus and Claudius.

4 The Fourth Empire: Diocletian and Constantine

The final chapter in the history of imperial Rome, the empire's last struggle for survival and its ultimate collapse is a story with three features. The first, entirely predictable, was Diocletian's division of the empire into two, a western empire with Rome, the residence of the senate, for its nominal capital while its effective capital, which for strategic reasons had to be further north, was the western emperor's residence for the moment – Trier (Augusta Trevirorum), Milan (Mediolanum), Ravenna or Sirmium; the eastern capital was first at Nicomedia (Izmit) and then at Byzantium, renamed Constantinople when Constantine rebuilt it as a great Christian city. It had senate, magistrates and officials copying, though on a lower scale of wealth and eminence, the senate, magistrates and officials in Rome, and its new walls, stouter by far than those which Septimius Severus had destroyed, were themselves to be made stronger still in the fifth century. In the Balkans, the line of division between the two empires was not, it seems, firmly fixed and in rare periods of friction between east and west, this became an issue, as it did between the bishops of Rome and Constantinople.

The second feature was utterly unpredictable: the conversion to Christianity of a Roman emperor and the imposition on the entire empire of Christianity as its single official cult.

The third feature which, if not predictable, must have been universally apprehended, was the overwhelming of the imperial defences by the barbarian peoples who, after the chaos of the third century, had by the time of Diocletian's accession been driven back beyond the frontiers. When would they strike again and where, and in how great numbers?

The division of the Empire

As has been seen, the division of the empire into east and west may have been suggested as a device for separating Geta from his brother Caracalla. It was in fact operative between 253 and 260 with Valerian in the east and Gallienus in the west and, indeed, in the year before Diocletian's proclamation, when Numerianus cam-

Augusta Trevirorum (Trier), originally capital of the Treveri in Gaul, became   219
a Roman colony, probably under Claudius. It was the most important
city in north-east Gaul, and centre of the Moselle wine trade. From the
time of Maximian it was frequently the residence of the western Augustus.
Very extensive Roman remains survive, including a large amphitheatre
and the late Roman gateway, the *Porta Nigra*, illustrated here.

paigned against Persia in the East and his brother Carinus held command in the West. Diocletian planned something more radical, a permanent division of the empire and a separation of rule to prevent the military riots and promiscuous proclamations by soldiers of their generals which had caused such havoc in the previous century.

Not only was there to be an Augustus of the east, the senior Augustus, Diocletian himself, and an Augustus of the west, Maximian, an Illyrian of low birth like himself, who was proclaimed Augustus in 286, but after 293 each Augustus was underpinned by his own Caesar; Diocletian by Galerius and Maximian by Constantius, both of Illyrian parentage, though later fiction, requiring more illustrious origins for Constantius, as the father of the first Christian emperor, claimed descent for him from the emperor Claudius II. This was the system of the tetrarchy. Four rulers should be sufficient to provide commanders for every campaigning army and so the danger of ambitious upstarts should be avoided. At the start, each Caesar married his Augustus' daughter, Constantius being forced to discard his wife – or mistress – Helena, the mother of his son Constantine. Here were firm links. Each of the Caesars might anticipate succession when his Augustus died and then there would in turn be other Caesars, selected for their merit and adopted. Hereditary succession was no part of Diocletian's plan. It was a splendid scheme on paper, but after his resignation, it did not work at all. In 309, four years after he and Maximian resigned, there were – including an upstart in Africa – six Augusti. The basis of the system however, stood firm until the last emperor of the west, Romulus Augustulus, was pushed into retirement by the German king Odoacer in 476. One Augustus, the senior Augustus, ruled the eastern empire, the other the western.

Diocletian's reorganisation of administration

Diocletian, who was born with the soul of a true bureaucrat, systematised the whole structure of government in novel form and imposed regulations of iron-like rigidity which not only determined

The Empire: division into
dioceses under Diocletian.

221

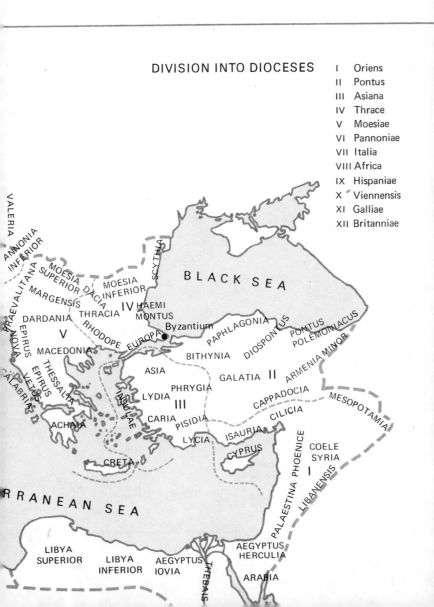

DIVISION INTO DIOCESES

I Oriens
II Pontus
III Asiana
IV Thrace
V Moesiae
VI Pannoniae
VII Italia
VIII Africa
IX Hispaniae
X Viennensis
XI Galliae
XII Britanniae

VALERIA
ANNONIA INFERIOR
MOESIA SUPERIOR
DACIA
PRAEVALITANA
MARGENSIS
MOESIA INFERIOR
DARDANIA
THRACIA
RHODOPE
IV HAEMI MONTUS
EUROPA
SCYTHIA
NOVA EPIRUS
MACEDONIA
V
Byzantium
PAPHLAGONIA
DIOSPONTUS
PONTUS POLEMONIACUS
THESSALIA
EPIRUS VETUS
CALABRIA
ASIA
BITHYNIA
GALATIA II
ARMENIA MINOR
PHRYGIA
LYDIA
III
CAPPADOCIA
MESOPOTAMIA
ACHAIA
INSULAE
CARIA
PISIDIA
CILICIA
LYCIA
ISAURIA
CYPRUS
PHOENICE
COELE SYRIA
CRETA
PALAESTINA
LIBANENSIS
I

BLACK SEA

RRANEAN SEA

LIBYA SUPERIOR
LIBYA INFERIOR
AEGYPTUS IOVIA
THEBAIS
AEGYPTUS HERCULIA
ARABIA

Table 6 Emperors from Diocletian onwards

West	East
Maximian, AD 286-305	Diocletian, 285-305
Constantius Chlorus, Caesar, 293-305 Augustus, 305-6	Galerius, Caesar, 293-305 Augustus, 305-11
Severus, Caesar, 305 Augustus, 306-7	Licinius, Augustus, 308-24 Maximinus Daia, Caesar, 305-8 Augustus, 308-13
Maxentius, Augustus, 308-12	
Constantine, Caesar, 306-8 Augustus, 308-337	
Constantine, Emperor of West and East, 324-37	
*Constantine II, Caesar, 317-37 Augustus, 337-40	Licinianus, Caesar, 317
*Constans, Caesar, 333-7 Augustus, 337-50	*Crispus, Caesar, 317-26
	*Constantius II, Caesar, 324-37 Augustus, 337-61
Magnentius, usurper, Augustus, 350-3	†Dalmatius, Caesar, 335-7
	†Gallus, Caesar, 350-4
Constantius II, Emperor of West and East, 353-61	
†Julian, Caesar, 355-60 Augustus, 360-3	
Julian, Emperor of West and East, 361-3	
	Jovian, Augustus, 363-4

*Son of Constantine   †Nephew of Constantine

West	East
Valentinian, Augustus, 364-75	Valens, brother of Valentinian, Augustus, 364-78
Gratian, son of Valentinian, Augustus, 367 (aged 8)-83	Theodosius I, Augustus, 379-95
Valentinian II, Augustus, 375 (aged 4)-292	
Magnus Maximus, usurper, 383-8	Arcadius, son of Theodosius, 383 (aged 6)-408
Eugenius, usurper, 392-4	
Honorius, son of Theodosius, 393 (aged 8)-423	Theodosius II, son of Arcadius, 408 (aged 7)-449
Valentinian III, nephew of Honorius, 425 (aged 6)-455	Marcian, 450-7
Eparchius Avitus, usurper, 455-6	
Majorian, 457-61	Leo, 457-74
Libius Severus, 461-5	
Anthemius, sent from East by Leo, 467-72	
Olybrius, 472	
Glycerius, 473	Zeno, 474-91
Julius Nepos, nominee of Leo, 473-5	
Romulus Augustulus, 476	
	Anastasius, 491-518
	Justin, 518-27
	Justinian, 527-65
	Justin II, 565-78
	Tiberius Constantine, 578-82
	Maurice, 582-602

retail prices of goods and froze wages and incomes, but also chained vast numbers of his discontented subjects in their existing employment. Officials multiplied, glorying in a profusion of new grandiloquent titles.

At the head of all, both in the East and the West, was the Augustus, who ruled by the grace of god (Diocletian as Iovius, Maximian as Herculius), ornately costumed, burdened by jewels, approached with the gesture of *adoratio*. His top advisers constituted the sacred consistory, with its innumerable secretaries, *notarii*. The Augustus depended on his *magister officiorum*, the head of all the administrative bureaux, the *scrinia*. He had his finance ministers as before and his secret service, now called *agentes in rebus*.

Partly for the sake of efficiency and partly because men in small commands are less dangerous than men in big ones, the empire was reorganised in smaller units – fifty provinces. Asia and Africa were under consulars; Sicily, Achaea and Italy (which lost its superior position and, excluding the district within a hundred miles of Rome, now constituted two provinces) were governed by *correctores*, senatorial or equestrian; other provinces by equestrian governors, *praesides*, who were *viri perfectissimi*. The *praeses* was occupied in judicial and financial matters, no longer having, like earlier provincial governors, the services of a special financial officer. The provinces were grouped in twelve dioceses, each under a deputy (*vicarius*) of the prefect of the praetorian guard, also a *vir perfectissimus*; and so, since appeals from the vicars went straight to the emperor, the power of the prefects of the guard was greatly weakened. Public officials had vast clerical staffs, the vicarius about four hundred, the praeses a hundred.

The division between the frontier and the field army remained and was to be strengthened by Constantine. The imperial field army consisted of the *comitatus* (including the Iovii and Herculii, which were crack regiments) and the existing *Protectores Divini Lateris*. The two top officers were the *magistri praesidiales*, one of the cavalry, one of the infantry, though the two posts might be combined and held by a single man. Armies on the frontier and in the provinces were commanded by *duces*, of which there were about twenty or by *comites*, while high commands over large areas were held by *magistri militum*. The duces depended for their commissariat on the civilian provincial governors, but were otherwise independent of them. The size of the army was vastly increased. The Severan army consisted of 33 legions; Diocletian raised the number to 67.

The expense of the enlarged army and of the new bureaucracy was huge. Lactantius observed cynically that the number of men who were supported by the taxes was larger than the number of those who paid them.

The new tax system was frightening in its results. On paper it was splendid, a masterpiece of bureaucratic expertise. The burden fell most heavily on the countryman who, the empire over, submitted to a tax-assessment which was for the future to be revised (upwards, generally) by periodical re-assessments – at first after five, later after fifteen years – on the basis of land (*iugatio*) and employees (*capitatio*), the latter what is today called selective employment tax. A *iugum* consisted of between 14 and 40 (modern) acres of arable land, according to its quality, just over three acres of vineyard or a certain number of olive trees.

The units were counted. The imperial budget was drawn up by the *censitores*. The praetorian prefect apportioned it to each province. By simple division the tax for each unit was calculated, not in money but in kind: wheat, barley, meat, wine, oil, clothes, recruits for the army, labourers for public works, animals and waggons for the public post – everything, in fact, that the greedy armies required. On large estates, the system may have been workable; on small units it can hardly have been workable at all. If the calculations proved to have been wrong, there was a supplementary budget, a *super-indictio*. The poor *curiales* had to see that it was all collected – corn, wine, oil, clothes, labourers and the rest. If it was not forthcoming, they had to meet the deficit from their own resources. And it was not forthcoming, for bad land naturally went out of cultivation.

The decurions and the farm-workers, on whom the scheme depended, were tied to their posts, and if discovered by the censors to be absent from their homes they were forced to return. The sons of decurions were doomed to succeed their fathers; they could not enlist in the army, even if they wanted to. Later, if decurions became senators, they had to leave a representative or to continue themselves to discharge their responsibilities as decurions.

Merchants and shopkeepers were not taxed as heavily as country-men. Constantine therefore introduced a *collatio lustralis*, a quin-quennial levy of gold and silver on merchants and craftsmen, which proved an oppressive levy, for urban craftsmen were often very poor. Constantine also introduced something like a graded super-tax on the owners of very large estates, a *collatio glebalis*.

Administered with integrity, the tax system would have been harsh. Its impact was in fact made worse by the universality of corrupt practices in its administration. When Julian investigated

these in Gaul in 360, he was able to reduce the standard levy under the *capitatio* by something like 75 per cent. Julian did his best, too, to reduce the inflated number of civil servants – the notaries of the sacred consistory who by this time numbered over five hundred, and sinister government officials like the *curiosi*, hated inspectors of the public post.

The coinage was restored by Diocletian, with dependable gold and silver pieces, though the issues were woefully inadequate from lack of precious metals, and with a billon issue for small change, the largest billon coin being the *follis*. Constantine's gold *solidus*, which survived to the eleventh century, was a further improvement, though it too, was issued in very small quantities. The loss of Dacia in the third century had meant the loss of the Dacian gold mines. From Diocletian onwards, compulsory gold purchases were made from cities and these were the source, presumably of the huge subventions in gold which were paid to the barbarians.

Diocletian's edict fixing prices for every commodity and also fixing wages, which must have occupied an enormous amount of a great many civil servants' time in its drafting, and of stone-cutters in cutting copies for public display all over the empire, had almost at once to be abandoned. Traders and merchants refused to pay attention to it. As the fourth century ran on, there were state factories, even monopolies, as there had been in Hellenistic Egypt. No department of socialist state planning was unexplored.

In the economy of the later empire great poverty existed side by side with great wealth. As always in the ancient world, wealth was predominantly invested in land and there were, all over the empire, vast imperial estates and vast estates belonging to the senatorial class, many of them acquired by new men whose fortunes had been made, however corruptly, in government service. There were still some rich land-owning decurions; and there were the increasingly large estates of the Church. The small owner-farmer disappeared, killed by taxation. Perhaps a fifth of the land of the whole empire went out of cultivation, partly through devastation by invaders, partly as a result of deforestation, whose evils the ancients seem never properly to have understood, partly because it was marginal land and, under the oppressive taxation system, could not be farmed profitably. On the large estates there were free tenants, and *coloni*, many of whom were *adscripticii*, descendants of men registered under Diocletian's census, serfs, unable to leave the land, little different from agricultural slaves – unless they had a number of sons and the estate-owner found himself with a surfeit of labour.

Christianity

Though the first measures against the Christians since Valerian were taken when Diocletian was emperor, they were taken when he was old and ill and he may have disapproved. The chief responsibility lay with that friend of neoplatonists Galerius, first as Caesar in 303 and then, after Diocletian's retirement in 305, as Augustus in succession to Diocletian, and by his Caesar, Maximin

Daia. The persecutions were almost entirely restricted to the eastern empire, lasting for eight years in its European provinces and ten years in Asia.

The number of victims is uncertain. There were a hundred altogether in Palestine, in Egypt a hundred in a single day. Britain and Gaul were unaffected and Italy, Africa and Spain suffered only for a year, under the first edict.

Though Origen and Tertullian disapproved in the third century and Lactantius in the fourth, there were Christians in the army. At a pagan sacrifice attended by Diocletian and Galerius the entrails of the sacrificed animals were hideously unpropitious; it was said, because Christians in the ranks had invoked their own hostile devils by crossing themselves. Soldiers were then given the option of pagan sacrifice or dismissal, and the storm blew over for the moment. Then in February 303, the first edict was issued, forbidding Christian worship and ordering the destruction of Christian churches and books; soon afterwards a fire broke out in the palace at Nicomedia and sinister use was made of the fact, as the burning of the Reichstag was to be exploited in this century for the Nazi persecutions of the Communists and also of the Social Democrats.

By a second edict bishops and clergy were arrested and the prisons filled to overflowing; by a third, the prisoners were made to sacrifice under force, and so the overcrowded prisons could be emptied. By a fourth edict, when Diocletian was seriously ill, all citizens of the empire were compelled to sacrifice under pain of death. Then Diocletian retired. A fifth edict instructed provincial governors to enforce sacrifice. The next edict, issued by Maximin Daia in 306, ordered the rebuilding of pagan temples with the compulsion on all citizens to be present and taste sacrificial meat and gave instructions that all goods in the markets should be sprinkled with sacrificial blood.

Galerius and Maximin were by their lights commendable fanatics, believing in the true Roman tradition that the empire's welfare depended on the *pax deorum*, which Christianity contravened; but people at large, who by this time had little personal dislike of

On the arch of Constantine in Rome,
see page 124. The relief here illustrated
is of Constantine seated on the
platform (rostra) of the Forum in Rome.

Christians as individuals, were sick of it all. Galerius fell horribly
ill and the seventh edict of April 311 called the persecution off.
Christianity was to survive on toleration.

The Christians were still only a small proportion of the inhabitants of the empire and there is no easy explanation of the miracle
by which Constantine was converted to the conviction that theirs
was the one true god. That the emperor was the servant of *a* god
was already accepted belief; Diocletian of Jupiter, Maximian and
Constantine, in the succession from Maximian as Augustus, of
Hercules. Then Constantine had his first conversion, regarding
himself, as Aurelian and Constantius had done, as the servant of
the sun, *Sol Invictus*. Later in Gaul he had a vision, the sign of the
cross against the afternoon sun. He invaded Italy to depose
Maxentius, the son of Maximian who had been proclaimed
Augustus; in his sleep on 28 October 312, he was bidden to mark
the shields of his troops with the Christian monogram, the letter X
with a vertical line drawn through it and turned at the top. On the
following day he won the battle of the Milvian Bridge outside
Rome. Maxentius was killed and Constantine entered Rome in
triumph. The last flicker of persecution, a caprice of Maximin Daia,
was extinguished and in 313 Maximin died a natural death more
horrible even than that of his fellow-persecutor Galerius. Licinius,
who had defeated him, himself inspired, it was said, by Christian
intimation of victory, was the new Augustus of the east. Constantine
had already restored to the Church its destroyed buildings and
Licinius issued an edict granting complete freedom for all religions.
Constantine's favours to the Christians were such as to surprise
even his Christian prefect of the guard. Christians were now
allowed to appeal from a secular court to a bishop, as a court of
final appeal. Christian soldiers were given time off to go to church.

After Constantine had disposed of Licinius, he ruled as sole
Augustus from 324 to 337. The new Constantinople, the first
Christian city with no pagan temples, was inaugurated in 330. And
now Christianity began to show its seamy side; a religion bedevilled
by schism and a conflict of bishops. Donatism in Africa had already

been condemned. Now, far more serious, came Arianism, the doctrine of a dissident priest of Alexandria, the question of defining the nature of God the Son in relation to God the Father. Was He of one substance or two? The great oecumenical council of bishops which Constantine as head of the Church – for in the tradition of paganism and from the circumstances of his own conversion he had no doubt that this was his position – assembled at Nicaea in 325 and over which he presided, reached agreement on *homoousia*: the Son was co-substantial with the Father, *consubstantialis patri*, a solution which was said to have been devised by Constantine himself. It was acceptable to the western church; to the eastern church it was distasteful and accepted only from general hostility to Arius himself.

Constantine's thirtieth year of rule, 336, was celebrated by a Council at Jerusalem and the consecration of the great church of the Holy Sepulchre. In the next year, Constantine died leaving his handsome legacy of great churches; Hagia Sophia (Holy Wisdom) at Constantinople and a number, including the first basilica of

St Peter, in Rome. The church of Hagia Sophia in Constantinople was later destroyed and the present magnificent building, later a mosque and now a museum, was erected by Justinian in the sixth century. In Rome, the only surviving near-contemporary Christian monument is the lovely church – originally the tomb – of S Constanza, probably the grand-daughter, not the daughter, of Constantine; she founded the original church of S Agnese which is beside it.

Julian's rule (360-3) was not long enough to impede to any great degree the march of Christianity. He was an over-enthusiastic pagan, ascetic, a believer in magic, a student of neoplatonism, who scorned the Christian religion. He cancelled state grants and other privileges which Constantine had made to the Church and forbade Christians to teach literature in schools. He issued an edict of universal toleration, sacrificed extravagantly and even tried to set up a universal priestly structure for paganism with pagan bishops and metropolitans. Then he embarked on his reckless war against Persia and was killed.

The Corbridge *lanx* (silver dish) was perhaps the work of an artist in Asia Minor at the time of Julian in the fourth century AD. It shows the worship of Apollo, the last flicker of paganism under Julian. With other silver objects it found its way to Northumberland in Britain and there was buried at the time when the settlement at Corstopitum (Corbridge) was overrun; it was dug up again in 1735.

Paganism received the *coup de grâce* from Gratian who abandoned the title Pontifex Maximus in 382 and, in the last years of his rule, from Theodosius I, Augustus in the east from 379 to 395. Influenced by Ambrose, bishop of Milan from 374 to 397, Theodosius ordered the closure of all pagan temples and forbade sacrifice in 391 and 392, and the ban which he imposed was never lifted. Not, of course, that paganism was killed at a stroke. It survived strongly in the west and was still a part of the inherited culture of the senatorial class in Rome, a fact well illustrated by the tug-of-war which went on between the senate and successive emperors in the fourth century over the retention of the altar of Victory, at which senators made offerings in the senate. Removed by Constantius II in 337, it was restored in the pagan revival; Gratian removed it – Ambrose winning his battle against Symmachus – in 382, but ten years later it was back again. Particularly paganism survived, a focus of superstition and magic, among the peasants.

Christianity continued to confront emperors with its problems. In the east they involved foreign policy, for Armenia was converted in the early fourth century, and Persian attempts to impose Zoroastrianism on it provoked pious emperors to war. There were incessant issues of doctrine, as the rulings of Nicaea were challenged by one heresy after another. There were conflicts and crises in the appointments of bishops; 137 persons killed in Rome in a holy place in a contest between two candidates in 366, and the appointment by Theodosius of a bishop in Constantinople who was found never to have been baptised. And there was the conflict in the hierarchy, with Rome eclipsing Milan after the death of Ambrose and retaining the primacy in all the empire's sad dissolution, with Constantinople after 381 in second place.

The centre of gravity in the Church was most markedly in the East with, in the sixth century, primates at Constantinople, Antioch, Jerusalem and Alexandria and a papal vicar at Thessalonica, as against the Pope at Rome and a primate at Carthage.

Between the third century and the sixth the Christian Church, generously excused such taxes as *collatio glebalis* and *capitatio*, acquired enormous wealth by gift, bequest and, in the west, partly by the introduction of tithes; it organised charities and developed a hierarchical paid priesthood; episcopal powers grew, with glaring inequalities in episcopal stipends, so that of the Roman see a witty senator could say, 'Make me Bishop of Rome and I will become a Christian tomorrow', and the exposure of simony was not infrequent. There was not yet a universal celibate priesthood, but by the early fifth century, the rule of clerical continence was in theory at least universally acknowledged in the West.

Barbarian invasions

Barbarian pressure was on all sides: Alemanni, Franks, Burgundians, Vandals, Sueves and Alans from across the Rhine; Alans, Quadi, Sarmatae, Ostrogoths, Visigoths, with Huns on their tails, over the Danube. Large invading bodies numbered something like 80,000, roughly a quarter of them warriors. The Roman army of defence in the West in the early fifth century was about a quarter of a million strong, with some 135,000 on the frontiers and 115,000 in the field army. When things went well, the barbarians were driven back across the frontiers; when things went less well, they were persuaded to go home on terms, an ample annual subsidy paid by the Romans in gold. If the payment failed to arrive in any year, they were liable to return to claim it. Sometimes the Romans agreed to their leaving a portion of their people to settle on deserted or uninhabited Roman land, particularly in the Balkans.

With every year the proportion of barbarians serving in the western Roman army was on the increase until by the late fourth century the army was almost entirely barbarian. The soldiers were either 'federate', supplied under the terms of Rome's agreement with tribes across the rivers in exchange for the subsidy of gold, or else they were recruited from barbarians who had been settled in Roman territory or from barbarian prisoners. Not only troops but, to a steadily increasing degree, officers.

In 376 an agreement was reached with the Visigoths that a large number, something like 200,000 – 50,000 of them fighters – should cross the Danube and be allowed to settle, on the promise that they would provide the Roman army with large numbers of recruits. The settlement was hideously mismanaged by the Romans; no proper arrangements were made to feed the settlers on arrival, and they were quite shamelessly exploited. Ostrogoths crossed the river to join them, and they had recourse to arms. At the disastrous battle of Adrianople in 378, the eastern emperor Valens was killed and in 382 a sinister new chapter was written in the history of the Roman decline when Theodosius agreed to their settling in Northern Thrace, not as Roman subjects, but as a politically independent people under their own kings. The subsequent aggressions of their king Alaric could twice have been arrested if there had not, after the death of Theodosius, been an acute conflict between the civilian ministers of the eastern Augustus, Arcadius, and the Vandal Stilicho, the great general who had been sent by Theodosius to the West, over the question of boundaries, whether Macedonia and Dacia, south of the Danube, belonged to East or West. The eastern government, therefore, built Alaric up, appointing him *magister militum* in Illyricum, out of jealousy of Stilicho. Thus inflated, Alaric invaded Italy with an army of some 40,000 fighters and, after failing to blackmail the western emperor Honorius, whom he blockaded in Ravenna, to make him his supreme military commander, he captured and sacked Rome in 410.

In the first half of the fifth century Britain was eventually overrun by the invading Saxons. The Vandals were ravaging Gaul and moving into Spain, from which they crossed into Africa, where in 442 they agreed a settlement by which Mauretania and Numidia remained Roman and the Vandals possessed the rest. Between 434 and 453 came the invasion of the Huns under Attila, over the Danube and into Italy, where in 453 Attila died; and this, miraculously, was the end of the Huns. They evaporated, a menace no longer. A number of them were absorbed by the Bulgars.

The circumstances in which the rule of the western emperors

Barbarian invasions of the
Empire in the fifth century.

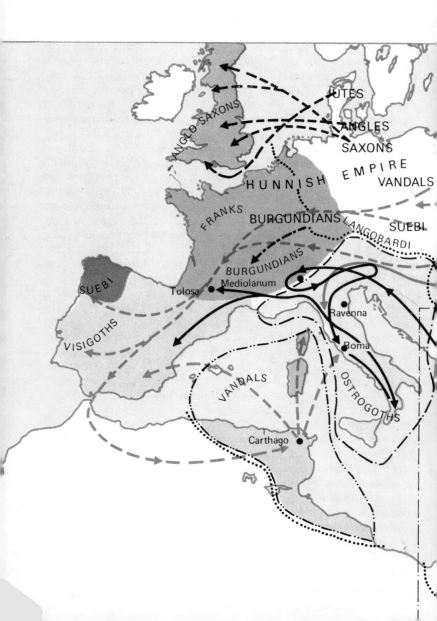

JUTES

ANGLES

SAXONS

ANGLO-SAXONS

E M P I R E

VANDALS

H U N N I S H

FRANKS

BURGUNDIANS

LANGOBARDI

SUEBI

SUEBI

BURGUNDIANS

Mediolanum

Tolosa

Ravenna

VISIGOTHS

Roma

VANDALS

OSTROGOTHS

Carthago

OF ATTILA

AVARS

ALANI

OSTROGOTHS

VISIGOTHS

GEPIDAE

● Constantinopolis

EASTERN
ROMAN EMPIRE

EMPIRE
OF THE
SASSANIDS

Medallion on the Certosa
of Pavia supposedly
representing Attila.

collapsed are these. The Vandal Gaiseric did what seven hundred years earlier Romans had professed to fear that the Carthaginians might do: he took Sardinia and Corsica and from them as a springboard, invaded Italy and in 455 captured and for a fortnight sacked Rome. After which he retired. The expedition sent against him by the eastern emperor Leo in 468 was a disastrous failure; as a result Gaiseric acquired Sicily.

In 476 the troops in Italy, entirely German, elected one of their officers, Odoacer, as king and he deposed the young Romulus Augustulus, freshly appointed emperor, settling him in well-paid retirement in Campania. After this there were no more emperors in the west. The complaisant senate dispatched the imperial regalia, for which there was no more service, to the eastern emperor Zeno, stating that Rome had no more need of emperors, and suggesting that Odoacer should rule as king and be honoured with the title of patrician which by this time indicated the supreme military commander. Odoacer rented Sicily from Gaiseric, acquired Dalmatia and decided to abandon Noricum, evacuating its inhabitants to the south of Italy. Zeno, who had returned a noncommital reply to the senate's earlier request, in 489 commissioned

Theoderic, King of the Ostrogoths in the Balkans, to recover Italy for the eastern empire. Instead, after killing Odoacer and taking Ravenna, Theoderic had himself proclaimed king by the Goths. He ruled with great enlightenment from 493 to 526. The senate was happy; so was Zeno and, after him, Anastasius. Theoderic recovered Visigothic Spain which he ruled through nominees. Gaul by this time was in the hands of the Franks and the Burgundians.

In Italy and the western provinces the invaders acquired land from the earlier owners on the basis of what was euphemistically called *hospitalitas*; landowners were forced to surrender a third of their property to the newcomers, who on their freshly acquired land were liable for tax. Indeed, in taxation, the administration of law and government generally the existing Roman practices survived. The barbarians took over the Roman system just as in the first conquests of eastern provinces the Romans centuries earlier had taken over the systems of the Hellenistic kings.

In the sixth century Justinian, that devout Christian and proud Latin, who was responsible for the publication of the great corpus of Roman law between 529 and 533, launched an expedition under Belisarius in 532 to recover the West to be an appendage to the surviving eastern Roman empire. By 552, after prolonged and heavy fighting, Dalmatia, Italy, Sicily, Sardinia, Corsica, Africa and most of Spain south of the river Baetis were recovered. This at the expense of the Danube frontier, which was weakened; and, with receipts from taxation now inadequate to meet the cost of administration, the value of the achievement may be questioned. There were Moorish inroads on Africa to be countered and mutinies of the troops, who were inadequately paid.

The end of the sixth century saw the invasion of the Avars across the Danube, who broke through to Constantinople, and the penetration of the Lombards into Italy. In the seventh century Syria, Asia Minor and North Africa were overwhelmed by the Saracens.

Epilogue

For Rome in its turn the moment came to which, with tears in his eyes, Scipio Aemilianus had looked forward when he made a bonfire of Carthage in 146 BC. A long history, which started with Romulus and received a fresh fillip from Augustus, ended with the deposition of a boy, Rome's last emperor, himself ironically named Romulus Augustulus. Though even this, as has been seen, was not quite the end of Rome. In the West Theoderic described himself as King of the Ostrogoths and Romans. In the East Byzantium lived on.

For centuries Rome had constituted the nearest thing to a world-state known to history. How splendid if it had gone on for ever, developing and making adjustments to take account of one fresh new factor after another, in the way in which it succeeded in taking account of Christianity. This is a pipe dream of some historians who disregard the fact that history is volcanic, always erupting where eruptions are least expected and erupting often in a catastrophic manner. And it leads historians to ask the kind of question which nobody ever asks when a very old person dies. Why did it happen? Why did the Roman empire collapse? Or, better perhaps, why towards the end did it not put up a better fight?

Did it collapse from internal weakness or from external pressure? Must we go to Rome itself for the answer, or to the barbarians? In the view of the distinguished French scholar Piganiol, the Roman empire did not die a natural death; it was assassinated.

The question, 'Would the empire have collapsed if there had been no barbarians?' is not perhaps a very meaningful question. To ask, 'Why were the defences in fact overwhelmed?' makes better sense.

The overwhelming of the defences could have two explanations: the military and numerical superiority of the attackers or the technical or numerical weakness of the defence. About numbers, in the absence of good evidence, it is hard to speak with any certainty. It was once thought that the invaders succeeded because of their great superiority in cavalry, and Sir Charles Oman considered the battle of Adrianople in 378 one of the world's decisive battles on that account: 'The Goth found that his stout lance and his good steed would carry him through the serried ranks of the Imperial infantry. He had become the arbiter of war, the inaugurator of that ascendancy of the horseman which was to endure for a thousand years.' Yet the tactics of the battle do not bear out this generalisation. Though at Adrianople the Visigothic horsemen were in at the kill, they were not numerous, and they were not an important element in respect of attack or defence in the dispositions of either side before the battle. The saddle certainly arrived as a barbarian innovation in the first century AD; stirrups, which revolutionised cavalry attack, came from the East, but not before the end of the seventh century AD.

From the point of view of the defence of the frontiers, some have thought that Rome's mistake was in allowing the development of what in the end was in effect a mercenary army and an army which controlled and coerced civil government instead of obeying it, for emperors were all too often its servants, not its masters. So Augustus is blamed, and it is suggested that he should have reintroduced compulsory militia service. Alternatively it has been held that he should have retained a larger army. The first suggestion was clearly impracticable. As regards the second, the Augustan army of between twenty-five and thirty legions proved itself large enough for two hundred years. As for the failure to man the army adequately with good Romans (except where the Balkans were concerned), was this in part the result of a steady decline in the population of the empire? Was there no recovery from the toll taken by the great plagues of the second and the third centuries AD?

No country or empire can fail to be weakened by recurrent civil strife, and civil wars did infinite harm to the Roman fabric, even though the first civil war, which destroyed the Republic, created the new, efficient and imaginatively organised empire of the Caesars. Subsequent civil wars were between pretenders to the purple. Would the destructive anarchy of the third century have been avoided if Marcus Aurelius had passed over the claims of his son Commodus and had instead followed the system which had worked so well from the moment when Nerva adopted Trajan? Should he have adopted as his successor not his own son but 'the best man'? Yet, given the power of the armies, such action would surely have sparked off another civil war; for the army had a sentimental attachment to emperors' sons.

Or was there a general weakening of the Roman fabric, of the will to resist? Was there the feeling that Roman civilisation was no longer a civilisation that was worth fighting for?

We lack the material for a confident answer.

Christianity, of course, was a catalyst of traditional *Romanità*. For centuries it had preached hostility to principalities and powers; its eyes were set on the New Jerusalem – 'There shall be a new heaven and a new earth'. It persuaded men who might have played a constructive part in public affairs to turn their backs on public life and enter monasteries. And its triumph was an uneasy triumph. Christian fanatics were for iconoclasm and the destruction of all pagan literature. On the other hand the world was full of nominal Christians who, at heart, were as pagan as ever.

Yet Christianity opened up an absolutely novel field of thought, and the heresies and schisms were anything but deplorable in themselves. They produced intellectual excitement and kept men thinking. Universal orthodoxy can be a stifling sedative. And Christianity was the stimulus to a new art, one which turned its back on classical tradition.

In the East, where wars were religious wars, it gave men something to fight for. This as well as the sturdy character of the Anatolian soldiery is a reason why the Eastern empire survived. There was no such religious conflict in the West. If the invaders were not Christians already, they were soon converted.

It was a weakness of the ancients that they looked back to a golden age and never forward to a millennium. They had none of the excitement of material progress. They had not the economic *expertise* (for which it was easier to blame them a hundred years ago than it is today) to arrest inflation and the collapse of the currency in the third century. The acquisition of Roman citizenship was no longer a goal since Caracalla had given it to everybody who was free. And the horrors of existing society were in the end omnipresent and, it seemed, inescapable: loss of personal freedom, iniquitous taxation which only the very rich, somehow or other, avoided; administrative inefficiency; corruption everywhere.

To quote from Juvenal and consider race-admixture the cause of Roman disintegration is to emulate the stupidity of Hitler. The Greek East gave Rome its doctors, its architects, its teachers and many of its best thinkers. Every part of the world made its admirable contribution to Roman administration and government from the first century of the Empire of the Caesars onwards. This absorption first of Italians, then of provincials, was at its best a slow process; at the end, with the Germans, Rome was required to absorb too many and too fast.

And so the general standard of culture fell; so that Rostovtzeff rightly confronted the modern reader with one of the most frightening challenges that a historian has ever thrown down:

The ultimate problem remains like a ghost, ever present and unlaid: Is it possible to extend a higher civilisation to the lower classes without debasing its standard and diluting its quality to the vanishing point. Is not every civilisation bound to decay as soon as it begins to penetrate the masses?

Looking at the success of the fourth-century Gallic empire and at the achievement of the Palmyrene sheikdom of Odenathus, anyone may ask whether a greater development of regionalism might not have strengthened loyalties and strengthened resistance. But this might only have been an invitation to greater fragmentation. Zenobia was not content with the boundaries which had satisfied her husband. Regionalism inevitably rebels increasingly against central control.

Yet to the end among good men hope never died. There was Justinian's sanguine attempt to recover a great section of the western empire in the sixth century. Before that, the soldier-historian Ammianus Marcellinus, a contemporary, was not daunted by the disaster of Adrianople: 'People who know no history say that Rome was never overwhelmed by such disaster, but they are wrong. A consideration of ancient, even of recent, history will show that such calamities have often happened. Yet, despite disastrous losses, there has been a complete recovery' – but only, on earlier occasions, thanks to a spiritual resilience which, as Ammianus described it, he must have known to exist no longer.

There are no parallels to be drawn between the collapse of the western Roman Empire and the liquidation of the nineteenth-century empires in the modern world. While a few colonies have accepted with luke-warm enthusiasm an independence which has been forced on them, the great majority have grasped independence with a heady intoxication – even though, as with all intoxication, there has inevitably been a morning-after. Some have plunged into the disaster of civil war. Many – whether temporarily or not – have discarded the democratic system which was the legacy of the nineteenth-century Utopianism of their imperial rulers in favour of a more or less stark form of autocratic government. The alternative of communism can present itself as a live issue. Every one of the new countries needs money for reasonable and ambitious development schemes and in one way or another the money which once came – sometimes generously, sometimes not – from the imperial ruler is available, mainly in the form of loans (sometimes with labels attached) from one or other of the great powers in what is generally considered to be to its own political interest, or from an international source.

What is important is that, despite frustrations and initial set-backs, every one of these newly independent countries has the challenge and excitement of building its own future. There are few which should not be grateful for much that they have inherited from the days of imperialism and some do not hesitate to express their gratitude. But it is to be doubted if in any case, given a free choice, they would choose to return to the status from which they have been emancipated.

When the western Roman Empire disintegrated, on the other hand, only a bigoted fanatic like Salvian could rejoice in its disintegration, claiming that the savage barbarian was a noble savage and that the Roman civilisation which he destroyed was the civilisation of Sodom and Gomorrah.

A strong feeling of security pervading the whole Roman Empire had in its heyday been the Empire's strength, and in the period of the collapsing Empire every Roman alive, if given the choice, would have opted for a return to the days of such security. The third century, when those who had experienced security themselves felt the shock of its loss, must have been the worst time of all. Once the disintegration started, when the vigour went out of that city life which had been the pride of Roman civilisation and the strongest focus of the individual's loyalty, the dark clouds rolled up and the sun never came through again. Everybody, it seemed, was an enemy, set to get out of you all that he could: your own soldiers, imperial agents, tax-collectors, the government itself. Then there were barbarian marauders. Security had gone, and safety too. You were best on the land, even if you were chained to it, for the land, as long as you were able to till it, would supply you with food. If you lived in a town, it might be occupied, whether by your own soldiers or by the barbarians, and under siege. Siege meant starvation and, at the end, more likely than not, pillage, arson, rape. These are the vivid horrors which in the sixth century Procopius' history depicts. What did it matter? One side was as bad as the other.

Or sometimes, not often, as good. At all ranks there were bad barbarians and good. The whole Roman senate would have gone into the witness box on Theoderic's behalf. And there was the Gothic ruler Theodatus, Theoderic's nephew, who was ready to make any concession to Justinian for the sake of peace and who wrote, 'I have been devoted to philosophy since my young days, and am to this day a stranger to the din of battle. The last thing I could want is to live the dangerous life of a king.' But, not un-naturally, his 'noble savages' thought him better dead.

The prospect of life generally in the dark days was the same or worse. A new – medieval – world was destined to grow out of the ruins of the old; but nobody was to know then what the future had in store. Pure contentment was reserved for those devoted Christians, particularly the monks, who were putting into practice the precepts which pagan Stoicism had once preached, precepts which constitute the whole burden of Seneca's writing. Such men had turned their backs on the world, happy in the salvation of their own souls. If, instead, with all their fervour, they had gone out into the world, they might have done something to save it.

Bibliography

What follows is necessarily a very selective bibliography and does not include biographies of individual emperors. Admirably complete bibliographies, comprising more than 1,200 items, are to be found in Paul Petit, *La Paix romaine*, Nouvelle Clio, Paris, 1967 and R. Remondon, *La crise de l'empire romain*, Nouvelle Clio, Paris, 1964.

Histories of the period

H. Bengtson, *Grundriss der römischen Geschichte* I, Munich, 1967 (up to AD 284).

Cambridge Ancient History, VII-XII, Cambridge, 1928-39 (up to AD 324).

Cambridge Medieval History, I, II, Cambridge, 1911-3.

H. Dessau, *Geschichte der römischen Kaiserzeit*, Berlin, 1924-30.

A. Garzetti, *L'impero da Tiberio agli Antonini*, Bologna, 1960.

L. Homo, M. Besnier and A. Piganiol, *Histoire Romaine*, III, IV, i and ii (*Histoire Générale*, ed. Glotz), Paris, 1933-47.

M. A. Levi, *L'impero romano dalla battaglia di Azio alla morte di Teodosio* I, Turin, 1963.

R. Paribeni, *Italia imperiale* (*Storia d'Italia* II), Milan, 1938.

H. M. D. Parker, *A History of the Roman World from AD 138 to 337²*, ed. B. H. Warmington, London, 1958.

E. T. Salmon, *A History of the Roman World from 30 BC to AD 138*, London, 1944.

H. H. Scullard, *From the Gracchi to Nero²*, London, 1965.

A. Solari, *L'impero romano*, Genoa-Rome, 1940-7.

A. von Domaszewski, *Geschichte der römischen Kaiser*, Leipzig, 1909.

Ancient sources in translation

N. Lewis. M. Reinhold, *Roman Civilisation Sourcebooks*, I, *The Republic*, II, *The Empire*, Harper Torchbooks, New York, 1966.

A. H. M. Jones, *A History of Rome through the Fifth Century*, Harper Paperbacks, I, The Republic, 1968; II, The Empire.

General

E. Albertini, *L'Empire romain*, Paris, 1938.

J. P. V. D. Balsdon, ed., *The Romans*, London and New York, 1965; Penguin

248

Books, 1969 (tr. *I Romani*, Milan, 1969).

G. Bloch, *L'Empire romain*, Paris, 1922.

V. Chapot, *Le Monde romain*, Paris, 1927.

M. P. Charlesworth, *The Roman Empire*, Home University Library, London, 1951.

Michael Grant, *The World of Rome*, Weidenfeld and Nicolson, 1960.

L. Homo, *L'Empire romain*, Paris, 1925.

H. Mattingly, *Roman Imperial Civilisation*, London, 1957.

S. Mazzarino, *Trattato di storia romana*, II, *L'impero romano*, Rome 1956.

Fergus Millar and others, *Das römische Reich und seine Nachbarn* (Fischer Weltgeschichte, Bd. 8), Frankfurt am Main, 1966; (tr. *The Roman Empire and its Neighbours*, London, 1967).

M. P. Nilsson, *Imperial Rome*, London, 1926.

P. Petit, *La Paix romaine*, Paris, 1967.

R. Remondon, *La Crise de l'empire romain*, Paris, 1964.

A. N. Sherwin-White, *The Roman Citizenship*, Oxford, 1939, and *Racial Prejudice in imperial Rome*, Cambridge, 1967.

Chester G. Starr, *Civilisation and the Caesars*, Cornell U. P., 1954.

R. Syme, *Colonial Elites, Rome, Spain and the Americas*, London, 1958.

The Republican Empire, to Augustus

E. Badian, *Roman Imperialism in the late Republic*, Oxford, 1968.

F. B. Marsh, *The Founding of the Roman Empire*, Oxford, 1927.

R. Paribeni, *L'Età di Cesare e di Augusto*, Bologna, 1950.

R. Syme, *The Roman Revolution*, corrected reprint, Oxford, 1952.

Middle and late Empire

A. Alföldi, *Studien zur Geschichte der Weltkrise des 3 Jahrhunderts n. Christus*, Darmstadt, 1967.

Franz Altheim, *Die Krise der alten Welt*, Berlin, 1943, and *Niedergang der alten Welt*, Frankfurt, 1952.

J. B. Bury, *History of the later Roman Empire*, London, 1923.

A. Calderini, *I Severi, la crisi dell'impero nel III secolo* (Istituto di Studi Romani, *Storia di Roma* VII), Bologna, 1949.

Edward Gibbon, *The History of the Decline and Fall of the Roman Empire*, ed. J. B. Bury, London, 1896.

Michael Grant, *The Climax of Rome*, Weidenfeld and Nicolson, 1968.

A.H.M.Jones, *The later Roman Empire, 284-602*, Oxford, 1964, and *The Decline of the Ancient World*, London, 1966.

F.Lot, *La Fin du monde antique et le début du moyen âge²*, Paris, 1951.

(tr. *The End of the Ancient World and the Beginnings of the Middle Ages*, London, 1931).

Ramsay MacMullen, *Enemies of the Roman Order: Treason, Unrest and Alienation in the Empire*, Harvard U.P., 1967, and *Soldier and Civilian in the later Roman Empire*, Harvard U.P.., 1963.

S.Mazzarino, *La fine del mondo antico*, Milan, 1959.

(tr. *The End of the Ancient World*, London, 1966), and *Aspetti sociali del quarto secolo*, Rome, 1951.

R.Paribeni, *Da Diocleziano alla caduta dell'impero d'Occidente*, Bologna, 1941.

K.Pfiister, *Der Untergang der antiken Welt*, Leipzig, 1941.

O.Seeck, *Geschichte des Untergangs der antiken Welt*, Berlin, 1897-21.

J.Vogt, *Der Niedergang Roms*, Zurich, 1965.

(tr. *The Decline of Rome*, London, 1967.)

F.W.Walbank, *The Awful Revolution, the Decline of the Roman Empire in the West*, Liverpool, 1969.

Particular provinces and districts

A.Alföldi, *Der Untergang der Römerherrschaft in Pannonien*, Berlin-Leipzig, 1924.

G.W.Bowersock, *Augustus and the Greek World*, Oxford, 1965.

O.Brogan, *Roman Gaul*, London, 1953.

T.R.S.Broughton, *The Romanisation of Africa Proconsularis*, Baltimore, 1929.

V.Chapot, *La Province romaine proconsulaire d'Asie*, Paris, 1904.

G.Charles-Picard, *La Civilisation de l'Afrique romaine*, Paris, 1959.

H.Dessau, *see under* 'Histories of the Period'.

S.S.Frere, *Britannia, a History of Roman Britain*, London, 1967.

L.Hahn, *Rom und Romanismus im griechisch-römischen Osten*, Leipzig, 1906.

J.J.Hatt, *Histoire de la Gaule romaine*, Paris, 1959.

A.H.M.Jones, *The Cities of the Eastern Roman Provinces*, Oxford, 1937.

B.Levick, *Roman Colonies in Southern Asia Minor*, Oxford, 1967.

D.Magie, *Roman Rule in Asia Minor*, Princeton, 1950.

R. Menéndes Pidal, *Historia de España* II², Madrid, 1955.

Th. Mommsen, *The Provinces of the Roman Empire*, London, 1886; also (the Western provinces only) ed. T. R. S. Broughton, University of Chicago Press (paperback), 1968.

M. Pavan, *La provincia romana della Pannonia Superior*, Rome, 1955.

I. A. Richmond, *Roman Britain²*, Harmondsworth, 1963.

A. L. F. Rivet, *Town and Country in Roman Britain*, London, 1958.

C. H. V. Sutherland, *The Romans in Spain*, London, 1939.

Administration

F. F. Abbott and A. C. Johnson, *Municipal Administration in the Roman Empire*, Princeton U. P., 1926.

J. A. Crook, *Consilium Principis*, Cambridge, 1955.

Mason Hammond, *The Augustan Principate²*, New York, 1968, and *The Antonine Monarchy*, American Academy in Rome, 1959.

H. Mattingly, *The Imperial Civil Service of Rome*, Cambridge, 1910.

H. G. Pflaum, *Les Procurateurs équestres sous le haut-empire romain*, Paris, 1950.

J. S. Reid, *The Municipalities of the Roman Empire*, Cambridge, 1913.

A. N. Sherwin-White, *Roman Society and Roman Law in the New Testament*, Oxford, 1963.

G. H. Stevenson, *Roman Provincial Administration*, Oxford, 1939.

Architecture

Gilbert Picard, *Living Architecture: Roman*, London, 1965.

G. T. Rivoira, *Roman Architecture and its Principles of Construction*, tr. G. McN. Rushforth, Oxford, 1925.

Mortimer Wheeler, *Roman Art and Architecture*, London, 1964.

Armed service

G. L. Cheesman, *The Auxilia of the Roman Imperial Army*, Oxford, 1914.

H. M. D. Parker, *The Roman Legions²*, bibliography by G. R. Watson, Cambridge, 1961.

E. Ritterling and A. Schulten, s.v. 'Legio' in Pauly-Wissowa, *Realencyclopaedie der klassischen Altertumswissenschaft*, XII, 1186-1837.

C. G. Starr, *The Roman Imperial Navy, 31 BC-AD 324*[2], Cambridge, 1960.

A. von Domaszewski, *Die Rangordnung des römischen Heeres*[2], ed. B. Dobson, Cologne, 1967.

G. Webster, *The Roman Imperial Army of the first and second centuries AD*, London, 1969.

Economic and social life

A. E. R. Boak, *Manpower Shortage and the Fall of the Roman Empire in the West*, Ann Arbor, 1955.

M. P. Charlesworth, *Trade Routes and Commerce in the Roman Empire*[2], Cambridge, 1926.

Tenney Frank, ed., *Economic Survey of Ancient Rome*, Baltimore, 1933-40.

J. Innes Miller, *The Spice Trade of the Roman Empire*, Oxford, 1969.

M. Rostovtzeff, *Social and Economic History of the Roman Empire*, rev. P. M. Fraser, *Oxford*, 1957, (*Gesellschaft und Wirtschaft im römischen Kaiserzeit*, Leipzig, 1929; *Storia economica e sociale dell'impero romano*, Florence, 1946.)

Law

V. Arangio-Ruiz, *Istituzioni di diritto romano*[2], Naples, 1927.

J. A. Crook, *Law and Life of Rome*, London, 1967.

J. Declareuil, *Rome et l'organisation du droit*, Paris, 1924.

P. de Francisci, *Storia del diritto romano*, Rome, 1926-38.

P. F. Giraud, *Manuel élémentaire de droit romain*[7], Paris, 1924.

Raymond Monier, *Manuel élémentaire de droit romain*, I[6], Paris, 1947; II[4], Paris, 1948.

Barry Nicholas, *An Introduction to Roman Law*, Oxford, 1962.

Fritz Schulz, *Prinzipien des römischen Rechts*, Munich, 1934 (tr. *Principles of Roman Law*, Oxford, 1936), and *History of Roman Legal Science*, Oxford, 1946, and *Classical Roman Law*, Oxford, 1951.

Religion and thought

A. Alföldi, *A Conflict of Ideas in the late Roman Empire*, tr. H. Mattingly, Oxford, 1952, and *The Conversion of Constantine and Pagan Rome*, tr. H. Mattingly, Oxford, 1948.

C.N.Cochrane, *Christianity and Classical Culture*, Oxford, 1940.
W.H.C.Frend, *Martyrdom and Persecution in the early Church*, Oxford, 1965.
A.Momigliano, ed., *The Conflict between Paganism and Christianity in the Fourth Century*, Oxford, 1963.
A.D.Nock, *Conversion*, Oxford, 1933.

Acknowledgments

I am grateful first to a wonderfully sympathetic audience at Cambridge which listened a few years ago to the lectures out of which this book is constructed; to Colin Haycraft who encouraged me to write the book; to the translators, particularly Mrs Ursula Margotts who corrected more than one mistake; and, very particularly, to Pat Farrar-Hockley who typed the manuscript against time, and to two of my old pupils and friends, Dr Andrew Lintott of Aberdeen University who read the galleys and greatly improved the book by so doing and Sir Arthur Benson GCMG who took the first draft of the Introduction and showed me how to improve it.

Acknowledgment is also due to the following for the illustrations (the number refers to the page on which the illustration appears). Frontispiece, 84 Adolfo Tomeucci; 18, 23, 28, 31, 39, 45, 54–5, 58, 60–1, 112–13, 116, 125, 153, 169, 178–9, 187, 204, 226–7, 231, 238 Mansell Collection; 21 Museum Calvet, Avignon; 52 Soprintendenza alle antichità di Ostia; 83 British Museum, London; 118 J.Allan Cash; 121 Gabinetto Fotografico Nazionale; 123 (Crown copyright), 173 Ministry of Public Building and Works; 133 Turkish Tourist Office; 146 The Louvre, Paris; 209 Fototeca Unione; 232 University of London, Warburg Institute.

The maps and diagrams were drawn by Design Practitioners Ltd.

Index

accensus 50
Achaea 139
Achaean League 28ff., 164
administration 20-3, 26-8,
  43ff., 62ff., 69-78, 82-7,
  126ff., 210-16, 219-28
aedile 21, 69
Aetolian League 28ff., 164
Africa 26, 33, 47, 107, 129,
  170, 235
Agricola 114, 127, 146
agriculture 27, 148-9, 152,
  207, 225, 228
Agrippa I 92, 94, 106
Agrippa II 176, 182
Alaric 17, 235
Albinus, D. Clodius 196
Alexander 16
Alexander, Severus 135,
  197, 208
Alexandria 130, 175, 187,
  193, 233
Amminius 101
Anastasius 239
Antioch 193, 196, 206, 233
Antiochus of Syria 30,
  31-2
Antoninus, M. Aurelius
  see Caracalla
Antony 42, 95
Apollodorus of Damascus
  117
Arabia 107, 117
Archelaus 105
Armenia 38, 95, 103, 104,
  117
Arminius 94
army (Roman) 19, 41-2,
  45-6, 49-50, 56, 78-81,
  87ff., 98, 208, 214-15,
  224-5, 234, 241
art and architecture 35,
  122, 165, 171, 189, 192-3

Asia 38, 170
Athens 193, 203
Attila 235
Augustus 42-3, 68-9, 76,
  82, 87, 92-3, 96-7, 105,
  175, 213
Aurelian 201, 204, 208,
  210
Aurelius, M. 122, 124, 203
Aureolus 208
Ausonius 190, 206
Avars 239

Balbinus 197
Balbus, Cornelius 67
barbarians 17, 115, 123,
  173, 203, 204, 217, 234ff.,
  240
battles: Actium 43, 68,
  175
  Adrianople 235, 378-9
  Bedriacum (1) 109
  Bedriacum (2) 112
  Cannae 26, 30
  Carrhae 40, 62, 95
  Cynoscephalae 30
  Issus 196
  Magnesia 32
  Philippi 79
  Pydna 32
  Teutoberg Forest 94
  Trasimene 164
  Zama 26, 30, 33
Beneventum 167
Bithynia 38, 43, 168, 170
Bohemia 94
Boudicca 102, 184
Britain 79, 93, 97, 101-2,
  114, 196, 203, 208
Brundisium 66
Brutus, M. 50
Burebista 93
Burrus 141

Caesar, Julius 38, 40, 42,
  49, 54-5, 60-1, 68, 94, 95,
  175
Caligula 99, 102, 106, 107
Cappadocia 104
Caracalla 154, 175, 196
Caractacus 101-2
Carinus 202, 218
Carteia 66
Carthage 16, 24-5, 33-4,
  193
Cartimandua 102
Carus 202
Cassius, Avidius 124, 133
Cassius, C. 62
Cato 33
Caucasus 108
cavalry 95, 115, 208, 240
Cerealis, Petillius 113
Chosroes 117, 119
Christianity 17, 143, 162,
  187, 201, 210-11, 217,
  228ff., 242
Cicero 12, 49, 54, 55, 66,
  136
Cicero, Quintus 66
Cilicia 38, 43
citizenship 9, 11, 42, 58,
  63, 67, 78, 81, 154, 160,
  161-2, 189
Civilis, Julius 113, 186
Claudius 81, 97, 99, 102
Claudius II 201, 205, 208
Cleopatra 38, 175
Cogidumnus 102
coinage 96, 106, 154, 176,
  186, 203, 205-6, 227
comites 50, 155
Commodus 124-5, 133,
  135, 203
Constantine 224, 227-8,
  230-1
Constantinople 17, 193,

230, 233, 239
Constantius 219
Constantius II 233
consul 22, 26, 44, 47ff., 69,
  74-5, 128-9, 131
Corbulo, Cn. Domitius
  102, 104-5
Corinth 24, 33
corn 28, 82, 148, 157
Corsica–Sardinia 25, 26,
  33, 43, 70, 77
Cottius, M. Iulius 93
Crassus 40, 62, 95
Cunobelinus 101
Cyprus 38, 119
Cyrenaica 119
Cyrene 38, 138, 170

Dacia 93, 115, 116, 124,
  203-4, 235
Daia, Maximin 228-9
Dalmatia 95, 99
Danube 82, 94-5, 108,
  114, 115, 117, 124, 203,
  204, 234
Decebalus 115-6
Decius 201, 210
Diocletian 143, 202,
  217-19, 228
Domitian 114, 115, 213
Domna, Julia 196, 216
Drusus 93, 94, 97
Dyrrachium 66

Ebro 25
Egypt 16, 28, 38, 71,
  107-8, 119, 147-8
Elagabalus 135, 196
Elbe 94, 98
equites 64, 77, 78, 86, 131,
  135, 213
Ethiopia 107-8
Etruscans 18, 24

Eumenes, king of
  Pergamon 32
Euphrates 105

fasces 48
finance 27, 51, 56, 137,
  140, 152-3, 242
Flaccus, Hardeonius 112
Florian 202
Florus 99, 184
Florus, Gessius 106, 176
Fuscus, Cornelius 115

Gaetulicus 99
Gaiseric 238
Gaius cf. Caligula
Galatia 96, 105, 122
Galba, Ser. Sulpicius
  108-9
Galerius 143, 219, 228-9
Gallienus 201, 208, 210,
  217
Gallus, Aelius 107
Gallus, Cornelius 107
Gaul 18, 24-5, 40, 92-3,
  94, 108-9, 113, 128-9, 148,
  208
Germanicus 97-9, 102
Germany 76-7, 93, 108,
  113, 114-15, 123
Geta 175, 196
Gordian I 197
Gordian II 197
Gordian III 135, 197
Goths 123, 201
governor 47-50, 53ff., 71,
  74-5, 77, 85, 126, 137,
  153ff., 213, 214-15, 224
Gracchus, C. 46, 51
Gratian 233
Greece 16, 30ff., 96, 130-5,
  163ff.

Hadrian 119-22
Hannibal 25-6, 30
Herod 105
Honorius 235
Huns 234ff.

Illyricum see Dalmatia

Jerusalem 107, 114, 119,
  230
Jews 105-6, 114, 119,
  186-7
Josephus 107
Judaea 77, 105, 114
Jugurtha 42
Julian 232
Julianus, Didius 126, 196
Justinian 239

Langobardi 123
law and justice 27, 36, 46,
  47, 56, 58-9, 62-6, 138,
  155, 190, 214, 215, 239
legate 49, 50, 74-5, 76
Lepidus, M. Aemilius 99
Leo 238
lex provinciae 27, 44
Licinianus, Piso 109
Licinius 230
lictor 37-8, 48, 57
Livy 40
Longinus 216
Lucullus, L. 46

Macedonia 12, 28, 32-3,
  43, 47, 124, 139, 235
Macrinus, M. Opellius
  196-7, 214
Marcellinus, Ammianus
  206
Marius 42
Maroboduus 94
Masada 114

Mauretania 107, 170, 235
Maximian 219, 229, 230
Maximinus 197
Mesopotamia 95, 117, 119, 202, 204
Messina 25
mines 28, 40, 52
Mithridates 38
Moesia 95, 115, 139

Narcissus 101
navy (Roman) 24, 49, 82
Nero 102, 104-5, 108, 130-1
Nerva 115
Nicomedia 217
Nicomedes 38
Niger, Pescennius 126, 196
Noricum 77, 93
Numerianus 202, 217-18
Numidia 33, 107, 170, 235

Octavian see Augustus
Odenathus 201, 210, 243
Odoacer 219, 238
Origen 216, 229
Ostia 82
Ostrogoths 234ff.
Otho 108

Paetus, Caesennius 104-5
Palestine 119
Palmyra 117
Pannonia 94, 95, 115
Papinian 215
Parthia 38, 95-6, 103-4, 117, 122-3, 196, 203
Paulinus, Suetonius 102, 107
Paulus 215
Pergamon 28, 30, 32, 38
Perseus of Macedon 32

Persia 123, 203-4, 232-3
Pertinax 126, 196
Petronius, C. 107
Philip v of Macedon 30, 164
Philip (emperor) 135, 197, 201
Phraates 96
Pius, Antoninus 122, 142
plague 123, 205, 241
Plautius, A. 101
Pliny 12, 140
Plotinus 216
Polybius 19, 30, 32, 34, 165-6, 181
Pompey 38, 43, 49, 60, 67, 82
Poppaea 108
Postumus 208
praeses 213, 224
praetor 21, 26-7, 46, 48-9, 69
praetorian guard 79, 99, 111-12, 196-7, 214
Prasutagus 102
prefect 86
Primus, Antonius 112-13, 129
Probus 202
proconsul 27, 47, 69, 137
Procopius 207
procurator 77, 86, 137
province 10, 26-7, 46, 48-9, 55-62, 71ff., 137-9, 158-62, 224
Ptolemy Auletes 38
publicanus 51-3, 56, 77
Puteoli 82
Pyrrhus 18-19, 25, 33

Quadratus, Ummidius 104
quaestor 21, 27, 48-9, 51,

53, 61, 69, 74-5
Quintilian 190
Quintillus 201

Raetia-Vindelicia 77, 93
religion (pagan) 19-20, 22, 106, 180-1, 210, 212-13, 230, 233
Rhine 40, 76, 94, 99, 108, 114, 117
Rhodes 30, 32
roads 22, 66, 189
Romulus 18
Romulus Augustulus 219, 238
Rufus, Rutilius 64
Rufus, Verginius 109, 112

Sacrovir 99, 184
Samnites 18, 24
Scipio, Publius 26, 35
Scribonianus, Furius Camillus 101
senate 42, 43-4, 57, 62, 71, 74-5, 85, 126-8, 131-3, 135-9, 213-14
Seneca 141
Sertorius 67
Severus, Septimius 119, 126, 193, 196, 208, 213
Sicily 25, 26, 43, 46, 51
Spain 25, 26, 43, 46, 51
Stilicho 235
Strabo 181
Sulla 42, 47, 63
Syracuse 48, 193
Syria 28, 43, 62

Tacfarinas 80, 107
Tacitus 12, 97, 114, 127
Tacitus (emperor) 202
Tarentum 18, 66
taxation 27-8, 51-5, 77,

256

81, 122, 153-4, 177, 183-4, 207, 215, 225-6, 239
Tertullian 229
Theodoric 239
Theodosius 233, 235
Tiberius 87, 93, 94, 96, 97-8, 139
Tigranes 96
Timgad 160-1
Tiridates 104-5
Titus 107, 114
Togodumnus 101
trade 24, 101, 148-9, 159, 175-6, 189, 205, 226-8

Trajan 12, 97, 115-19, 140
tribune 21, 69
Tunisia 24, 33

Ulpian 214, 215
Utica 33

Valens 235
Valerian 201, 210, 217
Vandals 235ff.
Varus, Quinctilius 79, 94, 98
Vercingetorix 92
Verres 12, 60, 63, 64, 137

Verus, L. 122, 124
Vespasian 101, 105, 107, 109, 112-14
villa 35, 163, 193, 207
Vindex, Julius 108, 109, 129, 186
Virgil 19, 24
Visigoths 234ff.
Vitellius, L. 102, 109, 112-13
Vologeses 104

Zeno 201, 210
Zenobia 238-9, 243